D0889902

BEYOND SHAME

Beyond Shame

Reclaiming the Abandoned History
of Radical Gay Sexuality

PATRICK MOORE

Beacon Press

BOSTON

Beacon Press
25 Beacon Street
Boston, Massachusetts 02108-2892
www.beacon.org

Beacon Press books
are published under the auspices of
the Unitarian Universalist Association of Congregations.

07 06 05 04 03   8 7 6 5 4 3 2 1

This book is printed on acid-free paper that meets the uncoated paper
ANSI/NISO specifications for permanence as revised in 1992.

Text design by Elizabeth Elsas.
Composition by Wilsted & Taylor Publishing Services.

Library of Congress Cataloging-in-Publication Data
Moore, Patrick
   Beyond shame : reclaiming the abandoned history of radical gay
sexuality / by Patrick Moore.
       p. cm.
"Commissioned by the Estate Project for Artists with AIDS (a project of
the Alliance for the Arts)."
   ISBN 0-8070-7956-1 (cloth : alk. paper)
   1. Homosexuality, Male—United States—History—20th century.
2. Gay men—United States—Psychology. 3. Gay men—United States—
Sexual behavior. 4. Gay men—United States—Attitudes. 5. AIDS (Disease)
—United States—History. I. Title.
HQ76.2.U5M64 2004
306.76'62'09730904—dc21   2003014313

FOR DINO, WHO I ONLY THOUGHT I HAD LOST,

AND FOR JOAQUIN, WHO I WILL NEVER LOSE.

BEYOND SHAME: Reclaiming the Abandoned History of Radical Gay Sexuality was commissioned by the Estate Project for Artists with AIDS (a project of the Alliance for the Arts). This commission was made possible through the generous support of the Royal S. Marks Foundation Fund, the Peter Norton Family Foundation, and the Robert D. Farber Foundation.

Research assistance for this book was provided by Brennan Gerard.

If you want to feel empowered, feel the richness of your past.

—ARNIE KANTROWITZ
"LETTER TO THE QUEER GENERATION"

The eventual disappearance of gay culture constitutes a significant loss, not just for gay people, but for American culture in general ... turning us into a drab and homogeneous mass of identical citizens.

—DANIEL HARRIS
THE RISE AND FALL OF GAY CULTURE

CONTENTS

ACKNOWLEDGMENTS

When I sent the manuscript of this book to my friend Carolyn Dinshaw, the director of New York University's Center for the Study of Gender and Sexuality, one of her many excellent suggestions was that I show it to Gayatri Patnaik at Beacon Press. I could not have hoped to find a more decisive, fearless advocate than Gayatri for this book and I am forever indebted to Carolyn for making that connection.

It is a great privilege to have my first nonfiction book published by a house as respected as Beacon. To have my work presented at the level of intellectual discourse represented by Beacon is, frankly, more than I had hoped for. Aside from Gayatri being the champion for my book and helping it take final shape, I am also grateful to Brian Halley at Beacon for making the process so effortless, as well as the rest of the Beacon staff for their professionalism and kindness.

Michael Bronski pioneered the concept that sex, politics, and culture are inextricably related. I can think of no one whom I would rather have introduce this book to readers, and I thank him for his generous foreword.

Many people gave generously of their time during the interview process for this book. Felice Picano and Sarah Schulman are particularly important to me as interview subjects, valued readers, friends, and mentors. Thanks also to my friend Betty Prashker for her support and guidance.

I am grateful to the One Institute/International Gay and Lesbian Archives at the University of Southern California for access to their collection. It is a treasure trove of historic publications from the 1970s. Thanks also to the New York Public Library and the Fales Collection of New York University.

This book would not exist without the generous support of the Royal S. Marks Foundation Fund, the Peter Norton Family Foundation, and the Robert D. Farber Foundation. All three foundations were an important part of my time as director of the Estate Project for Artists with AIDS and I am so grateful that they have also supported this culmination of my work with the Estate Project. In his role as both a funder and a valued adviser, Vincent McGee has been particularly generous.

In this book, I identify the lack of generational contact between gay men as a key factor in our losing a sense of identity. So it is interesting that this book represents three generations of gay men working together toward the shared goal of reclaiming our history. My research assistant, Brennan Gerard, is in his twenties, and our daily work together has shaped my beliefs dramatically. If Brennan represents the future of gay America, then I remain hopeful about our prospects. On the other end of the spectrum, my friendship with Randy Bourscheidt has taught me everything about the power of maturity; he has, quite literally, reshaped my life over the ten years we worked together in creating the Estate Project for Artists with AIDS. I feel bracketed by the integrity of these two men. As the three of us stand in the present, this book embodies our rich past and our hopeful future.

Finally, I need to say that, while I write about some very sad things in this book, I am blessed with a happy life built on the support of my beloved Joaquin, my parents, and our extended family here and in Spain. I am one of the fortunate few with no doubts that I am loved.

by Michael Bronski

At the beginning of the twenty-first century, it is difficult to shock readers with a radical idea. Most of the progressive, radical concepts that have been dreamed of and implemented since the Enlightenment—and I would include here such diverse and groundbreaking concepts as the demise of the divine right of kings, the idea of feminism and human integrity for women, the advent of a labor movement, the disassociation of reproduction from heterosexual activity, the desacralization of the concept of "whiteness" in Western culture, and the rise of the idea of same-sex orientation as a distinct and commendable identity—have gained some public acceptance. Yet, at the end of his amazing examination of late-twentieth-century life and culture, Patrick Moore presents us with a concept so radical, so transgressive, that it will startle most readers, perhaps even those who have been prepared for it after reading the two-hundred-plus pages that have preceded it. Quoting Dr. Lynn Ponton, a psychotherapist practicing in San Francisco, Moore asserts that "a vibrant sexual culture stimulates other types of creativity."

The first problem that many may have with this statement is the existence of such an entity as a "vibrant sexual culture." Many Americans consider sexuality, by which they almost always mean heterosexuality, as a private issue, and of culture as a public activity, with no common, shared ground between them. But the idea that heterosexuality is private is a myth. Obviously there are multitudinous ways in which heterosexuality is glaringly public all the time. The idea that heterosexuality is "private" only occurs because heterosexuality is viewed as normative, thus "natural" and unremarkable, unseen. When people do consider "sexual culture," it is usually in negative terms—the widespread presence of sexual images in television, film, and advertising. And most particularly, those images that the mainstream judges to be nonnormative sexuality—heterosexual prostitution or promiscuity, sex involving youth, "fetish" sex, and, obviously, homosexuality. (Indeed, one of the major objections to the advance of gay liberation and gay rights in the United States has been that homosexuality should be secretive, "private"; a widespread social form of "don't ask, don't tell.") But the idea that a public sexuality can be "vibrant"—i.e., positive—is alien to most Americans.

The second problem that some readers may have with Moore's declaration is the easy connection between sex and "other types of creativity." Certainly, American culture holds that sex can (and in many cases, should) be pro-creative. And, thanks to the changes that have occurred over the past forty years, a substantial number of Americans grant that sex can be rec-creative. And while many people will understand that sex can be stimulating, I believe very few will actually make—or can even be convinced of—the leap that sex can stimulate, animate, or encourage other types of creativity. For centuries Western culture saw sex, and sexual pleasure, as solely a means of reproduction. We have come a long way to the understanding, yet to be overwhelmingly acknowledged, that it is permissible for sex to be an end in itself. We still have much further to go to comprehend that sexual activity and pleasure can be not just an inspiration, but the source of creativity.

While this is perhaps the most profound, startling, and important thesis of *Beyond Shame*, Patrick Moore has far more to say. The book is full of vital history—much of it already forgotten not only in the wake of AIDS, but as a victim of our overwhelming cultural indifference and antagonism toward open, experimental, and outré sexuality. His early chapters on *Fag Rag*, the first national gay-male-liberation publication, famed sex clubs such as New York's Mineshaft and San Francisco's Catacombs, the sex art films of Fred Halsted, and the Saint and St. Marks Baths in New York are some of the most critically significant historical uncovering of queer history that has occurred in the past decade. But reading these chapters, at least for me, prompted sadness and loss, as well as excitement. Not sadness because these institutions were no longer available to men (although that is cause enough for grief) but because even the memory of them is now fading. Of course, this is partly because many of the people who created and attended them are now dead, but also, as Moore points out, because of a sense of community shame, which erupted at the advent of AIDS, that such flagrant sites of "vibrant sexual culture" existed in the first place.

I know the truth of this firsthand. As someone who was a habitué of the Mineshaft, and many other sex clubs, who went very occasionally to the Catacombs, who worked for just under a year at the Club LaGrange (part of the national Club Bath chain) in Boston, I personally felt their loss, and also received criticism when I later wrote positively about my experiences there. After AIDS, the idea that one might still promote a gloriously promiscuous gay male sexual culture was thought by many safe-sex educators, gay politicians, and even some writers who were involved in such progressive groups as ACT UP to be in poor taste, even potentially destructive to the community who, we were told, had "grown up" and moved out of its sex-obsessed adolescence.

But there is another way that I know, and understand, the sense of cultural shame over 1970s sex that continues to exist today. For the past few years I have been Visiting Scholar in Women's Studies at Dartmouth College, teaching Introduction to Gay, Lesbian, Bisexual, and Transgender Studies as well as an advanced class called Contemporary Issues in Gay, Lesbian, Bisexual, and Transgender Studies. We spend several classes on post-Stonewall, pre–AIDS lesbian and gay life and discuss sexual cultures at length. We watch *Cruising* and I pass out copies of lesbian sex magazines such as *Bad Attitude* and *On Our Backs*. This year some students, women and men, voiced a curiosity about gay male magazines, especially *Drummer*, the most famous of the S/M, fetish gay male publications of the 1970s and 1980s. It was a reasonable enough request—we were discussing this material in class, and who doesn't want to look at porn?—but I hesitated, and in the end did not bring the magazines to class. I decided that there was no demanding pedagogical purpose for them to see *Drummer*, and the explicit nature of the magazines could conceivably have caused some slight stir in the deanery (although the likelihood of this was very small). But after reading *Beyond Shame*, I have had to question my decision. While I have never shied away from talking or writing about my sex life in the 1970s and 1980s (or now), I was not at all prepared to show my students magazines that were formative to my sexuality and identity from that time. It wasn't about sex—I had no problems giving them *Bad Attitude* to examine—it was about me.

I couldn't blatantly say that it was shame that made me decide not to bring *Drummer* magazines to class. Still, if I'm being completely honest, I can't rule shame out as a contributing factor either. Did I want my students to have some entrée into my own sexual and emotional life—to see images and stories that I might have masturbated to? Clearly, I had enormous reservations about circulating materials that related too closely to my own sexual life.

Shame—from childhood to one's last days—is a first-rate form of social control. Shame is what keeps us in line, and what prevents us from discovering not so much who we are, but what we might become. One of the most important aspects of *Beyond Shame* is that Patrick Moore has not simply written a vital book that points out the presence of shame in gay male (and mainstream) culture, but he has instigated new ways to conceptualize how we think and talk about shame.

This is an important, and profoundly necessary, task in our

current sociopolitical culture. But *Beyond Shame* does something else, as important, as well. It makes clear and convincing links between sex—*eros* might indeed be a better word here—and creativity. In the opening chapters Moore writes about sex clubs, such as the Mineshaft, as theater. This assertion disrupts our ideas about both sex and art. To equate the Mineshaft with theater is to imply that the sex there was, to use a slightly out-of-date word, playacting. This is an apt and useful term for what occurred at the Mineshaft and other sex clubs, as it emphasizes the twin aspects of this enactment of sexuality: it was both playful and highly intentional. It wasn't simply that some men dressed up as a cop, fireman, construction worker, or (using a collar and leash) animal, but that, as in professional theater, the heightened emotional and psychological effect came as much from imagination and craft as from endorphins.

Reading the opening chapters of *Beyond Shame* brought back, with some vividness, images I hadn't reflected on very much over the past twenty-five years. In 1978 I spent several months in San Francisco visiting a close friend who had moved there. Most of my nights were spent going out to the fairly new and thriving bars and sex clubs South of Market that catered to a burgeoning S/M and leather scene. My two favorites were the Black and Blue and the Handball Express. (These names were descriptive, not metaphoric.) The Black and Blue was a "heavy" leather bar—people were serious about their commitment to their performance here, there was no nonbutch behavior, no queeny talk, no overt camping—and its atmosphere was solemn, even forbidding. It was not a large bar: you entered through an open door, and then passed through some leather curtains into a medium-large room, with a full, old-fashioned wooden carved bar, maybe even turn of the century, to your left. The floor of the bar was part wood, part small black-and-white tiles; it may have been a restaurant in the 1920s or 1930s. The very high ceiling was classic 1930s hammered tin. The far right corner led to a men's room (with urinal troughs; very hot) and next to that was a closed-off "back room" for sex. Aside from some framed posters of motorcycle club runs and benefits, the main ornamentation in the bar was a large Harley that was hung by chains from the ceiling. Suspended high above the crowd, it was both ever present and magically elusive, as though it was a fantasy of outlaw masculinity that hovered in the collective minds of the patrons.

A full-size Harley hanging from chains in a leather bar is theatrical enough, but the Black and Blue, being a gay bar, could not stop there. Once a night the music, usually a mixture of Motown, R & B, and some low-key disco, would stop, lights in the bar would be dimmed to near complete darkness, and perfectly on cue, stage lighting would illuminate the bike from the corners of the hammered-tin ceiling. It was a stunning sight, and when it happened a magnificent hush fell over the bar. Within moments of the silence falling, the music would begin: it was always the Gloria from Bach's Mass in B Minor. For those seven or eight minutes there would be nothing but Bach's transcendent music and the gleaming chrome of the illuminated motorcycle. The Black and Blue had become—as it always, in some dimension, was—a church. Every night this moment felt, to me, startling and sacred, even holy. I think it had less to do with sacralizing masculinity or male power and was, in essence, a moment of profound recognition and celebration of community and, in the best sense of the word, brotherhood.

While the power of this image and experience was tremendous, it can be better understood in light of what happened at the end of the evening at last call. After the lights came on, and there was the usual 2:00 A.M. hustle to find someone with whom to leave (or make plans to go to the all-night sex club, the Handball Express, or to Hamburger Mary's for something to eat), the bar backs would begin clearing and suddenly the speakers would very loudly begin playing either Judy Garland singing "Somewhere over the Rainbow" or Jeanette MacDonald singing "San Francisco." If Bach's Gloria was the high sacred moment in evening service at the Black and Blue, Garland or MacDonald was the recessional. When this music came on, it was as though the curtain had been lowered and the show was over—or at least slowly ending. The lights were now on, some of the butch attitudes were dropped, and there was a friendlier atmosphere. And while Garland's and MacDonald's songs were different—the first is imbued with a melodic sadness and longing of wanting to be safe, sung in a warm, comforting voice; the second begins as a Victorian-parlor song ballad that breaks into a frantic 1910 rag, sung in a pure, if somewhat hysterical, soprano—they delivered the same message: this was over the rainbow, this was San Francisco, this was home.

The power and the draw of the Black and Blue and other sex clubs, aside from the fact that you could easily and randily engage in any number of sexual acts there, was that they gave many gay men a sense of home, a sense of physical, emotional, and psychological safety. They were havens in an altogether heartless world. And their genius is that they were created by the men who went there because they knew what they wanted and what they needed. It is this level of creativity—that is, actually changing the physical world—which, to a large degree, fuels gay and lesbian culture. If these sex clubs were theater, it was in part because the creation of theater—of art—is, in many ways, a response to having to live in this heartless world. It is a release or flight from the harsh reality of everyday life.

I've written at length here about Patrick Moore's daring reclamation of sexual freedom—in film, sex clubs, art: all manifestations of the imagination—but *Beyond Shame* has one final point. Moore, along with the most progressive thinkers and theoreticians of safe sex and AIDS prevention, understands that if we, as a community and a common culture, are going to deal effectively with the AIDS epidemic, we are going to have to encourage not less sex, but more sex.

To some this may sound counterintuitive, and to others as simply glib, early 1970s sexual-liberation rhetoric. And it is true that in the 1970s we did believe that more sex was always better, that any sex was better than none, and that sex could fix just about everything. And, indeed, on some metaphysical level we were right. The world would be a better place if the people living in it had more access to their sexuality, to their imagination, to their fantasies. What we did not understand in the 1970s, and barely understand now as a culture, is how entrenched and intransigent shame can be. Nor did we realize—despite our best efforts to pursue a vision of sexual freedom that was both liberating and joyous—that we did not vanquish shame. We just managed to push it to the sidelines. But in the 1980s the shame about sex that we had seemingly maneuvered around came back full force as shame about AIDS—which was, of course, shame about sex squared. How can we, Moore asks, teach younger gay men to value themselves and their lives—and to have safe sex —if they do not value their sexuality? Sexual liberation, he is claiming, didn't cause the AIDS epidemic, but it may be the only way to stop it.

What Patrick Moore has done here is to force us to look not only at the joys of sexual liberation and the dire effects of shame on our lives but to see that the only way to fight shame is to return to an earlier vision of sex as liberation and as joy. The sex clubs and alternative cultures that were envisioned by and created by the queer world, and which only became possible after the gay movement created a public space for them, were, at heart, a form of political resistance to a so-called "normal" world that attempted to control queerness through shame.

The celebratory, liberationist intentions of the Mineshaft and of the Black and Blue, of Fred Halsted's movies, and of *Fag Rag* was that they created a public space of queer shamelessness—a "vibrant sexual culture." It will certainly take enormous effort and time to rebuild these cultural and physical structures. For the time being, it will be enough to remember and honor them. But it is imperative to remember that this is not a sentimental project of memorializing "how good the old days were" but rather the first step in creating a new culture—not only in the face of the devastation of AIDS, but as a way to combat it— that will once again attempt to ignite our imaginations, spark our sexuality and creativity, and replace shame with joy.

To the extent that my age, sexuality, background, political beliefs, and life experiences align me with a subset of the American population, the views expressed in this book could be said to be both personal and representative of a larger group. The problem is that the larger group with which I should feel an affinity no longer exists *as* a recognizable group. There are certainly other gay men in their thirties and forties who survived AIDS but were permanently changed by it. There are other such men who were politicized by the disease and have now reverted to more traditional lives. And there is most definitely a large group of men who have lived their entire adult lives with AIDS coloring their feelings about sexuality. But these groups of men do not form a community.

The word *community* is problematic in describing the wild diversity of gay people in America but I use it hopefully in this book, believing that it is still possible for gay Americans to have some sense of connection. When AIDS was still considered a gay disease in America, we were a kind of community, albeit one bound by regret. And before we began to see ourselves reflected in the mass media, we were a community drawn together because of our mostly secret lives as sexual outlaws.

Our connection at the moment is shame. We are a community of shame. Shame defines our view of a sexual past that segued into AIDS, confirming to us our worst fears about ourselves and lending the condemnation of bigots a truthful echo. Shame motivates our forward movement as we fearfully suppress images of gay people as sexual beings, encouraging instead non-threatening roles (parent, homeowner, or campy friend) that prove "we're just like you." In our community of shame, we believe that by actively forgetting the past we can erase it, and many important parts of our legacy are now being lost or willfully abandoned.

If the gay community's sense of itself is mired in shame, it will continue to be nearly impossible to reach young gay men with HIV-prevention messages that create the sense of self-worth necessary for them to make healthy decisions about sex. This sense of shame also reinforces negative messages that young black gay men, who are the group most at risk for HIV infection in the United States, are already receiving about the viability of living life as proud, openly gay men. Without a sense of pride in our history, the gay community will continue to produce a fatherless generation of young gay men, disconnected and unreachable during a critical period.

I want to acknowledge upfront that I do not come from the academy. Indeed, my career has been in the art world, while my thinking about gay issues has been informed from my work as an activist. If I have not referenced academics, it is simply because I am largely unaware of their work in this area. My hope is that this book, because it's written accessibly and employs a strong narrative, might reach a varied audience that includes general readers like myself who may not have read some of the fine academic writing that addresses similar issues.

While I have not written this book as a memoir, it is has been shaped by certain facets of my life. My fascination with the sexual culture of the 1970s derives largely from the fact that I did not experience it directly. Born in 1962 and raised in Iowa, I was not able to make my way to New York City until the early 1980s. By the time I arrived in New York, the sexual culture that I had heard so much about was already very much in decline and what remained was joyless. To my great disappointment, the ascendant culture of New York at that moment was the East Village art scene, which always seemed vacuous to me. My first real engagement with gay culture came with ACT UP (AIDS Coalition to Unleash Power), where I found, for the first time, gay men (and women of all sexual preferences) who served as aspirational models.

My concern with the AIDS crisis found its purest expression during my time in ACT UP. However, my critical thinking about AIDS and its cultural impact really began when I was hired by the Alliance for the Arts to create the Estate Project for Artists with AIDS. The Estate Project was an attempt to recognize the loss of artists and artworks during the AIDS crisis, to preserve some of that work, and to act as a catalyst in getting powerful institutions to present the work to a larger public. What I realized over the decade that I worked with my colleague Randy Bourscheidt at the Alliance is that judgments about the talent of a particular artist are almost always transitory and personally biased. I also began to realize that, for me, the excellence of a particular work of art was not the reason for preserving it. The reason to preserve art endangered by AIDS was that these artworks—"good" and "bad"—had the unique ability to capture a sensibility that was rapidly disappearing. For me, an AIDS activist videotape or a 1970s porno was as worthy of preservation as a painting or a ballet. A connection with these artworks and artifacts was a way for me to begin to dispel the sense of shame that had insinuated itself into my view of gay history.

Looking back, my years of preserving the work of artists with AIDS were an attempt to preserve a sexual culture that I was never able to directly experience. Edmund White has described the sensibility that was lost to AIDS as a kind of bohemianism. (In 2001 the University of Wisconsin Press published an anthology titled *Loss within Loss: Artists in the Age of AIDS,* edited by Edmund White for the Estate Project. White's introduction to the anthology provides an excellent overview of his concept of gay bohemianism.) From the perspective of someone who never lived that life, I see in the 1970s a willingness to live a life where one's sexuality was used as the tool for radical change. This book is an attempt to encourage gay people to see the sexual experimentation of the 1970s as a powerful and laudable part of our legacy rather than as an act of self-destruction. Perhaps naively, I also hope that the straight world will begin to see the sexual experimentation of gay men alongside the more radical elements of that era's antiwar, civil rights, and feminist movements—as part of a wide spectrum of sometimes threatening but historically important creative actions toward social change.

In the 1970s gay men used sex as the raw material for a social experiment so extreme that I liken it to art. I should be clear that I am using the idea of sex as art as a metaphor, a way of taking pride in a time that is now unfairly enmeshed in a web of grief and shame. Having worked in the New York art world my entire adult life, I am under no illusion as to the reality of what is considered art in this country. For my purposes, I am defining art as creative exploration and expression, and, therefore, I believe that gay men were at the vanguard of artistic life in America in the 1970s. The art that I describe in this book is more likely to be a man playing a role in a sex club than a man choreographing a ballet. In that context, I have included a profile of the filmmaker Fred Halsted, whose mind-bending S/M films played in both porno theaters and the Museum of Modern Art. I also talk at length about the nightclub impresario Bruce Mailman and his club, the Saint. Important gay art in the age of AIDS, I believe, was more often displayed during an ACT UP demonstration than in an East Village gallery or onstage. No artist better straddled this divide than David Wojnarowicz, and I write of his ability to create powerful works of art based on emotion rather than the crass trendiness of the East Village scene in which he was first discovered. Other artists such as Cookie

Mueller and Felix Gonzalez-Torres are also represented in these pages as creative people emblematic of an era influenced by AIDS. And I remember the poet Assotto Saint because he was my friend and a fine writer but also because I admired his fierce pride in being a black gay man.

My reference to some of the figures I write about as artists when they would not usually be considered so is not meant to denigrate the traditional view of art, but it certainly reflects my opinion that creative individuals themselves are as culturally significant as the works they produce. It is also reflective of my stance that the compartmentalization of art is one of the primary reasons for its irrelevancy to most of American life. Why must our definition of art be so narrow? Gran Fury, a design collective associated with ACT UP, was absolutely right when it stated in the 1980s, "With 42,000 dead, Art Is Not Enough." But I do think that to *live as an artist* is enough, and that artistic, ecstatic ways of living were available to a wide array of gay men in the 1970s. These lives of radical exploration, using the sexual self as an instrument, required a courageous willingness to risk absolutely everything. As a gay man who missed those years, I refuse to abandon their memory.

Despite our shame and exhaustion, the gay community must also, unfortunately, reclaim AIDS. In our rush to find compassion, we have willfully ignored the fact that AIDS in America remains a gay disease and, therefore, has special needs in terms of both treatment and prevention. (This statement is not meant only to be a provocative opinion; it is based on widely reported but much ignored epidemiological data that is detailed in this book.) So eager are we to be compassionate to those in the developing world afflicted with AIDS, we have lost sight of the reality of the disease in America. The reality of AIDS in America is that gay men of color—finding no home in either their birth communities or the highly commercialized, white gay world—represent the majority of HIV infection in America. The time has come for the gay community to take responsibility for reaching these gay men *as* gay men, insisting that their lives are as important as the first group of gay men lost to AIDS in the 1980s.

This book attempts to draw a line between two topics—the gay male sex art of the 1970s and current ownership of the AIDS crisis in America—that might not initially seem linked. Even to those of us who worked in the AIDS field and were proud of our activism, it was incredibly difficult to reconcile a sense of pride in our sexual culture with the overwhelming grief for loved ones infected with HIV through unprotected gay sex. For all of our bravado and sex-positive messages, we have carried with us a belief that we got what we deserved. For men of my generation there was the double bitterness of living constantly with death without having enjoyed an earlier era when sex was less associated with guilt and shame. Our task of reclaiming both the gay sexual past and AIDS as vital but *separate* histories is daunting but central to our hopes for a healthy future.

Even though infection rates continue to rise in our young men, exhaustion and the empty promises of seeing ourselves represented in the mass media have lured us, despite American statistical evidence to the contrary, into saying, "AIDS is no longer a gay disease." We desperately want to believe that the gathering storm clouds will break elsewhere this time. Inherent in our ability to ignore the continuing influence of AIDS on gay life in America is our systematic effort to strip gay life of all associations with the radical sexuality of the past. If there is no sex, no memory of sex, and no current sign of sexuality, then we can hope that AIDS will pass by our doorway this time.

As much as I admire the experiments of the 1970s, I regret that they included a loss of connection between gay men and lesbians. As I interviewed both men and women who lived through that critical male/female split, I have heard different reasons for it. Perhaps the only thing that people agree upon is that it occurred and that women are to be credited for healing many of those historic wounds through their incredible AIDS work. Much of this book pertains to the experience of gay men, and I often use the word *gay* to mean gay men. But I want to acknowledge that my political awareness has come mostly from women, and I thank them for their generosity in continuing to care about the lives of gay men.

In presenting a polemic on the gay male sexual culture of the 1970s, I am not implying that lesbians and heterosexuals were not embarking on their own sexual journeys at the same time. However, I don't feel the same need to revitalize those legacies, nor do I have the experience to speak about them authoritatively. I believe that gay male sex, now so entirely identified with AIDS, is in particular need of a corrective.

I hope that as we fight for the absolute surety of gay marriage, adoption rights, and the other hallmarks of traditional families to which many of us aspire, we can also embrace a more experimental past. Unless we want to create a world of "good gays" and "bad gays" we will need to make room for those who do not wish to lead lives that mirror a heterosexual model. I propose that we rip away the veil of AIDS that brings shame and regret to a past that deserves to be remembered, studied, and taught to new generations.

It is imperative that we find a way to move beyond shame. Because of a lack of continuity between generations and a disavowal of our sexual history, the gay community has arrived at its present state: disassociated assimilation that excludes all except those leading the most traditional of lives. This is not a call to rise up against straight America or a belief that we must return to sexual extremism; it is more a plea for the gay community not to abandon its own history in exchange for empty promises of assimilation. We should not mistake visibility for civil rights. While it is undeniably an important development, I do not see the recent Supreme Court ruling repealing sodomy laws as a panacea for the range of injustices gay people still face in the United States. Corporate America's recognition of our economic power as a consumer group is a matter of business, not respect. And it is a matter of life and death that we remember that we share a common legacy that includes the sexual artistry of the 1970s and the devastation of AIDS. The pain that we have gone through does not enfeeble us. We are not shamed by our explorations. We are strengthened.

Before

CHAPTER I

The Great Experiment

Let us think of time as a theater. In that theater, we, the audience, are seated in the auditorium of the present. We are looking at a stage hung with a scrim that is the public recognition of AIDS in 1981. In front of that scrim, on a narrow strip of stage, scenes are played out—the early hysteria, the scientific discoveries and setbacks, the activism, the struggles, and, of course, death—illuminated in the proper historical context of AIDS.

However, behind that scrim of AIDS lies another stretch of time that extends to the back of the theater. Let us say that the Stonewall Riots form the sturdy bricks of the theater's back wall. In between that back wall and the scrim, backstage, are the years 1969–1981.

It is very difficult for us to see those backstage years. They lie in shadow, hidden behind the scrim, illuminated only dimly by the light of AIDS. All scrims become opaque when they are lit from only one side and we, the audience, sit in the present, viewing those years through the lens of tragedy. If we turn to speak to our neighbors, they too see the dim backstage from the same vantage and our conversations inevitably reflect the present even though we are speaking of the past. When the houselights lower in the theater and we are left with our own thoughts, what do we feel? Many in the audience feel shame. The entirety of their past plays out with death in the foreground. From a seat in the present, the past always looks like a carefully planned march forward and we can no longer clearly see the motivations of those actors moving backstage because their strange actions are obscured by a massive scrim that has unexpectedly lowered itself.

If that scrim remains forever lowered, there will soon be a day when it is time for us to stand up from our seats and walk out of this theater, into another one. Perhaps in the next theater, a comedy will be playing rather than a tragedy. There will be another scrim, behind which AIDS will then lie in the darkness, unseen behind the farce played out under the bright lights. And soon, the audience will forget that backstage of the 1970s in the original theater ever existed. The tools and actors and scenery and script will lie in the murky darkness, forgotten and moldering.

We are in danger of forgetting what was interrupted, and perhaps lost, because of AIDS. We have lost the opportunity to complete a great social experiment initiated by gay men using their bodies and sexual creativity. We have lost the conception of sexuality as an art form created by gay men in the 1970s. We have lost the vanguard of American culture when the creators of the true sexual revolution, the *gay* sexual revolution, died before the rest of America could see clearly what they had created. We have lost a moment in history when gay male sexuality was so radical that it might have transformed America by creating entirely new models of sexual interaction. In the 1970s, gay men initiated an astonishing experiment in radically restructuring existing relationships, concepts of beauty, and the use of sex as a revolutionary tool.

To reclaim this history, we must at least illuminate the scrim from both sides. The more somber light at the stage's front will always color the clear light of revolution and youth behind the scrim. But at least we can bring some balance to our view of the stage. Without being time travelers, no more is possible. But if it were? Were it possible to lift the scrim and step backstage, we would no longer be audience but participants again in a great experiment.

★   ★   ★

Beginning in the 1940s, gay Americans became involved in organized social change that was sometimes specific to the cause of homosexual liberation and other times embedded in the larger agenda of left politics. However, the number of gay men and lesbians willing to risk visible involvement in political struggle remained small until the Stonewall Riots of 1969. This book recalls and contrasts two relatively short periods of time—the expansive years following Stonewall and the crisis years following the first cases of AIDS: a "before and after."

The history of the American youth revolt, the peace movement, civil rights, and feminism has been told many times elsewhere. In this book, I hope to recast the gay male sexual revolution as a similarly radical and complicated movement. It is my hope that we can see the sexual experimentation of gay men in the 1970s without the filter of AIDS as a series of individual actions and cultural creations that were liberating to some participants and destructive to others, influential in liberal popular culture and deeply threatening to conservatives. If the following pages seem a romantic endorsement of activity that was viewed by many as hedonism, their extremity is necessity as a corrective to the widely held negative views that AIDS has created.

Let us look back to a time when Huey P. Newton, the Supreme Commander of the Black Panther Party, told his comrades, "Maybe a homosexual could be the most revolutionary."[1] At the time of his statement, issued as part of Newton's essay "The Women's Liberation and Gay Liberation Movements, August 15, 1970," the Black Panthers still regularly referred to any male enemy as "faggot." Newton's essay was at least indirectly a response to Jean Genet's displeasure with the homophobia of the Panthers at the very time they were asking Genet to rally support for them among intellectuals. The forced nature of Newton's statement does not minimize the idea that gay sexuality could be positioned as a revolutionary tool.

Around 1974, a gay male sexual culture began to coalesce that was so revolutionary, it seemed that Huey Newton might be right. This revolution, distinctly male and sexual in tone, would take place in a cultural rather than a political arena as gay men began to develop a distinctive lifestyle in which masculinized representations of beauty, sexual experimentation, and drugs were central. The steady increase in the migration of gay men to urban centers such as New York and San Francisco following Stonewall created conditions where there were enough visible gay men to sustain a new kind of sexual separatism. The gay ghettos of the Village and the Castro were dependent not only on the numbers of men needed to attain some degree of safety but also the number of customers to economically sustain the commercial establishments that were the primary sites of gay revolution in the late 1970s—bars, sex clubs, bathhouses, resorts, and discos. Twice the number of gay men moved to San Francisco between 1974 and 1978 than had in the previous four years. The arrival of twenty thousand gay men in the gay ghetto and experiencing gay sexual freedom, perhaps for the first time, naturally created a thriving sexual culture.

Certainly, this lifestyle was made possible by society's increased sexual permissiveness and the greater acceptance of drugs as part of a liberated urban society. However, gay men were to take this experimentation to a new level, utilizing their creativity and emotional depth. As Carl Wittman wrote in his seminal "Refugees from Amerika," "We have to realize that our loving each other is a good thing, not an unfortunate thing, and that we have a lot to teach straights about sex, love, strength and resistance."[2]

One method of presenting the 1970s without filtering them through the lens of AIDS is to look at the publications of the day. Many of the early political successes of the gay movement owe a debt to the network and sense of community that large publications such as the *Advocate* created. In the context of the 1970s, however, it might be more interesting to look at smaller, more radical publications that should continue to provide inspiration for both new political thought and the rediscovery of past radicalism. The Boston cell of the Gay Liberation Front (GLF) created the most interesting of these small publications, called *Fag*

Rag, in 1971. Although GLF quickly dissipated, *Fag Rag* continued to publish until the early 1980s. Ironically, the term *faggot,* which had been denounced by Huey Newton, was picked up by gay radicals, in much the same way that Queer Nation would later revitalize its nom de slur. It would be easy to marginalize *Fag Rag* were it not for the fact that it was clearly not just operating on the fringes of the gay world and included interviews and writing by such prominent gay intellectuals as Gerard Malanga, Christopher Isherwood, Gore Vidal, Allen Ginsberg, William Burroughs, John Rechy, and Ned Rorem. From the beginning, *Fag Rag* presented a far more complicated view of gay life than the *Advocate*. In so doing, *Fag Rag* was more revolutionary, as well as more fun.

There were other widely read gay magazines of the day but they tended toward campiness, which reached its zenith in *Queen's Quarterly*. This particular mix of camp and Midwestern practicality would later be resurrected in the 1980s and 1990s to cloying effect in the form of drag shows, gay public-access television programs, and performance art. *Queen's Quarterly* included such features as "Goin' Crabbing—On You," "Turning On with Aphrodisiacs," "V.D.—The Gift of Love," "Tea Time at the Orgy or How Not to Throw a Gay Party," "Decorating a Stylish Apartment at Half the Cost," and "Poppers—The High Price of Turning On."

In contrast, *Fag Rag* was not camp. It melded a Gay Faerie sensibility with left politics, and didn't hesitate to throw in some good pornography as well. *Fag Rag* is of singular importance because it articulated a far more radical and isolationist view than the earnest coalition-building so common in gay politics. It also resisted a commercialized vision of gay life where the "correct" body, disco, gym, and vacation spots were carefully identified as markers of belonging. *Fag Rag* embraced gay male sexuality while insisting on critiquing it from a political perspective and denouncing a uniformity of male beauty.

An entire book could and should be devoted to the influential sensibility showcased in *Fag Rag*. It is worthwhile beginning a discussion of 1970s gay male sexuality with an extended look at *Fag Rag* because the magazine was one of the few places that presented the gay sensibility in all of its complexity. This was a gay sensibility that had little to do with practical legislative measures or the latest party on Fire Island. *Fag Rag* was addressed to the more "vulnerable" members of the gay community—"children, prostitutes, promiscuous, working class, transvestite."[3]

Fag Rag's most important writer was Charles ("Charley") Shively. Shively's "Acts of Revolution" series presented a political strategy that positioned gay male sexuality and sensibility as the central tools for revolutionary change in America. Shively's voice ranges from inspirational and spiritual to angry and despairing over the years as he brings forward promiscuity, cosmetics, cocksucking, self-indulgence, and even incest as "fagly" acts of revolution. In 1976's "Incest as an Act of Revolution," he paints a gloomy picture of each gay man making an inevitable, forced return to the biological family that had once rejected him. "As faggots we may leave the family, reject its values and choose to live entirely outside marriage, home or family life. Yet even the most independent are forced back during some crisis like imprisonment, illness or death. At such times, unless you're rich and famous, you have nothing if you have no family."[4] This gloomy assessment of gay life was proven eerily accurate a few years later as many gay men were forced to decide between ending their lives with their urban gay families or returning to their hometowns and biological families.

Far more often, though, Shively's writing for *Fag Rag* was simply exhilarating in its honesty and outrageousness. In "Cosmetics as an Act of Revolution," Shively again strikes home in his critique of objectified physical beauty in the gay community:

> Although I refused to ever be a man, I had no special desire to be a woman; in fact I had contempt of cha-cha shoes, bubble gum, hair curlers and make-up in general. I disliked these things not because they were effeminate but because they were middle-class. My mother had none of them. While I often deplored the fact that my mother was so ugly ... on a deeper level I admired her general indifference to beauty and society.[5]

Fag Rag defined the gay community as inherently revolutionary because of its sexual practices and the ability of those practices to bring into question the morals (monogamy) and institutions (marriage and the church) that were at the center of American capitalism. While blacks had been central to left politics because of external oppression, fags were the center of a new kind of revolution because of their internal nature. If gays (women disappear entirely from the equation in this more sexualized definition of community) were to be defined by their sexuality, then they would welcome that definition and utilize their sexuality to its fullest as a revolutionary act. "According to one account, the greatest empire in the world fell apart because of self-indulgence and lack of personal discipline. Now if cocksucking could bring down Rome, think what we might do to Capitalism and the American system of imperial terror.... SHOW HARD. MAKE DATE."[6]

Now that sex itself had been defined as revolutionary rather than shameful, lines of division became increasingly clear between gay male assimilationists and sexual activists. "These anti-indulgent faggots try to settle down, get a job, a permanent loving mate, go to church, give money to Globe Santa, wear the latest from either Sears or Bloomingdale's. They put down such indulgences as public sex, promiscuity, prostitution, pederasty and playfulness. (Although they often do these things privately, secretly.) Their ideal is to become indistinguishable from straight men."[7] Whereas a few years earlier, women had been seen as revolutionary comrades, there was suddenly an arrogant defensiveness about their presence in locations with a highly sexualized atmosphere. As gay men took center stage in a community notorious for its misogynistic door policies in gay clubs and bars (the only meeting places in an era before organized community centers), the relationship between gay men and women moved from an uneasy alliance to hostility. As accounts later in this book will show, the new arena of political revolution—the sex club—was almost entirely segregated, to the point that interested women had to resort to disguises if they were to witness the action. This, perhaps, is the most troubling aspect of the

politicization of sex that occurred in the 1970s. *Fag Rag* espoused
the belief that men should not follow women in terms of sexual
behavior. Interestingly, the publication pointed out that men
were often made to feel guilty for being promiscuous or participating in extreme sexual behavior because of "what they *imagine* to be women's desires."[8]

There were attempts by politically conscious writers to raise
the question of parallel concerns between gay liberation and
feminism. An unsigned editorial in *Fag Rag* in 1978 pondered
the issue: "It puzzles why gay men don't understand (or pretend
they don't, or want instead the safety of a flip answer), the connection between the sexism which women fight and the roles
into which gay men have historically been compelled to fit,
the sexism which makes sexual role models both possible and
enforceable."[9] The writer John Stoltenberg, who identified so
strongly as a feminist that he took pills to inhibit his ability to
have erections, which he found politically repugnant, also noted
this escalating division between men and women in the gay liberation movement:

> I think it's important to recognize that gay liberation began much
> closer to an understanding of the fact that queer men are stigma-
> tized because they participate in the inferior status of the female in
> a patriarchal, sexist culture. ... When I talk about the gay move-
> ment now, I'm talking about a movement that has really reneged
> on those revolutionary insights. The men are seeking enfranchise-
> ment from the dominant culture as men, and their civil rights as
> men are what they are agitating for.[10]

The radicalism and divisiveness of the ideas in *Fag Rag* express healthy political growth, a continuation of a process that
was leading newly politicized gay men through their adolescence. Unfortunately, this process too often involved derisive
judgments of one group of gay men toward another. Anyone
who has been to a gay pride parade can see this issue still being
worked out today as the "sweater queens" cringe at the appearance of the "leather queens," which encourages the "leather

queens" to intensify their sexual activities to further horrify the "sweater queens."

The men of the 1970s had clearly identified the question that was to persist through many years and tragedies—to pass or not to pass. As Shannon Austin wrote in *Fag Rag*, "To obtain any kind of acceptance we must show the middle-class that we pose no threat to them. To do this, gay men have stuffed their sexuality back in the closet to present the Gay Lifestyle ... and this trend of taking sex out of the Gay Liberation struggle is helping to make us a tolerated part of breeder society."[11] The late John Preston makes a similar point:

> Before, and even after Stonewall, the first impulse of gay activism, to be a form of progressive and even revolutionary politics, was left behind. In the place of that rebellious attitude there was an almost immediate plea for social acceptance. The first line of political defense was to proclaim our ability to have monogamous relationships.... The first line of moral defense was to declare that to have homosexual sex was no different than having any other form of sex.[12]

It is interesting to note that AIDS organizations were later accused of adopting some of the same strategies to "de-gay" the epidemic as a way of adding credence to the importance of the tragedy and obtaining additional funding for services and research. Had gay liberation enjoyed the luxury of another ten or twenty years of growth without the interruption of a terrible tragedy linked to these very acts of revolution, there may well have developed a culture that celebrated difference but insisted upon inclusion.

Many gay men who began the 1970s integrated into a political spectrum that included a broad range of left political struggles, found themselves finishing the decade in their own newly developed ghettos, where concerns of class struggle seemed not only far away but beside the point in the more personal explorations of the baths and clubs. Their explorations had become cultural rather than political and included openly gay theater, art, and writing that served to explicitly represent the sexual experience to a growing audience of gay men newly arriving in the gay ghettos. (Lesbians, who were more committed to political action, albeit in a feminist context, would later also turn to the cultural arena—in the shape of twelve-step programs, women's music festivals, and women's studies programs—where personal growth was valued over political change.)

When Huey Newton proclaimed that gay men might end up being the most revolutionary group of all, he may have envisioned activists who saw gays as simply another "oppressed group" (and perhaps not the most important one) fighting for change. Or could he have imagined a more loosely focused culture that was revolutionary through its inherent ability to threaten mainstream America? It would be entirely too easy and too depressing to say that the second half of the 1970s was defined by a selfish, isolationist embrace of sexual hedonism. Was it hedonism? As gay liberation became gay *male* liberation, it quite naturally became focused on sexuality. (These were, after all, men in their twenties and thirties for the most part.) The sexual culture that developed in the mid-1970s was not simply physical, nor was it overtly political. It was fueled both by subconscious needs and conscious acting out.

When we look to the history of early gay liberation, there is a tendency to valorize the tangible accomplishment of the movement in building institutions, networks, and political power. And it is absolutely true that without the institutions put in place between 1969 and 1974, the sexual explorations that followed would have been much more difficult. In spotlighting the sexual explorations that began in the mid-1970s, one need not minimize the groundwork that they were built on. However, the very nature of gay life between 1974 and AIDS makes it more vulnerable to being lost or being recast as personal indulgence.

We will, I believe, remember our institutions, the legislative battles, the fiery speeches, and the marches. It is our cultural, sexual legacy that is most at risk and needs to be reclaimed. We need to redefine the sex of the 1970s to capture its power and intent. These men were using flesh and spirit and sexual energy as their artistic tools. The sex of the 1970s was creative; it was art.

Sometimes new behavior is so revolutionary, so unlike what came before, that it is more appropriate to examine it in terms of art rather than social interaction. The concept of sex as art is helpful in that it can encompass both the acknowledged, romantic definition of sexuality as well as the uncontrollable, even destructive power of sex. The men of the 1970s seemed to be reaching for something that was beyond both physical release and political freedom. Theirs was a pleasure that brings to mind the Indian goddess Kali, with her terrible beauty and promise of redemption through destruction. Other artists have toyed with utilizing the body as an artistic medium. Artaud's Theater of Cruelty forced participants toward catharsis through extremity. Certainly artists such as Chris Burden, who had himself shot, or stuffed into a small storage locker, viewed their bodies objectively as tools. Other body artists such as Stelarc have explored Native American rituals using pain to achieve states of transcendence. But all of these other experiments took place primarily in theaters or art galleries, so unthreatening that they ultimately became something of a cliché. The limitation of this kind of body art is that the body is the only thing at stake, and the body is extraordinarily resilient. Manipulating the body quickly becomes rather tedious, whereas using one's body to threaten and change society as a whole is truly frightening.

Gay men in the 1970s took the radical step of removing the line between life and art, insisting that the performance not wait for the audience to arrive. People who are repressed tend to respond creatively, but that same repression also creates emotional damage, meaning that the sexual explorations of the 1970s, while creative, would also be marked by extremity. This is the most complicated and exceptional kind of art that knows no boundaries and is driven by urges that are not fully understood, even to the artist. Before AIDS, many of the gay men participating in the sexual experiment of the 1970s had already paid the high price of loneliness and addiction in exchange for their participation. The fact that the experiment included risks undertaken by emotionally conflicted men does not minimize their actions' importance as art or revolutionary practice.

If we define the sexual world of the 1970s as art, then the men who were visiting the Everard or stalking the piers or coming out of the Mineshaft into the morning light were artists. These men were artists using sex as their medium. The gay male community in the late 1970s might be seen as a collective engaged in an unprecedented exploration of their own minds and bodies. The very radicalism of this experiment, and its dependence upon drugs and extreme emotional states, ensured that some members of the collective would find spiritual ecstasy while others would find degradation. Because the experiment necessitated gay men isolating themselves from mainstream America in a way that reinforced the view of gay men as deviants, the stakes were very high.

Was this performance worth the risk? We cannot know, because the performance was never finished. It was a rehearsal that will be forever judged as opening night. And this, ultimately, is the cultural impact of AIDS. In addition to the loss of individuals and what they might have achieved, the investment in the great sexual experiment of the 1970s was forfeited and the behavior that made it possible was forever cast in the shadow of self-destructive indulgence. There was no time to integrate organized political work with personal, sexual explorations. The best that we can do is to remember, from their vantage point, the time when gay men lived as artists. When we speak of the cultural impact of AIDS, we need to talk about the loss of painters, filmmakers, writers, directors, actors, choreographers, and composers, but we also need to remember that there were few lines drawn between life and art during the period. (The Estate Project's primary work centered on the preservation of artworks in all disciplines as a way of remembering both the artist as a person and their artistic contributions. You can see and hear many of these artworks by visiting www.artistswithaids.org.) In a way, it is too simple to remember these men by their artistic production. We need to remember them by the culture that they created. We need to remember the gay men who led a life that, to them, was an inspirational, artful experiment.

CHAPTER 2

Theater of Pleasure

The Mineshaft

It seems a basic human inclination to remember important times in our lives by remembering physical locations. This can range from the "Where were you when …" way of remembering trauma to a more generalized remembrance of good times—"I remember that I was living on University Place and would go to the Jefferson Market." The enormity of certain periods in our lives makes discussions of ideas and emotion seem inadequate, almost trite. When remembering the sexual arts of the 1970s, it might be most effective to talk about the physical settings in which they took place.

Men who lived in major urban centers in the 1970s love to tell sex stories from the era. These stories inevitably have to do with a physical location, usually public to some extent. These stories are rarely romantic but tend toward awe, as if the participant had traveled to an exotic locale that no longer exists. And indeed, many of these foreign lands have disappeared. From the dangerously public cruising grounds of parks and restrooms (tearooms) to the decaying piers along the Hudson River, these spaces have either been repurposed for "legitimate" use or demolished. However, these types of public sex spaces are somewhat too public to fit into the category of art or theater. More interesting is the activity that occurred in the enclosed, controlled environments of private clubs, discos, and bathhouses. In these spaces, sheltered to some extent from the hostility of the outside world (which, of course, public-sex proponents would say adds to the sexual charge), patrons were free to explore with the aid of theatrical props, stylized gestures, and preselected interests. Simply by entering a bathhouse or a club, one was making a statement of interests and beliefs. The person entering the Continental Baths might also patronize the Mineshaft, but they had to adopt different personas for each—an actor performing different roles in two shows. This seemed to many like a kind of duplicity and still results in the snide accusation that the man who goes to a leather bar often also has an interest in floral arranging. This sort of observation, aside from being driven by fear, lacks an understanding of how people participate in art and ritual—an actor does not forever become the character that he portrays, the writer does not always participate in the behavior he describes, and the shaman is not constantly in a trance. The point of art and ritual is to leave the world for a prescribed amount of time, not abandon it forever.

In the 1970s much sexual exploration took the form of sado-masochism (S/M) and leathersex. One need not value leather-sex any more or less than vanilla sex to recognize that it represents the most extreme expansion from traditional American sexual behavior, and is inherently important as an exploration. S/M and the leather culture had been actively explored by a small group of gay men for years before becoming common in the gay world. In the anthology *Leatherfolk*, editor Mark Thompson outlines this history:

> Men in black leather—and *into* all that that implies—have been a visible part of the urban scene for the past 50 years. Immediately after World War II, a loose-knit fraternity of men who recognized themselves as social outcasts began to organize.... A new type of community, one based on intense masculine sexuality and the fulfillment of a previously unmet need, was created. This audacious escape from prevailing norms defined the leather image in the '50s and '60s. And along with this newfound freedom came further liberation from sexual taboos.[1]

The morality of extreme sexual exploration and the S/M world was strongly questioned by those who overtly identified with left politics or feminism. Although semipublic S/M sites such as the Mineshaft were still six years away when Ray Ryan wrote "Advice to the Wartorn" in *Gay Sunshine* in November 1970, he warned of the emotional and political implications of S/M, even as a private act, in relation to gay liberation: "We should cultivate a strong sense of dignity about our person, our bodies, rid ourselves of the repressive sexual habits which kept us down in filth—masochism . . . and sadism. . . . Sexual freedom is not freedom to degrade oneself. We should learn to love fraternally, honestly, in a comradely fashion which is befitting to revolutionary men, not as sexual objects."[2]

Leathermen would argue that their sex is, indeed, comradely and forms fraternal, honest bonds. And despite the criticism from within certain quarters of the gay world, leather culture was taken up enthusiastically by gay men who were coming out in the relative safety of gay urban playgrounds, eager to experiment. The extent to which leather became a part of gay male life in the 1970s, though, indicates a deeper connection between gay men and practices that were so thoroughly at odds with the traditional sexual norms that they had grown up with. The superficial trappings of leather are easily melded to stereotypical gay male interests—theatricality, costuming, and, of course, a worship of all that is masculine. However, the widespread interest in leather culture seems to indicate a deeper need on the part of gay men for rituals that make sense of their lives and that transform shame into acceptance. The writer and therapist Guy Baldwin has long been a vocal proponent of the positive powers of leather sex: "I came to learn that an S/M experience is my chance to have an intense physical and psychological experience that is mixed with primal sex energy. . . . When leather and S/M scenes were done in a certain way, we achieved a different level of awareness—we felt transformed into someone whom it felt better to be. Also, a kind of bonding occurred between S/M players that had been missing in our more usual sexual encounters."[3]

Baldwin, however, rejects the idea that this type of ritual was limited to contemporary urban gay men, preferring to put the leather experience on a continuum that stretches back past recorded history. He writes that "anthropologists have long told us about religious ecstasy being achieved by means of physical and mental stress. The institution of transformation through ritual ordeal is an established fact dating back from before the development of writing."[4]

As an arena for gay liberation, the leather bars and S/M clubs were mostly closed to lesbians. Baldwin was very much part of the leather scene of the early 1970s and is now acknowledged as one of its elders. Baldwin explains that he was not so much opposed to the presence of women (indeed, he supported the inclusion of kinky women) as to the presence of outsiders. However, many of the men whom Baldwin describes as the old guard of the era were from a military background: "As such, they were used to being in a homosocial environment, away from women. Part of the male ritual bonding stuff that takes place on the battlefield ... there was a real desire to preserve that. Add to that, these were gay men who wanted some distance from women because in their regular lives they had to pretend to be interested in women."[5]

Perhaps the most famous S/M club that ever existed was New York's Mineshaft. Opened in October 1976, the Mineshaft operated continuously until 1985 at 835 Washington Street (the corner of Little West Twelfth) in the Meat District. Other clubs and private parties catered to even more specialized tastes, but the Mineshaft epitomized the sexual frontier. Although it was always rumored to have been Mafia-owned, the Mineshaft was managed by the godfather of leather sensibility, Wally Wallace, who died of heart failure in 1999. In the *New York Blade*'s obituary of Wallace, Arnie Kantrowitz is quoted as saying, "He taught us all what it is to act like a man. He was the set designer for exposing the beautiful, darker side of our sexuality."[6] The Mineshaft seems to have functioned as a sort of main "set" for the playing out of powerful fantasies.

From John Rechy's carefully articulated trails in LA's Griffith Park to the endless descriptions of the Everard Baths, gay men have always tended to imbue their sex sites with special powers. Laud Humphreys noted this in his landmark study, *Tearoom Trade: Impersonal Sex in Public Places,* in 1975: "I have noted more than once that these men seem to acquire stronger sentimental attachments to the buildings in which they meet for sex than to the persons with whom they engage in it."[7] The physical space of the Mineshaft, as well, has taken on mythic qualities as gay writers try to explain the powerful atmosphere of the club.

In his novel *The Golden Age of Promiscuity,* Brad Gooch describes the music that was so much of the atmosphere, "music that included Philip Glass, Steve Reich, and many other minimalists ... music that was labeled 'sleaze.'... By dawn there would always be full electronic Vangelis chords mixed with Mahler while attendants stuffed black hankies and paper towels into ... cracks in the wood and cement that were admitting offensive rays of morning's early light."[8] Gooch goes on to describe the lights of the club: "He felt he'd walked into a pumpkin, black inside but artificially lit by red and yellow glows. It was that amber again, the amber of the movies, but mixed with coal dust."[9]

In his forthcoming essay "Staging Masculinity at the Mineshaft," the architect and scholar Ira Tattelman looks at the Mineshaft and other sex clubs as "an arena for the masculinization of the gay male."[10] Rather than gay men turning to gritty clubs housed in old warehouses because they had no other choices, Tattelman believes that the participants responded to these clubs because they were carefully constructed to re-create physical settings such as parks, docks, alleys, trucks, and garages that carried with them a sense memory of sexual excitement for men who had previously been forced to enact their rituals in dangerous public spaces. Tattelman describes commercial (these were businesses, after all) settings, where "within the safety of a male domain, men questioned the reality of sexual categories and the stability of a single identity. They were willing to take on different personas and positions depending on the moment and desire." As Tattelman points out, these spaces were public in the sense that participants acted out their rituals observed by fellow participants and, in so doing, the clubs also became spaces for education:

> Men gained confidence by seeing other men engage in sexual behavior. They became bolder, their activities heightened and intensified.... The clubs used the conceptual apparatus of theater and spectacle in order to form space and facilitate activity.... With self-sustaining and self-defined codes, postures and clothing, men acted by themselves or with the crowd. By playing with their appearance, they changed self-perceptions and stretched their limits.

There were other theatrical sex venues in New York at around the same time as the Mineshaft. Arnie Kantrowitz remembers a bathhouse called Man's Country on Fifteenth Street, where "they had a setup on the top floor which looked like the back of a truck and a fake jail cell, so you could act out fantasies in a very clean, pristine environment."[11] The owners of the bathhouse had simulated half of a truck on the top floor, which evoked for many men the experience of having sex in the trucks parked in the streets of the Meat District or on the West Side Highway when it was covered by an elevated roadway.

The Mineshaft's layout seemed intended to take one very literally on a journey. Even the walk to the club, through the Meat District, was dramatic. The Meat District was, at the time, largely deserted at night, with the processing plants shuttered, scraps of meat and fat laying on greasy streets, and sharp hooks swaying empty on tracks used during the day to transport carcasses from trucks into the shops for disassembly. Burning trashcans, industrial buildings, and the shadow of the abandoned High Line (the elevated railroad tracks) all added to the sense of adventure and potential violence. One reached the black wall of an industrial building punctuated by an unmarked door that opened directly onto a flight of stairs. Either waiting in line silently with men dressed in jeans, leather, uniforms, or, if there was no line, climbing toward the entrance, one had already be-

gun the experience before entering the club proper. There was
a doorman at the top of the stairs who dispensed the first exercise in humiliation for those dressed in sweaters, dress pants, or
smelling of cologne. These potential patrons were either rudely
rejected or made to remove an offending item of clothing.

Thus, one arrived on the second floor of the building that
served as the first floor of the club. The design could be compared to a roller coaster or a log ride at an amusement park
where one creeps slowly up the first incline, turns onto a short
level stretch, and then plunges into oblivion. The "first" floor of
the club contained the necessary elements of transition—a bar
where conversation was allowed, a bathroom, and a coat check
for those who wanted to be nude or further costumed. Moving
back away from the front bar, one approached slings, restraints,
and a "glory-holed" wall. Extreme sexual activity including
fisting could be found here but it seemed, somehow, a prelude
to what lay below.

Having climbed one set of stairs to enter the club, one had
to plunge back down either another set of stairs or a kind of lad-
der into what seemed to be a basement but was, in reality, street
level. Here conversation largely stopped, except for whispered
commands and guttural sounds. In earlier types of public sex in
truly public settings such as tearooms, silence was essential for
maintaining the fragile environment of unreality that allowed
for acts that were literally dangerous, imbued with the fear of arrest or violence. In sex clubs those fears had been largely eliminated, but the environment remained a theatrical construct that
could not be sustained in the presence of "casual" conversations.
Carefully assembled music had replaced silence and only words
that fit within the "roles" of the participants could safely be in-
jected into the environment.

This carefully modulated atmosphere of the "basement,"
reached after passing through a series of checkpoints and small
journeys, readied one for sights and sensations that would otherwise have been so jarring as to jolt one out of the experience.
This was the reason that the bathtubs were located on the lower

level, carefully lit and beyond the reach of reality. The cluster of bathtubs was an otherworldly sight, and the piss pigs lying in them, ready for use, seemed to have reached an altered state not just from whatever drugs they might have been using but from the act in which they were absorbed. Their pleading eyes looked elsewhere. Having reached a place in themselves so deeply identified with ancient wounds and desires, they took part in a ritual that seemed to many to be one of the final rites of passage. Until the next weekend.

Although this layout is how most patrons remember the Mineshaft, the club was actually simpler and filthier during its first few months of existence. Originally, the club occupied only the second floor of the building and included a scat room (soon abandoned as too intense even for the Mineshaft patrons) and a piss room sans bathtubs that also proved to be hygienically challenging. A bartender wielded a grease gun filled with actual motor grease that prepared those who were to be fisted. With the club becoming more and more popular during its first few months, the club's management decided to avoid some legal liabilities by bringing down the raunch quotient and providing additional space downstairs, where most patrons were in reach of fire exits. It is fascinating to find that even the most extreme of the sex art sites had an earlier, smaller, more extreme incarnation that most initiates never experienced.

What happened in the Mineshaft and in other extreme sexual settings is often described as "play," a word that seems completely inadequate to describe what was a deadly serious ritual, replete with physical and emotional danger long before AIDS was identified. These rites, at least in public, were not undertaken with a sense of transformative joy. Rather, they were enacted by grim-faced men who knew in their hearts that they were embarking on a journey from which they might never return. Surely to call this "play" shortchanges an experience that was the highest form of participatory art, creativity, and ritual—the kind of ritual that gives and takes without permission. I have never spoken to a man who, whether they loved or hated the

Mineshaft, was not changed forever by seeing the darker side of their sexuality within its walls.

In "The Mineshaft: A Retrospective Ethnography," anthropologist Joel Brodsky makes the case for the club being more than simply an erotic indulgence but "a place of transformative experience and possibly awesome rituals."[12] Brodsky identifies S/M as a type of performative art but correctly notes that sociologists have pointed out that, in theater, most performers maintain a distance between themselves and the roles that they play. Herein seems to lie the potential danger in the Mineshaft experience for those who were perhaps too fragile or not prepared for the extreme trip they were about to take. The danger was probably greater for casual visitors who had not been vetted and prepared by the old guard system that Baldwin describes. For the men who became regulars, the old guard system not only validated their qualifications but also provided a support system for their explorations. However, in the world of bars, many participants operated in isolation, perhaps never even speaking with another man. The intensity of the experience, for the unprepared and unsupported, could make the rest of life seem beside the point, leading to more and more extreme participation that could either be liberating or addictive, depending upon the person. However, in the end, observers such as Brodsky tended to consider the Mineshaft and other similar clubs as relatively safe alternatives to the alleys and piers for sexual exploration. Because there were many men generally exploring the same theme in the club, it provided a supportive forum for a wide range of men to participate in a collective activity that otherwise may have seemed to them shameful and isolated: "The ability of the Mineshaft experience to accommodate the individual homoerotic realities of hundreds, if not thousands of gay men, was its most interesting feature. While each participant performed his own ritual with his own meanings, the Mineshaft functioned somehow to hook up all these performances with a common set of facilities, rules, symbols, and emotions."[13]

Sex clubs were also a venue for men who were not, in the

larger society, considered attractive because of age or appearance. Kantrowitz talks of the appeal back rooms had for these men: "Especially in dark back rooms, you could actually be pretty much nothing more than a shadow. Even the homeliest of men could have what they wanted. Maybe not if what they wanted was adoration and love, but they could certainly have sexual experiences."

The hypermasculine look of the leather scene eventually became commercialized and reached a mass-media presence in the form of the Clone. The Clone look was described by Edmund White as "a strongly marked mouth and swimming, soulful eyes (the effect of the moustache): a V-shaped torso by metonymy from the open V of the half-buttoned shirt above the sweaty chest; rounded buttocks squeezed in jeans, swelling out from the cinched-in waist, further emphasized by the charged erotic insignia of colored handkerchiefs and keys ... legs molded in perfect, powerful detail; the feet simplified, brutalized and magnified by the boots."[14] Add a leather jacket and a cap and you're at the Mineshaft. There was, however, a further distinction between the Clone look that reached all the way to Middle America via the Village People and the redefinition that was going on at the Mineshaft. The mainstream Clone was a commercialized emblem of masculine sexuality, which still depended upon beauty. The late porn-star Al Parker typified this kind of Clone. Al Parker would have been a strikingly handsome, beautifully built man regardless of his style of dress and facial hair. His sexual appeal was still dependent upon his beauty.

The Mineshaft and the world surrounding it took a far greater step in redefining sexual appeal. In the world of the Mineshaft, masculinity replaced beauty as the prime determinant of sexual appeal. In the dark caverns, an ugly lug with a beer gut, bald head, and hirsute back could be the hottest guy in the place. This butch realness, of course, often did not translate fully to the light of day, but in the silence of those dark caverns, it was beyond real, it was a transformation close to magic. There was a beauty and power bestowed on the masculine tops by their submissives, in defiance of the outside world. The worship of that considered ugly by the straight world was another kind of revolt against traditionalism, made all the more powerful because it was predicated on deep emotional needs rather than passing styles.

Genet thoroughly mined this territory in which exchanges of masculine power supplant the usual expressions of romantic love. Genet's *The Maids*, the story of two maids role-playing in a room temporarily vacated by their mistress, is sometimes presented with men playing the roles in drag because it so accurately expresses the pathos of the oppressed creating private rituals to compensate for their lack of power in the real world. The atmosphere of the Mineshaft was not so different from that of *The Maids*. In the carefully constructed unreality of the club, men were given rigid roles that satisfied their creative need to respond to the oppression of being a gay in an unaccepting world. Bottoms would abandon themselves to the exhilarating release of brutality and violence, while tops would grab back the authority they lacked in the outside world, dominating others in the darkened rooms. It was a world in which masculinity replaced beauty, and brutality was a kind of love. But, as in Genet's world, morning always waited. No matter how the men of the Mineshaft stopped up the cracks in the walls or painted the windows black, the knowledge that their magic did not work in the sunlight beyond the thin divide adds a note of sad complexity to their creative accomplishment.

CHAPTER 3

Another World

San Francisco and the Catacombs

One need not fetishize the Mineshaft to find evidence of transformative (one might call it religious) experiences in the sex art of the 1970s. Essay after essay in *Leatherfolk*, edited by Mark Thompson, is an ode to this experience. In his introduction, Thompson articulates the view of S/M (and nearly all of the sex in clubs like the Mineshaft was of the S/M variety) that has long been used as a positive explanation of these rituals: "S/M actually means 'sex magic.' It is their art and craft and means of taking a shamanic journey into the 'other world' of personal and collective myth. It is in that secret inner place where the healing occurs."[1] Thompson identifies a range of social clubs such as gay biker groups, gatherings in people's homes, and yearly invitation-only gatherings such as Chicago's Hellfire as well as more public clubs as sites for such explorations. The participants in rites of sex magic should be given a special place in the avant-garde of gay liberation, as Thompson explains: "It occurred to me that what had been marked as excessive or at fault was perhaps no more than a necessary stage of behavior and identity formation in the liberation process. No one can ever really say how much is 'too much' on the path of freedom until the farthest reaches have been touched."[2] At the end of Thompson's introduction to the book, he quotes a section of a Robert Chesley play. (Although Chesley was best known as a writer, he was also a composer. Chesley, along with hundreds of other composers

and performers, is included in the Estate Project music archive.)
These lines, spoken by a character looking out at the dawn,
comprise surely the most articulate possible description of the
creative journey embarked upon in the 1970s:

> I left my body for a while a few hours ago. Call it a waking dream
> if you want. You can discount it; I don't. I floated above myself,
> right up to the ceiling, and I looked down on everything that was
> happening; and it was beautiful. It was men making love so in-
> tensely and so courageously that all the barriers were down, and a
> connection existed above and beyond the boundaries which sepa-
> rate one human being from another: above and beyond the bound-
> aries of time, the boundaries of life and death.... There's a greater
> truth in visions.[3]

Although sexual artists were performing across the country
by the mid-1970s, there were important differences in how this
art manifested itself in different regions. Because New York and
San Francisco had the two largest scenes, it is interesting to compare them. In the *Black Sheets* "Sex Pioneers" issue, Bill Brent
asks a man identified only as Lewis to talk about the two cities:

> It seemed to me that the focal point of life in San Francisco was
> sex, whereas in New York, the focal point of life was having an ex-
> tremely complex, busy life, in which sex was as intense as one's
> work.... My impression was that one's sexual life here [San Fran-
> cisco] was the defining, central occupation.... They'd fuck all day
> long, and were stoned all the time, and no one ever seemed to
> work.[4]

Guy Baldwin agrees with this assessment and proposes a theory for the more compartmentalized nature of gay life in New
York. He thinks that there is a certain truth to the idea that New
York is a careerist culture and California a leisure one, and "to
the extent that careers need to be protected, people have a
greater need for secrecy."[5] As gay mecca, San Francisco presented
sex not as a component of life but as life itself. By the end of the
1970s, because of their sheer numbers, gays in San Francisco
were not only able to create a strong and separate subculture,

they had the political clout to protect their establishments from police interference.

One of the most fascinating essays in *Leatherfolk* is by the anthropologist Gayle Rubin and describes the most famous of all fisting clubs, the Catacombs, which operated from 1975 until 1982 in two different locations in San Francisco. If we think of the Mineshaft as the apotheosis of the New York experience and the Catacombs as an exemplar of San Francisco, interesting comparisons of the clubs and the cities they represented can be made. Of course, neither club was typical of its city, but neither are the best museums or restaurants of those cities; they represent something extraordinary about the city's spirit. There were, of course, similarities between the clubs. Both clubs were shaped by the sensibility of a gay or bisexual man (Wally Wallace for the Mineshaft and Steve McEachern, who founded the Catacombs). By all reports, the music tapes compiled by these men formed much of the atmosphere inside the clubs, leading participants through a progressively more intense journey as the night wore on. Both clubs were also carefully designed to provide an area of rest and transition before entering the more heady areas of the club. In the Mineshaft, this was the bar area on the "first" floor, whereas at the Catacombs, it was (in the club's first location) the front room:

> The front room was the social area of the Catacombs.... An extraordinary collection of male erotic art graced its walls.... Many of the pieces were artifacts of leather bars already by then old and gone.... The front room contained a "bar," although no alcohol was sold.... The front was where people would come in, sit down, greet their friends, do their drugs, finish their manicures, and make the transition from the everyday world into "play space."[6]

Already one can see key differences between the coasts. New York favored commercial or industrial locations marked by a theatrical grittiness. While the New York clubs had regulars, membership was little more than a legal strategy to protect the club from more stringent enforcement. Ownership of the club was obscure: although the Mineshaft was closely identified with

Wallace, he is alternately described as owner and manager. While the interior space was carefully conceived, it was not particularly comfortable. And the atmosphere in New York certainly did not lend itself to chatting while doing a manicure at the bar. The atmosphere at the Mineshaft was one of defensive, anonymous mindfuck rather than camaraderie.

The Catacombs, on the other hand, was built by a gay man in the basement of his Victorian home. Steve McEachern was the visible and proud owner who fostered a sense of friendship and community among the regulars. The club's membership was originally limited to McEachern's friends and he maintained a careful screening process even as the club grew larger. He took care to build a space that was adequately heated and provided amenities such as cans of Crisco hanging next to each sling for easy access. These may not have been the kind of home improvements most gay men were making to their restored Victorians, but they do indicate a level of pride that comes from ownership and a care for the participants.

Warmth and community, of course, are not necessarily attributes in the world of S/M sex art. One might make the case that New York's cold theatricality was the very thing that made it so exciting. However, San Francisco's sense of connection may have provided the kind of setting that would have allowed for continuity and growth had the sexual revolution continued. This is especially true in the single most striking difference between the coasts—in very limited instances in San Francisco, women began to become part of the radical gay male sex scene and, later, this experiment was extended to the bisexual and straight world. As one looks at the contemporary trends of tattoos, piercing, and the new practice among college-age girls of "hooking-up" (basically, having anonymous sex), one wonders how pervasive the seemingly marginal rituals of the Catacombs might one day have become were it not for AIDS.

This furthest step in the 1970s sexual revolution, the breaking down of gay male barriers against women in the sexual arena, seems to have begun in the relationship between the owner of the Catacombs and a woman named Cynthia Slater.

Slater, who is reported to have called herself a gay man with a cunt, had an affinity for the sexual culture of the gay male leather scene and pursued access to it with an astonishing lack of fear. Slater and a few other women began to walk brazenly into leather bars on Folsom Street despite harassment. (Guy Baldwin was initially one of the few men who supported Slater's presence in the bars.) Their outrageous behavior and lack of fear soon earned them a token slot in the gay male sex world. In her essay on the Catacombs, Rubin describes the route that brought Slater into the Catacombs: "In 1974, she founded the Society of Janus, which quickly became a point of connection between straight, bisexual and gay sadomasochists in the Bay Area. Through Janus, Cynthia also made contact with Steve and the Catacombs. By 1977, she and Steven were lovers. Steve eventually decided to allow Cynthia into the Saturday night parties."[7]

Guy Baldwin points out another important reason that Slater was able to broach the barriers to her presence in the club: "Remember that the Catacombs was largely a fisting palace and an interesting partition was beginning to be seen in the radical sex scene between S/M guys and people exclusively into fisting. The reason that Cynthia was able to so successfully insinuate herself into that situation was that she had a little hand and she could be a sort of cherry popper."

As one might imagine, the appearance of a woman in an all-male fisting club initially caused some distress among the participants. Perhaps because of her singular appreciation of gay men, Slater overcame this resistance and became a regular feature at the club. In 1979 Slater began a women's night at the club that later opened the doors further to a "mixed-gender/mixed-orientation S/M party" in 1980. Rubin describes the widening effect of those early experiments:

> The successors to these early mixed parties would eventually become a local tradition. While the mixed parties included both men and women, they included too many gay men and lesbians to be straight and too many heterosexuals to be gay. Although they provided opportunities for experimentation, they were not about getting people to abandon their different orientations. On the con-

trary, by fostering an attitude of respect for difference, the parties created a comfortable atmosphere in which diverse populations could observe one another, appreciate their mutual interest in kink, and discover what they did have in common.[8]

While McEachern and Slater were both gone by the end of the 1980s—he of a heart attack and she of AIDS—their experiment did seem to yield some lasting results. One of the most notable was the late 1980s/early 1990s sex and art scene in Los Angeles typified by Ron Athey, Catherine Opie, Bob Flanagan, and other Club Fuck participants. Again, gay men, lesbians, and heterosexuals came together in a creative environment (albeit a more self-consciously arty one) to break boundaries.

Not all women were willing to wait to be invited into the male sexual laboratories of the day. In her "Queen for a Day: A Stranger in Paradise," Rita Mae Brown tells of penetrating New York's Club Baths on First Avenue in 1975. Wearing a disguise including a moustache, Brown is taken into the baths by a male friend, and her account of the experience provides a fresh viewpoint. She is constantly aware of her otherness in the setting: "Naked I would become frightening to some of these men. Their sexuality depended on my absence. Men are terrified of being women; they don't want to identify with us in any way— and gay men are no exception. We still aren't people."[9] Perhaps Brown's most important observation, however, has to do with class:

> Since class peels off with clothing you might think a democracy of nakedness and need would develop. But here in the cubes [cubicles] a new hierarchy took place among these lawyers, artists, grocery clerks, stockbrokers, movement activists, professors, and cab drivers. Rank now came through size of penis, condition of body and age.... The irrationality of the flesh commands. Here the great American principle of competition and performance keep those on the make hungry, frightened, and slightly savage.[10]

Perhaps Brown's observations would have been different had she been able to visit a club like the Mineshaft, where definitions of sexual attractiveness were more sophisticated. She surely would have found a different hierarchy in a club like the Catacombs. Brown criticizes the fact that, although the usual class rules are subverted in a sexual environment, a new class structure quickly takes its place, with the young and the hung ranking highest regardless of their financial, social, or intellectual standing. While her criticism is accurate, it misses Samuel Delany's sexualized concept of interclass "contact" described later in this book. Brown would do well to acknowledge that, despite the inherent cruelty toward those who are not traditionally beautiful, the gay bathhouse (and other sites of gay male sexuality) brings together different classes and enables interaction between them. While it is true that the stockbroker might only approach the cabdriver in the bathhouse because of his penis size, it is also true that they would have an intense physical and, perhaps, emotional interaction. They might also talk afterward and actually come to know something about each other's lives. Surely, the opportunity for men of different classes to know one another and maybe even form relationships, no matter how tentative, is a positive addition to the functioning of the world. Beauty is no fairer than birth in determining access, but at least different determinants were at play in the sexual world of the 1970s.

Arnie Kantrowitz describes an atmosphere of friendly decency that evolved out of the mixing of people at the baths:

> Almost every single encounter ended with, "You're a hot man. Ciao." It was that kind of very friendly anonymity. I remember once at the Everard Baths somebody coughing as he was walking down the hallway. I wasn't thinking germs, I was thinking, "Hello, somebody in distress." So I slapped him on the back, he said thank you, and we went our way. You couldn't do that on the street with a stranger, but there was a sense of brotherhood [at the baths]. We were outside the margins; we were living in a protected environment. You could be *anyone* in a towel. They couldn't tell if you were a garbage man or a professor or an astronaut or whatever.[11]

CHAPTER 4

The Saint and the Beginning of the End

The S/M experience of the Mineshaft and the fisting experience of the Catacombs were only half of the sexual experiment that was played out in a more social way by the men of New York's Fire Island. The two groups had members in common, certainly, and visited one another's haunts, but the way that they manifested the ideals of sexual liberation could hardly have been more different. The lives of Fire Island men, whom Felice Picano describes as the group that could fit into the Ice Palace on any given Saturday night, appear to have been more holistic in defining a gay life that included the socializing of the beach and dinner parties, as well as the sex and drugs that connected all of these activities. And most of all the men of Fire Island were defined by dancing. As Picano recalls, "It was the age of the Tenth Floor, The Loft, Twelve West, Flamingo, and then The Saint. They were all private gay clubs. You had to be a member to get in."[1]

Indeed, the Fire Island experience seemed to many to be the pinnacle of an idealized way of living and partying. Kathy Watt is the executive director of the Van Ness Recovery House in Los Angeles. The Van Ness House is the longest-serving drug-treatment program for the gay community in the world, and Watt is uniquely qualified to speak of the special role that drugs have in gay life. She talks admiringly of the continuing influence of the scene: "Fire Island was an incredible place then. It was almost like there were no identities. It didn't matter whether you were gay or straight—you did the drugs and had the sex.... I think our sense of how you party started in Fire Island and we still try to re-create it."[2] Watt raises an interesting point about the influence of Fire Island for straight people and, potentially, as an intersection between the tastemakers of the heterosexual world and the gay artists, performers, writers, architects, and fashion designers that made Fire Island their home each summer. Certainly, it was easier for the straight world to appreciate this "done" world of beach houses and elegant dinner parties than the roughness of a sex club no matter how aesthetically innovative it might have been. The tentative moves of the straight world to explore the gay clubs and bathhouses tended to be interactions of prurience rather than participation, whereas Fire Island had a long history of straight communities that bordered gay Cherry Grove and the Pines, as well as a regular influx of straight weekend guests.

Picano is the great chronicler of Fire Island in his novelistic memoirs *Like People in History* and *A House by the Ocean, A House by the Bay*. He describes a classless society, mixing the rich and famous with those whose admission price was paid in beauty. This was not a completely hedonistic world devoid of the political consciousness of the early 1970s. Picano remembers many of the early politicos of gay liberation vacationing on Fire Island, although many of them were later based in Cherry Grove as the Pines became increasingly expensive. However, Arnie Kantrowitz, who spent several summers in Cherry Grove in the 1970s, saw a limit to even that community's openness:

> We were a group from GAA [Gay Activists Alliance] and we shocked Cherry Grove. They don't have addresses there; they have names of houses. One house was called "White Swallows." Another one was called "Wounded Knees." Some of them were just cutesy, like a purple house called "Catherine the Grape." We called our house "Gay and Proud," and it upset everyone. It just said so much that in Cherry Grove, which was the gay fantasy come true, they still didn't like it said out loud.[3]

Picano, and the men of Fire Island, saw the beauty and pleasure of their lives as a political act in and of itself: "As soon as you got on the Long Island Railroad to go to Sayeville, you were making a statement." Indeed, the lives of these men were a political statement, and the culture they were actively creating must have seemed revolutionary. As Picano asserts, these were men who had grown up in an extremely repressive society and took incredible risks emotionally, financially, and physically to participate in an entirely new culture.

> It's so hard to see what life was like before the revolution because the revolution was won.... To grow up in the '40s and '50s, you were in a repressed, completely homogenous society where children and women were objects. It is very difficult to explain what life was like then because it was so repressed. Those of us who rebelled were actually a very, very tiny minority. To get involved in any of these things, it was social death for you; it destroyed your academic career. You were taking enormous risks just by being in SDS [Students for a Democratic Society]. So to go from the civil rights movement and SDS into gay rights, you really had to cut off all ties in your old life.

The men who were identified with Fire Island also had their destinations in the city during the winter. Picano was a devotee of the Flamingo, a private gay dance club downtown. He points out that an important aspect of clubs like the Flamingo, the Loft, and the Tenth Floor was their size. Because they were intimate clubs, Picano remembers, the experience included the warmth of knowing almost everyone there: "People from out of town who went to the Flamingo had a fabulous time and said that they felt that they'd been to a gay political rally the night before. Just being able to do what you were able to do there was political."

In 1980 a consummate businessman with a talent for commodifying and packaging gay sexuality provided a climax for the sexual experimentation of the 1970s. The downside to any climax is that it indicates an ending, and Bruce Mailman's nightclub the

Saint provided a showy conclusion to the sexual exploration that was truncated by AIDS. In 1979 Mailman reopened the St. Marks Baths, which had since 1915 served as a gathering place for the Lower East Side's male immigrant population. In the way of many New York bathhouses, the St. Marks had gradually become primarily a site for gay sex by the 1960s, and by the 1970s it was a dirty, unsafe establishment. When the Everard Baths burned in 1977, Bruce Mailman realized that the S/M crowd that had patronized the Everard was without a bathhouse and he purchased the St. Marks Baths with the intention of creating a new kind of stylish, masculine setting for sexual exploration.

As influential as the New St. Marks Baths was to gay life in New York, Mailman's club, the Saint, was a far more important creation. Mailman was the gay-nightlife impresario who successfully commercialized the Clone lifestyle and brought it to new heights through the Saint and the New St. Marks Baths. Picano and many other gay men of the era have an ambivalent view of Mailman's contributions:

> The Saint was much colder, much bigger. With the Tenth Floor and Flamingo, you pretty much knew everyone there. It was that condensed of a group. We looked at the Saint as the commercialization of the scene; it let in too many outsiders. I'll say one thing for Bruce, though. He was, in his way, a visionary about gay liberation and equality. When he created a clean sanitary bathhouse, he gave a vision of gay life that was very positive. Did you ever see the poster for the New St. Marks Baths? That man on it was triumphant, triumphant!

Mailman did indeed see the cleanliness and high style of his establishments as hallmarks of a newly open society where gay men could demand, and deserved, certain standards. Mailman himself was a shadowy figure, rarely photographed and mostly unknown to the patrons of his facilities. Marisa Cardinale, who is currently a consultant to the Robert Mapplethorpe Foundation, met Mailman in the early 1980s when she worked at the Civilian Warfare Gallery. (Mapplethorpe's lawyer, Michael

Stout, was an investor in the Saint and Mailman's confidant.) Mailman was a collector who, Cardinale says, could be "counted on to buy the toughest work—Greer Langton sculptures and Wojnarowicz."[4] Cardinale also says that the aesthetic of the baths and the Saint came directly from Mailman—"metal, muted colors, black and red. Very Halstony. Silhouettes of orchids."

Mailman was a brilliant businessman who scolded Cardinale about using her own capital when creating a business. Mailman's ability to attract a range of investors for his seemingly marginal businesses was astonishing—Janice Ian was an investor in the New St. Marks Baths. He also counted such unlikely figures as Larry Kramer among his inner circle. (Kramer and Mailman were later to fall out over the fight to close the baths in New York because of AIDS.) As with many famous people, Mailman was also known for a certain amount of self-invention. Cardinale recalls hearing short, bald, and furry Mailman boast to new acquaintances that he was "a child model."

It is important to note that Mailman was not just an investor in his establishments, he was a participant. He would have his room at the baths on a Saturday night. He went to the Saint and summered on Fire Island. As both creator and participant, Mailman insisted on environments that reflected his taste and suited his needs.

While the Saint is often seen as a commercialization of the Fire Island Clone lifestyle, it was more accurately a commercialization of the aesthetic developed at the Mineshaft and leather bars, which was then grafted onto a dance club. Boundaries between the Fire Island group and the men of the Mineshaft were fluid. While there was naturally a sort of rivalry and cattiness, there was also a curiosity about what was going on in other quarters. Picano remembers he and his Fire Island friends visiting the Mineshaft and appreciating its existence: "The Mineshaft was part of gay liberation. You had to come up with your particular set of beliefs or dogma. It was sort of a walk on the wild side if you did that. I didn't really utilize it but I was glad it was there. Every time that we heard something new was going on we went to take a look. 'Oh, they're pissing on people in bathtubs. Oh, look at that. Next.'"

It is interesting to note, however, that by the time Picano and the other men of the Pines went to dance at the Saint's Black Party in 1982, those same bathtubs were adorning the ramps leading up to the dance floor, along with motorcycles and bondage racks. (Flamingo had hosted a Black Party in 1978 for its smaller, more tightly knit membership that set a precedent for the larger event at the Saint.) What had been the tools for sexual experimentation had become the props for theatrical abandon. The Saint brought a high-style masculine sensibility into a disco environment dripping with sex, which became an entirely new gay creation. The work that had begun in bathhouses and leather bars coalesced into a more public venue that could accommodate thousands of the world's most powerful and beautiful men, bringing them together on a Saturday night for a celebration that was, simultaneously, the culmination of the 1970s and the inexorable slide into the 1980s.

The Saint opened in September of 1980 in the East Village. The Saint's building had an impressive pedigree, having housed the Fillmore East—site of legendary concerts by the likes of Hendrix, the Doors, Jefferson Airplane, and Joplin. Mailman had looked at other venues on the West Side as well as around Union Square, but the Fillmore East made brilliant business sense because, after a night of dancing, members could walk the few blocks from the Saint to pay another cover charge at the Mailman-owned St. Marks Baths on a Sunday morning and then later wander back to the club for the Sunday movies and tea dance. The Saint's building was originally built by the Loews Company and opened as the Commodore Theater. Given its theatrical past, it is appropriate that the Saint's physical environment shared, on a much grander scale, some of the theatrical tricks employed by clubs like the Mineshaft. One entered not into the main auditorium of the club but a lounge area that provided visual preparation as well as amenities such as a coat check and a place to do the night's drugs as well as an area to retire to throughout the night when the experience became too overwhelming.

The first floor of the Saint typified Mailman's industrial design aesthetic, with gray carpeting on modular units, black walls, gleaming metal, and high-tech video displays. Towering floral displays provided notes of softness and drama. Mailman hired the architectural designer Charles Terrel and a team of decorators and lighting people to create a seamless environment. The dark surfaces provided the perfect backdrop for the hordes of muscled, shirtless men who had perfected the masculine theatricality of the Clone look. The dark gray and black environment was also endlessly adaptable, as the club was redecorated almost every week for a new theme. Mailman took particular interest in selecting the themes and delighted in outrageously expensive projects such as covering the entire downstairs in Astroturf for a football theme. Mailman and his partners poured nearly five million dollars into the club, which was initially budgeted at two million dollars. Much of the budget was invested in the second floor—a nearly five-thousand-square-foot circular dance floor under a planetarium dome illuminated by a professional star machine and powered by a sound system with five hundred speakers. Above the dance floor and behind the veil of the dome was an enormous, multisectioned balcony that served as the main sexual site for the club.

As opposed to earlier generations of piano bar patrons who tended toward cocktails that encouraged sloppiness as the night moved on, the Saint's men were highly skilled chemists who projected a cold power that was maintained right up to the moment when they overdosed. There was no staggering at the Saint, only collapse. Mailman's initial design for the club included a black dance floor, but management soon realized that a dark floor and a dark sky with rotating stars left the drugged dancers with no point of reference, and the floor had to be stripped to keep people from falling. The club had no liquor license, a calculated move to avoid city regulation, but also because Saint members preferred drugs to alcohol.

Richard Peters would later become known to the Saint's staff and patrons as Nurse Peters. In 1980, before the club had even opened, Peters was approached by a friend to become its maintenance person. Peters, a hard-core Mineshaft man, had little interest in working at a new club for Fire Island queens. It wasn't that Peters had anything against Fire Island; in fact, he "grew up there" with a series of "aunts and uncles."[5] It was just that the disco scene seemed to hold little appeal for a Mineshaft devotee. However, the prospect of employment eventually won out over disdain and Peters began working at the Saint shortly before it opened. Even in the daytime when Peters was picking up after construction crews, the club was undeniably impressive, but it took until the Saint's first Halloween party for Peters to actually return to the club after midnight, when it opened to the public.

Peters quickly came under the spell of the club as the man who wielded the wet-vac, cleaning the acres of gray industrial carpet, soiled from a weekend of sweat, and giving the dance floor a quick layer of baby powder in between the Saturday night extravaganza and the Sunday afternoon movies shown in the dome before a gentler Sunday night party. Although he became closely connected to the club, it took a change of top management before the Saint grew to be central to his life. Soon after the club opened, its first manager, Jack Stoddard, decided late one night that he could fly and took a test flight from the railing of the balcony above the dome. Stoddard (who died in 2002 from AIDS) was reassigned back into the Mailman organization and Mailman brought in one of his employees from the baths to manage the club. Peters says, "I was a Mineshaft guy. I liked sleazy and dirty. All of a sudden this new guy, Elliot, showed up to manage the club. He was a short, stocky bodybuilder with dirty fingernails. I just thought ... yes." Elliot Segal was well known in the leather scene and beyond. He had, in fact, appeared in a famous series of Mapplethorpe S/M photographs.

Peters soon became Segal's right hand in managing the club. Peters recalls that he, Segal, and others at the club during its first, greatest incarnation were all from the leather world. Their aesthetics were not only seen in terms of theatrics at the Black Party but in the general dress code enforced by "big leather queens" hired to do the door. Many of those Mailman hired to run the Saint came from within the ranks of the New St. Marks Baths, which was already a masculine, theatrical setting for S/M sex. Therefore, it is not surprising that the Saint would have been so heavily influenced by the S/M world.

The club reigned as the destination for the group Peters describes as "artists, lawyers, doctors, city planners, people who ran the world." Peters quickly developed a niche as the person who would help the influential patrons who had overindulged, either getting their clothes out of the coat check and helping them into a cab or laying them down "to relax" on a foldout cot in the nurse's station that had been improvised next to the staff lockers.

Peters gradually became identified with his niche at the club. Peters was vacuuming in the balcony one day before the club opened when a voice came over the loudspeakers, "Nurse Peters, Nurse Peters, you're wanted in the emergency room." The name stuck and Peters had found a role. He recognized nearly every face of the five or six thousand members who might fill the club on a Saturday night and genuinely cared for their welfare as they walked into steel beams or tumbled down staircases under the influence of coke, mushrooms, mescaline, acid, Quaaludes, and a variety of other substances. These substances sustained both the members and the staff. Peters had a team of ten or twelve young Puerto Rican men, recruited from the baths, who would assist him in maintaining the club. He and his team received "tips" in the form of dividing up the numerous joints, bottles, and other lost drugs that would be found in massive amounts after every party.

Nurse Peters's patients were soon facing a far more serious challenge than navigating the club's staircases. The membership of the Saint was one of the first groups to be decimated by AIDS; in fact, AIDS was known in certain circles as "the Saint's Disease." Because they were at the center of this group, the Saint's staff saw signs of danger long before the gay community in general. In 1982 word was coming in fast and furious about new casualties. Nurse Peters was working the balcony, trying to pry men apart and educate them about new sexual dangers; a thank-less and largely ineffectual task. By 1983, Peters and other mem-bers of the Saint staff were telling Mailman that he had to close the St. Marks Baths. According to Peters, Mailman, who died of AIDS in 1994, not only resisted the idea but fired the upper-level management at the Saint for suggesting it. Around 1984, with AIDS in full swing, new management and a new aesthetic were installed in the Saint—sexy sleazy S/M was out and a preppy polished look was in. Mailman had brilliantly built a commer-cial aesthetic that was no longer suited to the marketplace, and being a businessman, he naturally changed it to suit the new re-alities of business in the gay community.

Susan Tomkin was Mailman's assistant from 1980 until his death and she sees the transition of staff at the Saint differently. While she confirms the flying incident and others involving Jack Stoddard ("He tried to put me through a plate glass window one night"[6]), she feels that the Mineshaft crowd represented by Segal was never a real fit at the Saint: "Elliot was at the baths and Bruce brought him over when things happened with Jack. So Bruce brought Elliot over but I think he regretted it about two minutes later. Elliot didn't belong there. He never belonged there and Bruce fired him."

Tomkin relates the change in management not so much to a desire to "clean up" the image of the club as a need for a more efficient staff to manage a thriving business: "Bruce wanted peo-ple he could count on. When Joel Teitlebaum and Jason Mc-Carthy came in after Elliot left, they were totally devoted. Joel lived for the Saint. Elliot tended to give away a lot of Bruce's things, a lot of money. I don't think Elliot Segal ever wanted to close the baths."

It is unclear whether Mailman was uncomfortable with the leather crowd as AIDS began to spread. Mailman seems, above all, a pragmatist and one would assume that he simply looked for a staff that could continue to effectively run the club. What is clear is that the people who worked at the Saint in its early years and those who went there to dance were fiercely devoted to the club. There were clearly different factions who hoped to claim an ownership of the place but were frustrated to find that Mailman both literally and aesthetically owned the Saint. If the Saint utilized the masculinity of the leather world, it did not embrace the messy realities of small, poorly run clubs. Immense amounts of money were flowing though the club and Mailman ran a tight ship. He had perhaps learned a lesson from the travails of Steve Rubell and Ian Schrager at Studio 54; Tomkin relates Mailman's belief about money: "Everything was very honest in terms of money. There was so much cash. Every penny was accounted for. There were a lot of partners and they all wanted to see what was happening to their money. We couldn't take a chance. He didn't think it would be worth it. It was easier to be honest."

One can understand the Saint closing—the opening of the club to the straight world in the mid-1980s would dilute the experience, and Mailman himself had lost interest as his health began to decline. But the Saint did not just close. It is as if it were excised from the earth, along with the Hudson piers and much of the Meat District and the Times Square porn theaters and so many other sites of gay history. On a videotape in the collection of the New York Public Library, one can watch the artist and gay activist Copy Berg sitting in the window of his studio, talking about gay history and the vitality of the downtown leather scene. In the background, a wrecking ball slams into the side of the Saint, remorselessly erasing it from New York life, making way for another beige apartment building. Because there are so few opportunities to remember the gay male culture of the 1970s, it is doubly painful to think that even the physical settings so important to the time are now gone forever. In a final insult, a marble plaque has been attached to the bland exterior of the Hudson East apartment building that is perched upon the Saint's former site. It reads:

> On this site once stood the Loew's Commodore Movie Palace, the Fillmore East Theater and the Saint discotheque. Dedicated in celebration of all those who came to watch, rock and dance.

★   ★   ★

The Mineshaft, the Catacombs, the Saint, and the sleek houses of the Fire Island Pines are only some of the most visible sites that formed the map of gay male sexuality in the 1970s. Men were, of course, meeting in the streets, in tearooms, in bathhouses, and elsewhere. These settings were more common but less interesting in terms of defining sex as art because their physicality was diffused, less a staged coming together. However, the entire gay male sexual culture became incredibly influential as a vanguard in America's mainstream sexual revolution. This visibility would also lead to the scene's demise.

Gay men have always enjoyed a strange dual status in American society that *Fag Rag* identified: "We are considered animal/base because our only defining characteristic is sexual; at the same time we are paradoxically seen as an effete part of the ruling class—given over to music, philosophy, decoration, poetry and other intellectual pursuits."[7] American culture depends upon groups like African Americans and gays to continue the process of growth. One sees this cross-cultural movement most clearly today in the fascination of white suburban youth with rap culture. In the 1970s pop culture produced clear indications of gay influence through disco music ranging from Sylvester to the Village People. While this is a healthy aspect of American life, it inevitably leads to the dissipation of vital subcultures as they are consumed and commercialized by the wider public.

Herein lay one of the problems for the gay community in utilizing sex as a political tool in the 1970s—the experiment was so easily co-opted by the straight world. Because the gay community did represent these two apparently opposing traits—primitive animalism and high aesthetics—its sexuality was easily commercialized and added to a list of thrills for the straight world that might easily include skydiving, excessive drinking, and ... a trip to the gay baths. As early as 1973 *Rolling Stone* reported on the chic new trend of celebrities such as the Prince and Princess von Furstenberg and media mavens from *Women's Wear Daily*, the *Washington Post,* and the *New York Post* attending cabaret performances at the Continental Baths. "Gay men—and in the past year, straight men and women—have responded in numbers.... On a recent Saturday night, there were 1,400 customers at the baths."[8] The Continental Baths were perhaps the epitome of such a crossover hit, fueled by its owner Steve Ostrow, who apparently lived the lifestyle of an openly gay man while married to his wife, who was the manager of another branch of the bathhouse. *Rolling Stone* breathlessly reported that "about a year ago, Ostrow realized that his pleasure palace lacked a couple or three things: There was no live music and no women—except for the occasional visits by his wife and his mother."[9]

Arnie Kantrowitz feels that much of the power of the gay sexual world was sapped by the inclusion of outsiders: "People came to look at us like we were goldfish. And we lost our specialness, our privacy. The secrecy was part of gay culture and now gay culture was going to change by our very openness." Kantrowitz goes on to describe the complex emotions produced by being on display at the Continental Baths, in a world that was once entirely protected:

> So there was a kind of anger with which one would dance in front of straight people. I would try to make sure I would flop out or be particularly erotic until I realized I was some kind of freak show for them. I was the décor for their wild evening out. And I didn't like that.... It was like we were supposed to be thankful that they were willing to come in and sit next to us in our little den of iniquity.

More intense sex establishments such as the Anvil, a few blocks away from the Mineshaft in New York's Meat District, also enjoyed their straight chic periods. The Anvil was perhaps most open to allowing women into the club, at least the front section of the club where sex stage shows took place. Whispered reports after the weekend would tell of Lee Radziwill or Liza Minelli taking in the spectacle. In an article for the *Village Voice*, Kantrowitz recounts a straight couple in the audience greasing up with Crisco and fisting a performer apiece: "The married couple removed the audience one step further, rendering the whole thing not quite embarrassing but a little desperate, and certainly no longer exclusively gay."[10] Even the most extreme of the clubs, the Mineshaft, had become a tourist destination on Saturday nights. Kantrowitz remembers that regulars would no longer go to the club on a Saturday:

> The place on Saturday nights had become a tourist venue, people would come speaking lots of different languages. You knew that they were visiting the city and someone was showing off the lower depths to them. It became uncomfortable as it had at the Continental Baths. They were lightweights; they were vanilla people to the butch leather crowd that was supposed to be the mainstay of the Mineshaft. The original rules were you had to wear boots, not sneakers; they were really pretty intense to keep the mood they wanted. Eventually people were wearing all kinds of outlawed things, things the dress code did not observe on Saturday nights, and the real hard-core group wouldn't go on Saturday nights until four or five in the morning.

For all their power, the rituals that took place in the theaters of pleasure such as the Mineshaft were exceedingly fragile. The morning light, idle chatter, and prying eyes were sufficient to drain away the energy from what had been a closed world.

CHAPTER 5

Gathering Darkness

In addition to a sense of shame, for older generations of gay men, looking back to the 1970s involves nostalgia; for younger men, the '70s elicit envy. Both of these reactions tend toward a romanticism of the time that is as inaccurate as simply writing off the era as a time of excess that led to tragedy. It is important to acknowledge that, even if the intense sex art of the 1970s had not been co-opted by the mainstream and turned into a series of commercial enterprises, it would still have faced challenges other than AIDS. These challenges are reflected in the darkness that many participants observed coming over the gay male community around 1977 and intensifying through the end of the decade. Participants have identified many possible causes for the change of tone. Generally, America was in a somber mood, disillusioned with utopian left politics that had turned to violence in a country that had lost a war for the first time and witnessed the chaos of the Nixon administration. The golden age of American college life, where much political activity and social exploration had been centered, had also passed with the end of the student deferment in 1975 and the leveling off of population growth in the college-age demographic. Also, the gay male aesthetic was moving very quickly at the time, and new discoveries, as exciting as they were initially, soon became mundane routines. The wonder of sex palaces and dance clubs must have lessened after two or three years of almost constant attendance in them, after which the men had to consider them not as a novelty but as the central component of the rest of their lives. Because the lives that men lived at the time were so new, there had been no time to integrate the theatrical intensity into a fuller life that also included women and family.

From the vantage point of my generation, it is tempting to view the 1970s as emotionally uncomplicated because the participants had not yet experienced the trauma of AIDS. But in understanding the sometimes destructive choices made by these men within the larger context of a laudatory social experiment, it is important to remember that their entire lives had been shaped by oppression. With all their creativity, their social connections, and their relative wealth, these were men who had lived with the overwhelming sense of shame that was and is still a common denominator in gay life. The triumphant act of coming out and living an open life does not erase the damage done by living in fear during one's development.

I think, therefore, that it is important that we also look at the more destructive side of the 1970s sex scene but that we try to do so in the context of men who faced enormous emotional challenges. The excitement and pressure of the gay male sexual scene in the 1970s inevitably brings to mind the emotions of adolescence—for some the culture was one that finally delivered acceptance, even spiritual transcendence, while for others it was filled with cliques and cruelty. As in adolescence, there were many men who felt the pressure to belong to one or all of these groups but who simply fit nowhere. As Picano recalls, the writer George Whitmore might typify this group of men:

> Even though he wasn't a Flamingo person, George Whitmore moved heaven and earth to become a member. Two people had to recommend you and he went for the interview and he failed and I remember him saying that he couldn't understand what happened. So I said, "Well let's lay out what this private club is all about. It's about attractive people (and you are attractive) who like to have sex (you're bad sex), who like to dance (you don't know how to dance) and who take a lot of drugs (you can't take any drugs). Why would you be interested in joining this club? Three of the four things it's about, you're not."[1]

Picano's kind letdown did not seem to assuage the pain of Whitmore, who in 1982 penned a bitter denunciation of the sex scene for the *Advocate:*

> It is 1981 and I am in the basement of the Mineshaft. Like most everyone else here, I have come to prove a point. The point is that we can do this without flinching. Oh, we might say we come here to have fun or let off steam, but there is an undercurrent here, a subtext. It is the element of risk. It is not just risk of disease. It is that we have learned to witness certain acts with a jaded and skeptical eye.... It looks dangerous, but is it really? This is the phenomenology of risk, and we are expert at it.[2]

Whitmore looked at the triumphant figure that Picano described on the poster for the St. Marks Baths and saw a very different archetype:

> The Rebel is a consummate symbol of reaction, because that's all he does; his life revolves around rebellion, fury and denial ... an emblem of misdirected rage.... If society tells him the only way he can be gay is to crawl around on his hands and knees in a sewer five nights a week, the Rebel will oblige ... and having fervently embraced the role assigned to him—that of outcast and pariah—he must never relent, relax or weaken. He is, instead, driven to further extremities of alienation. Intimacy becomes impossible, even the one-night stand variety. The only actual relationship is a dim, ironic camaraderie with his fellows.[3]

There were also gay men in the 1970s who had little desire to participate in the cultural experimentation of discos and sex clubs but rather saw radical-left politics as the more important arena of social change. Not all gay men in the 1970s saw the creation of an openly sexual culture as a sufficient response to the oppression of a range of people in America, and it is interesting to look at one such man. Ferd Eggan recently retired as the AIDS services coordinator for the City of Los Angeles but his position as a government official seems unlikely after hearing him talk about his political history. Born in Michigan, Eggan was immediately aware of and drawn to the political arena; he was the youngest person at the state Democratic convention, working for John F. Kennedy. He also followed the civil rights movement and, when Kennedy was shot, Eggan's political interests focused on new issues:

> When I went away to college, it became pretty necessary to get involved in civil rights issues and the war in Vietnam.... I became involved in antidraft and antiwar work at the University of Chicago and going to civil rights demonstrations down South for voter registration projects in the winter of '65/'66. That summer, I spent the whole summer in South Carolina, got run out of town, and had my first adult gay experiences.... I returned [to Chicago] pretty disillusioned but began to meet people who were continuing the antiwar work in Chicago who later became the nucleus of the Weather Underground.[4]

Eggan speaks of his periodic disillusionment with the political scene but he also brings to life the appeal that the civil rights movement had for gay men in the late 1960s. Beyond the utopian political ideals, few people have Eggan's honesty in describing the sexual opportunities that presented themselves in the movement. Interestingly, these liaisons between people of wildly different economic and racial backgrounds would later be mirrored in the encounters that took place in gay sex clubs:

> It was dynamic, it was very vital.... We were included in the thoughts of black leaders as helpful friends. For me, there was also a typical exoticism and orientalism coming from a small town where I had never seen any black people. It was possible for me to have sexual liaisons with black men that I had never thought were possible.... I was being approached by them and it had never occurred to me that that was how people handled sexual affairs.... People were so different in terms of my life experience, they were so welcoming and so full of vitality and so full of courage and bravery that it made a space for the white gay boys who thought their lives were inauthentic.

In the early 1970s, after a brief sojourn in New York to do art projects and drugs, Eggan became reacquainted with radical politics through a Gay Liberation Front living collective in Chicago and embraced a radical agenda:

> By 1977, I had become convinced that we, as white people, owed unconditional solidarity and support to the black liberation movement whether they were homophobic or not. That movement was so important as a motor to bring revolutionary change to this country that we had to struggle and push for our own existence but that had to be secondary to the things that would bring revolutionary change.... Most of my set of people, from the Prairie Fire Organizing Committee, would have stood with black people in saying that gay and lesbian concerns were secondary.... I now believe that was a strategic mistake.

The Prairie Fire Organizing Committee was the above-ground presence of the Weather Underground Organization (aka Weatherman), which grew out of Weatherman's 1974 publication of the book *Prairie Fire: The Politics of Revolutionary Anti-Imperialism.* (The group has been described by others as cultish extremists.) With the nation's bicentennial at hand, it was a natural time for organizing a counterpoint to the blind patriotism that swept the country. Eggan's reengagement with the movement as a gay man took place around the same time, in San Francisco, where he had moved:

> Nobody [in the civil rights movement] wanted to deal with the fact that they might be gay within these really tight clumps of people. They weren't particularly good at women's issues either although there was a lot of talk about women's issues. I remember reading the Leary thing ["New Morning, Changing Weather"] in 1977 on Haight Street and it seemed like they were trying to be more in touch with us rather than us just following them.... By 1977, our principal work was trying to win gay support for solidarity organizations.

In light of the 2001 terrorist attacks, it is increasingly difficult to view the violent tactics of the Weather Underground in a positive light. One might wonder, though, at the lack of violence in the gay liberation movement (and later during the AIDS crisis). Although the movement seemed to have lost the sort of massive support it enjoyed in the 1960s, there were remaining ties between gay activists and groups such as the Weather Underground that were utilizing violent tactics. Eggan points out that there were thousands of bombings of military targets in the United States between 1974 and 1977 by the Weather Underground and other organizations and that "there were definitely gay men and lesbians involved in that work." However, that violence remained isolated within small clusters of people with far-left concerns and never manifested itself in the gay community. The murder of Harvey Milk, and the subsequent slap on the wrist of his murderer, Dan White, precipitated riots in San Francisco but did not lead to an organized campaign of violence. One of the few whispers of what such a campaign might have become can be seen in the 1979 issue of *Fag Rag,* where an unsigned editorial proclaims, "The stone that's in your hand, my dear, has a date with a plate glass window."[5]

Eggan's reinvolvement with the movement came at a time when he and many other activists were feeling disillusioned with a gay movement that had lost its early revolutionary tones and seemed increasingly like an all-male consumer demographic. Eggan particularly points to the separation of gay men and lesbians as a crippling factor: "I had pretty much stopped seeing my women friends by then [1976/1977] ... so almost all of the discourse was among men.... Most lesbians who came to gay radical formations had some deeper reasons for their politics and some more utopian hopes for the community.... That might have been a better grounding for what might have come next."

Eggan, like many men, also had to find a way to participate in the new gay lifestyle, where roles were more rigid and the androgynous look that he both admired and put forward earlier in the decade no longer worked: "It became necessary to butch up, to wear a leather jacket, to go to 'stand and model' kinds of bars.... To be a disco queen seemed too much of a commitment to one way of being and to be a leather fag seemed like too much of a commitment to another.... There was a lot of being left out." Because of the extreme climate change in the gay community in the mid-1970s, there were many gay men who had stood at the center of activity earlier in the decade only to find themselves adrift in a new apolitical, sexualized world that seemed incongruous given their beliefs. Says Eggan:

> Many of us had a utopian, anticapitalist vision of the world and, when disco came along, it seemed like we had just become another consumer demographic.... I felt that the gay world had become a place exactly as hucksterish and consumer driven as what we were trying to leave. It was disappointing to realize that our own bodies were on the marketplace and were consumer objects.... You had to look good to be on the marketplace and that was completely antithetical to things that we thought we were building.

By the end of the 1970s, there was another key factor contributing to the approaching darkness of the scene. As important as the clothing, the architecture, the music, and the lights were to the sex art experience, they would not have come together to make something more than an exotic location were it not for the drugs. Many establishments did not even have liquor licenses, so drugs were doubly reinforced as the method of maximizing the evening's activities.

Guy Baldwin talks about the effect of drugs on the gay male sex world as part of a larger shift in society that had an intensified effect on this relatively small subculture:

> By the time 1977 rolled around, those of us who were in the leathersex world knew that unprecedented levels of erotic exploration had been achieved and drugs were a part of that. There was a mood change by the late '70s but the mood change was something that had been coming for at least ten years. By the late '60s, using marijuana and hashish became part of one's movement toward erotic liberation. Hallucinogens were added to that next. That all bled its way into the gay male world and certainly into the leathersex world. The smaller a social organism is, the more vulnerable to changes it is and the more reactive it is to significant influences.[6]

It was not the drugs themselves that were the problem; it was the intention with which they were taken. With the exception of crack and the repackaging of speed into crystal methamphetamine form, the drugs of the 1970s were little different from contemporary substances—pot, hash, mescaline, acid, mushrooms, MDA, coke, heroin, speed, and, of course, poppers. (Felice Picano tells of dealers "test-driving" new substances like Ecstasy and Special K on the willing Fire Island population of the 1970s.) What changed, to a degree, was the intention of the users, as Kathy Watt of the Van Ness House points out: "They had speed on Fire Island but they did it to party and have fun. Drugs were taken later to shut off the voices and try to fit in. Those are two really different things."[7]

The social aspect of drug use in the early 1970s was still related to the experimentation of the 1960s, where the experience was often collective, meditative, or focused, rather than the drugs being used simply for their own isolated effect. One might argue that "raves" present the same forum for experimentation today were it not for the fact that they are so commercialized, controlled, and isolated from the larger life of the participants. It is very difficult to participate in rave culture 24/7 in the way that men lived in the gay ghettos of the 1970s. This was not a lifestyle relegated to Saturday night. It was, rather, a commitment that was integrated into the daily lives of the men living it. Watt again points to historic changes in the role of drugs in the gay community:

> Up until 1987 or '88, drugs were part of socializing and you had to be almost off the scale in terms of hurting yourself or your life becoming a mess before anyone would say, "Maybe you need to get help." We joke today about how guys plan their vacations around circuit parties. Well, in the '70s, everything was planned around parties.... Drug use was totally acceptable.... It wasn't until alcohol torched your life that you got help.... Poppers were for all practical purposes legal.... They were like carrying around a roll of Lifesavers.... I think it was much the same with speed. Speed wasn't a drug; speed was what allowed you to do life.

The ubiquitous French philosopher Michel Foucault (who was later lost to AIDS) seemed to have something enlightening to say about every aspect of gay intellectual life, and he spoke readily of how his sexual explorations were aided by drugs. The drugs were, he said, "really important for me because they are the mediation to those incredibly intense joys that I am looking for and that I am not able to experience, to afford myself."[8] Foucault explains perfectly the sexual effect of drugs in opening up possibilities. "The apologia for orgasm made by the Reichians still seems to me to be a way of localizing possibilities of pleasure in the sexual whereas things like yellow pills or cocaine allow you to explode and diffuse it throughout the body; the body becomes the overall site of an overall pleasure."[9]

Although drug use may have begun in a more lighthearted, experimental mode as gay men entered the sexual arena of the 1970s, those prone to addiction were finding the experience darker and darker toward the end of the decade. The very physical acts that often depended upon drugs—fisting, heavy S/M—could themselves be addictive and brought with them a limiting dependence. In an interview on the 1970s in the sex journal *Black Sheets*, Mark Thompson said of the time: "I do want to emphasize the shadow side of the scene. Drugs were so common. More and more people were coming, and doing drugs. It was like tumbling down into this dark rabbit hole, and some of us could integrate that into a daily life, whereas others got stuck down that hole."[10]

In the same interview, the legendary gay activist and writer Joseph Bean responds with more specificity: "It was the dedicated fisters who brought what I consider the dangerous drugs into the sex club scene. Because, in effect, fisting, looked upon the way they looked at it, can become just as addictive as those drugs. And yet, in order to do it in that addictive way, you need the drugs.... They also make you very willing to ignore pain which I would say you ought not to ignore."[11]

Patrick Califia looks at the link between extreme sex and drugs more sympathetically. Califia relates both activities to a spiritual impulse: "I think the impulse to get tied to a bench and flogged for two hours until you are flying out there with adrenaline and endorphins is no different than the impulse to snort a line of coke, or swallow a hit of MDA, and be someplace else. It's about looking for transcendence, it's about getting past fear, it's about being able to make a deep heart connection with other people that is not cluttered by all of this critical self-talk and self-consciousness that normally pollutes our experience of the world."[12]

Along with the wonder and experimentation of the 1970s, the decade produced an incredibly negative legacy in the form of the gay community's alarming rates of alcoholism and addiction today. (Most alcoholics eventually come to see alcohol and drugs as different forms of the same problem.) People who developed addictive lifestyles in the 1970s would not have found it so easy to simply switch back to social drinking. Looking back to a culture that was focused on bars and clubs where drugs and alcohol were central features, Kathy Watt traces the explosive growth of addiction and alcoholism in the gay world:

> The going rate of addiction and alcoholism for heterosexuals is about 10 percent. For the gay community, that rate is 40 to 50 percent. The reason for that is that our primary meeting places are still bars. In the '60s, when working people were drinking at lunchtime a lot and drinking alcoholically but not realizing it, the rates [of alcohol abuse between straights and gays] were more comparable, but not now. If you go to a gay restaurant in West Hollywood on a weekend night, the average table of four drinks an amount of alcohol that should serve a table of twenty.

CHAPTER 6

The Life and Films of Fred Halsted

In search of a narrative that captures both the exalted side of 1970s gay sex culture and its destructive power, I always return to the life and art of Fred Halsted. Halsted more or less created the world of gay sexual art and experimentation. He then watched it, and himself, be destroyed by AIDS, a sanitizing of gay sexual tastes and the power of addiction.

Fred Halsted didn't die of AIDS, but his world did. In early 1989 on a Saturday night, Halsted leaned against the wall in LA's famous leather bar the Gauntlet. For all his tough public image, Halsted was a shy man whose troubles showed on his face. Here was the ultimate leather top man in a corner, depressed and alone. Across the bar stood another leather icon named Durk Dehner. Dehner had made an effort to go out on that Saturday night, to meet new people, to try to start a new life in a world that had been ripped apart by AIDS. Dehner crossed the bar that night and spoke to Halsted:

> His emotions always reflected on his face and he looked really down. He acknowledged that he was out to see if he could inter-act with the world but it seemed like there was such a distance between him and other people. He was talking about how he couldn't seem to get anything going. We were deep into the epidemic at that point. I was out working at developing new rela-tionships because I had lost all of my old friends. I told him that the only way we would be able to go on was to remember what

we had done in our twenties—you have to work at developing
new friends and make dates and spend time with people. He acknowledged all of that but I knew I wasn't really reaching him.
He was lost and having a really difficult time finding meaning in
anything.[1]

Neither Halsted the person nor Halsted the sexual icon made
sense in the new world of AIDS. Six months later, Halsted was
dead of a deliberate drug overdose.

Fred Halsted is most commonly known as a pornographer,
yet prints of his films were shown at The Museum of Modern
Art and even today sit silently in the museum's storage vaults.
Although Halsted made a slew of forgettable sex films, he also
created a work of art that captured, and perhaps created, the gay
sex art world of the 1970s. In 1972 S/M and leather were a subculture within a subculture. One might say that a world cannot
exist until an image of it has been created. In 1972, when Halsted's *LA Plays Itself* opened at the Paris Theater in West Hollywood, the world of urban leathermen was created.

Halsted was an unlikely creator for a work of art so sophisticated that it could play both in a porn theater and MoMA. Fred
Halsted was more or less white California trash, born in Long
Beach in 1941 and raised in Oakland. He began lifting weights
made from railroad ties while he was growing up and developed
a magnificent body. Later he arrived in Los Angeles to go to college but never got around to studying film before dropping out
after three years. By 1969 he had developed and sold a chain of
wholesale nurseries and had become a landscaper. Not part of
the art world or any world, Halsted decided to create his own
world.

At twenty-seven, Halsted picked up a camera and shot *LA
Plays Itself* as an expression of his sexuality. He has been quoted
as saying that the film was highly autobiographical. Given its
nonnarrative structure, the film can be seen as a portrait of his
inner life and the development of a complex, frightening sexual
power.

Through looking at *LA Plays Itself*, one might develop an accurate profile of Halsted's life as well as the lives of many gay men entering the sexual explorations of the 1970s. As *LA Plays Itself* opens, the camera moves past a road sign stating "LA City Limit—Population 2,535,700" before the setting changes to the hills of Malibu. A vaguely oriental soundtrack plucks softly behind images of misty mountains and details of nature —a fossil in a rock, wildflowers, and insects. The pace is slow, tedious, enamored of the natural beauty; a viewer expecting a traditional porn film would already have become restless and uncomfortable.

The first of many disconnects in the film takes place in the form of a dialogue overlaying the music. The dialogue is hackneyed, bad enough to be irritating, nearly bad enough to be intentional.

> "The city, that's where it's happenin'. That's where the heavies are."
> "No man."
> "What happened out there in those Malibu mountains?"
> "I found somethin' awful nice out there."

The music becomes discordant as the camera follows a dark-haired man in a suede jacket, jeans, and a white T-shirt; masculine but not a leatherman. He meanders through the woods aimlessly until he comes upon a slack-haired California blond, naked and playing self-consciously in a stream. The brunette tells the blond, "I've got a heavy load on my mind today," and the blond obligingly asks, "Want some head?"

Hints of stereotypical top and bottom roles begin to occur as the brunette takes off his clothes and reveals that he has a tattoo on his arm—"U.S.N./Never Again." The brunette proves himself to be a halfhearted top as the blond blows him. The two carelessly change places as the camera moves in closer and closer on the vanilla kissing, fucking, and frolicking in the stream, layered with images of flowers. The layering of images is somewhat experimental, the extreme closeups unusual, but the sex is without any conviction or emotional charge.

Suddenly, though, the images of fucking are layered with more ominous creatures: a salamander and a spider. Without warning, images of a bulldozer are cut in. The bulldozer is powerful, ripping through the world of "natural" sex. The bulldozer, like what is to come, is unstoppable.

The viewer is next violently transported to the gritty streets of Hollywood. Halsted emerges from a garage and strides purposefully to a red Ranchero. He is extraordinarily handsome with his shaggy brown hair, his powerful body moving gracefully under fatigue pants and a T-shirt. His classic profile is roughened by muttonchop sideburns. Halsted bridges the gap that would later emerge between the beautiful Clones of Fire Island and the masculine Clones of the Mineshaft. His beauty and his masculinity are not costumed in the way of either camp. Seeing him on the screen for the first time, one senses that he exists as fully on film as he does in real life.

Nature is utterly vanquished now—cruising in Halsted's car, in his chosen world of Hollywood streets lined with low-rent hustlers, porno theaters, and careless shop fronts. A billboard advertises Mick Jagger in *Performance* with the slogan "Performance—Underground Meets Underworld." A building is scrawled with a graffito, "Gay Power."

The movement of the film is obscure but there is a constant sense now of momentum, of being taken somewhere, perhaps against our will. Another stilted dialogue begins as, over the images of streets, we hear the voice of a boy with a corny Texas accent reading aloud from a porno story. Joey Yale's face flashes briefly on the screen, still and beautiful with his clear white skin and dark blond hair. Joey disappears and the camera returns to the streets as the dialogue continues. Oblivious, or pretending to be, the boy tells a newfound friend that he found the porno on the bus he just got off from Texas. The boy's new friend suggestively says that he can show him around, help him. The friend also warns the boy to stay away from certain kinds of men: "You don't want to mess with guys like that."

The music moves into a trance-inducing beat, like a sound effect from an outer-space movie. Without transition, the film shatters into its final, powerful section with an image of a naked boy (Yale) at the base of a stairway. The dialogue disappears. Halsted, his body like a marble statue, stands shirtless in jeans and boots at the top of the stairs. He throws what appears to be a bottle of beer down at Yale, soaking him. Yale crawls humbly up the stairs to clean Halsted's filthy boots with his tongue.

Halsted then seems to break the hypnotic mood by cutting back to the streets, where the sun is setting. He inserts long shots of men lounging, half-naked in Griffith Park as Halsted prowls, dark and sexy among them. But the mood is not broken. It holds as one realizes that, in this new urban world, the power of sexuality is everywhere. The hypnotic, drugged mood courses through Halsted's entire world, whether it is the parks, the streets, or an abandoned building where he beats a slave.

The film wrenches back to the top of the stairway where Halsted is kicking Yale into a bedroom, throwing him on the bed, tying him before whipping, torturing, and fisting him. There are cuts to strange paintings, mounted insect collections, and a newspaper with the headline, "American kidnapped, tied, dead." Days seem to be passing in this room. Yale is now tied and sitting in a closet, desperately watching and wanting Halsted. Halsted, naked, displays himself, fully aware of his powerful presence. Halsted completes the film by jerking off, almost as an afterthought as Yale watches him with pleading eyes.

I describe *LA Plays Itself* in such detail because these images simply did not exist before Halsted. Here is a porno movie in which the sexual act is entirely beside the point, where the violent emotional climax is far more important than ejaculation. The "money shot" that Halsted offhandedly provides at the end seems to be an obligatory gesture toward the audience he has just topped.

The brilliance of *LA Plays Itself* was almost immediately recognized. Halsted was the only filmmaker working with porn images to be given a Cineprobe at The Museum of Modern Art. (Cineprobe is a forum for independent and avante-garde filmmakers.) Adrienne Mancia, who organized the Cineprobe, was the curator of film at MoMA in the mid-1970s. Although she warned the oddly mixed audience of wealthy art patrons and leathermen that the images they were going to see might be unusual, she never asked the museum administration for permission to show Halsted's work and received no flack for presenting his films. Mancia felt that Halsted's films were important because they showed an artist taking control of images, working at the edge. With her screening, Mancia elevated Halsted's films to a status that Halsted, with his healthy ego, was sure they deserved.

Halsted's MoMA Cineprobe is fascinating on a number of levels, not the least of which is its demonstration of a time when a major American museum could unquestioningly support work using extreme sexuality as a medium. It is also notable that a woman selected the films. Mancia, who is now curator-at-large for the Brooklyn Academy of Music Cinematheque, was the first of several women who would be central to Halsted's life and career. Most importantly, however, the presentation of Halsted's films at MoMA might be seen as mainstream culture's first opening to radical gay sexuality. Halsted's films never gained widespread distribution outside of the adult-film circuit, and his extreme S/M films were never commercially successful even within the gay porn industry. However, Halsted could never be dismissed once his films had received the blessing of high-art status.

While Halsted's life was mostly in Los Angeles, he did make a few appearances in the cultural capital of New York. Elliot Stein, the film critic for the *Village Voice* at the time, played host to Halsted during his trips to New York, showing him gay hotspots such as the Mineshaft. William Burroughs wanted to meet the filmmaker, and Stein arranged a dinner for the three of them, which was apparently calm and unremarkable. Stein describes Halsted as shy and gentle. He does say, though, that Halsted had an aggressive trait of never bathing and that his odor preceded him into a room and lingered long after he had left.

Halsted made two more notable films—*Sex Garage* and *Sextool*—before turning to more mainstream porn in an effort to make a living. *Sex Garage* is particularly interesting in that it opens with a long section of a girl blowing a garage mechanic before she inexplicably runs off, only to be replaced by a tough biker who seems more interested in having sex with his motorcycle than men. *Sex Garage*, shot in high-contrast black and white and containing a scene in which the biker literally fucks the motorcycle exhaust pipe, precipitated police raids in some theaters. (Both *LA Plays Itself* and *Sex Garage* originally contained fisting scenes that were later excised when the films were distributed on video.) In truth, Halsted made only one great film—*LA Plays Itself*. And he knew it. He felt that he had peaked at twenty-nine and the rest of his life was an inexorable slide to a pathetic end.

In recompense, there was Halsted's great love for Joey Yale. Their relationship became the central anchor in Halsted's life until Yale died of AIDS in 1986. Durk Dehner organized the first American shows of the drawings of Tom of Finland, which became totems of leather fantasy and later became fashionable in the art world. Dehner was living in Los Angeles at the same time as Halsted and describes Fred's relationship with Joey:

> Fred was part of a generation where it was part of the accepted norm that you did go out and have sex with other people and, if it worked out for you, you had a significant other you always came home to. That was the thing that broke him apart—when he lost that relationship and whatever it gave to him, everything else became meaningless. He was lost. He didn't seem to have the ability to pick it up. He didn't stick around long enough to complete the mourning process and see that there was life after.

Soon after *LA Plays Itself* was presented, other filmmakers began to present the S/M world, though mostly without the emotional power of Halsted's film. One film that did achieve a sexy, unflinching look at actual S/M sex is Roger Earl's *Born to Raise Hell*. Halsted was an important influence on Earl: "I saw *LA Plays Itself* at the Paris Theater on Santa Monica Boulevard.

I had been approached to make an S/M film but the atmosphere was a little frightening and I wasn't really brave enough to go out there. But then I saw Fred's film and I figured that he had broken the ice.... It was because of Fred Halsted that I made *Born to Raise Hell*."[2]

Earl's film shares certain traits with *LA Plays Itself* in that the sex itself is oddly unsatisfying. One rarely sees an actual erection in *Born to Raise Hell,* as the participants constantly snort poppers, enabling a level of physical exploration that would be very difficult without chemical aid. (Earl claims that other drugs were forbidden during the making of the film.) What is being explored in both films is a kind of sex that depends not upon erections or ejaculations, but rather on an emotional stretching that remains shocking today but must have been nothing short of revolutionary in the early 1970s. Huey Newton's predictions that gay men could be the most radical elements of society is brilliantly demonstrated in these films—films that are not afraid to be disturbing, even depressing. Refreshingly, these early representations of S/M do not present it as some easily packaged lifestyle or therapeutic activity. Rather, the door that Halsted opened and Earl flung aside offered the presentation of S/M as art, filled with messy, unresolved intentions. It is a mark of the impact of these images, though, that mainstream porn, both gay and straight, is today filled with S/M-themed videos. While these films involve only the most watered-down acts, they have a lineage that leads back to *LA Plays Itself.*

Halsted could be opinionated, often making inflammatory statements to see how others would react. He famously said that he could get any top man to submit to him. (Halsted bragged that in one encounter a pious Christian submitted to him, calling him Lord and demonstrating his faith by eating Halsted's excrement.) However, Roger Earl was one of the only people who realized that Halsted, the gay public's ultimate top, also had needs as a bottom:

> Fred and I were balling buddies but Joey didn't know. I topped
> Fred and Joey wouldn't have appreciated that. When he and Joey
> were together, he would call me up and want to get together. Af-

ter they broke up, he wasn't interested anymore. He told me that I was the first and only person to top him. How true that was and for how long, I don't know. Our little play sessions were very human, very beautiful.

Durk Dehner confirms this view of Halsted's sexuality: "Joey also topped him. Which doesn't mean anything except that Fred had a public persona and he couldn't go out and satisfy his needs." One must remember that Halsted's role as a sexual dominant was not only a personal point of pride; his films *depended* upon the public seeing him as a top. Publicly, Halsted was forced to play out the role he had created for himself on-screen.

Although most people describe him as a gentle, sweet person, there was the alcoholic side to Halsted that became so constant that Yale, his great love, finally left him. After Yale's death, Earl remembers, Halsted's drinking and drug use became more pronounced:

> Joey got Fred off of the bottle and various drugs. Fred slipped back and Joey pulled away to help him. Fred had a healthy ego. But that was destroyed when Joey separated from him. He lost his ego, his pride, and his persona. He got so bad that people didn't want to be around him. He ... was a sloppy, sloppy drunk.

Perhaps the only person who was constant in Halsted's life was a woman named Jeanne Barney. Barney is a figure of singular importance in gay and lesbian history who first came to public attention writing a bleeding-heart column for the *Advocate* in 1970. Her column, "Smoke from Jeanne's Lamp," became the paper's most popular feature. The *Advocate* was, at its beginning in 1969, an activist paper, and Barney enjoyed the camaraderie of working in such surroundings. However, she grew disillusioned when David Goodstein bought the *Advocate* in the mid-1970s and fired most of the staff. Rather than continue on with the newly commercial *Advocate*, Barney created *Drummer* with John Embry.

Barney, a straight woman, was an unlikely choice to be the editor of America's first leather magazine. However, she had high ambitions for it: "With *Drummer*, I wanted a gay leather S/M *Evergreen Review*. The leather people I knew were older, better educated, more affluent, intelligent, affable, and I felt that they deserved the best possible product."[3]

Barney may not have fit the stereotypical role of a leader in the leather community but she was definitely in sync with its spirit and her interest in S/M was not voyeuristic: "I was with the guys and I was sort of a Mother Superior. I would be lying if I said my interests weren't piqued. Just by chance I met a detective from the Hollywood Division. I used to get him in my living room and get him all lubed up with K-Y. And there is nothing in this whole world as satisfying as having your fist up the ass of the LAPD."

Barney first met Halsted when the Gay Students' Union at UCLA asked her if she would contact him to appear on a panel for a conference at the university. When Halsted showed up for the conference along with Joey Yale, Barney was struck by their incongruous partnership—Halsted in filthy jeans that Barney thought he must have "buried in the backyard to let age," and the blond-haired Yale in a blue cashmere sweater and white pants, the Super Twinkie personified. The bond between Barney and Halsted, whom she described as one of the few genuine people she has ever met, was immediate: "It was as if we were in a humane society and we adopted each other."

Barney was probably the closest person to Halsted and presents a complicated view of his relationship with Joey Yale. Yale, for all of his submission on the screen, was the driving force, one might say the opportunist, in the couple's business life:

> When Joey was alive, even after they broke up and were still doing business together, Fred produced because Joey was there to push him along. Fred had no head for business. When Joey finally died, Fred didn't have anybody to tell him what to do. He was kind of like the guy who comes out of the army and can't survive because there's nobody there to tell him when to get up.

Yale's adoration of the public Halsted was difficult to maintain in private when Halsted became all too human and fragile.

Barney describes Yale's quandary as finding out that Santa Claus does exist but that he has bad breath. She describes her offense at Yale's frequent and vicious diatribes against Halsted: "Fred cared for him as much as Joey would let him. Joey was a real shit, a real nasty little son-of-a-bitch. In all the years I knew him, I never heard Fred say a negative thing about Joey but Joey said some of the most vicious things about Fred. Joey was very emotionally stingy. I always liked Joey but you never knew where you stood with him."

Still, one must sympathize with Yale, who clearly had his hands full with Halsted's deepening alcoholism and addiction. For as long as Barney knew Halsted, he was on large doses of Thorazine and Valium, prescribed by his doctor just to keep him even. The drugs, and later the alcohol, helped Halsted to present a public persona that masked a deep insecurity: "He was very shy. He would always scowl in public because he was afraid people would find out that he wasn't what people thought he was— the best top, the best filmmaker. People always wanted him to be things that he didn't want to be, that he couldn't be."

Once Yale died, Halsted's career and personal struggle with addiction took a turn for the worse. Barney tried to help Halsted get sober but doubted his commitment to recovery: "I don't know if he sincerely wanted to get sober. When he'd stop drinking, he would go to the gym and he would get gorgeous again. But then he'd go on a binge and fall apart. The older he got the less easy it was to bounce back."

Toward the end of his life, Halsted, who made his living from sex, was having a difficult time making ends meet in a world beset by AIDS. He told Barney that he had decided that his meal ticket would be his memoirs, titled *Why I Did It*. Halsted showed Barney the manuscript, which she felt was strong but difficult. Halsted sent the manuscript to the New York porn publisher George Mavety, who quickly rejected it. With that single rejection, Halsted seemed to finally give up. Unwilling or unable to recast himself as a businessman trading on his previous successes, Halsted eventually moved to an apartment building in San Clemente owned by his brother, where he lived rent-free.

In San Clemente, Halsted was completely isolated from his previous life and the friends that remembered his glory years. Before he left, Halsted planted some jacaranda trees in Barney's yard. She called him frequently, joking that the trees were not blooming. Halsted told Barney, "Everything happens in its own time." The trees bloomed the day she heard that Halsted had committed suicide.

One must remember that in 1989, when Dehner and Halsted stood in the Gauntlet, the AIDS crisis was in full swing. An already troubled figure such as Halsted faced a world that he had helped create, only to watch it be destroyed, along with the one person he had loved. Dehner says of Halsted's decline: "We give creative people some extra leeway. They're extremely vulnerable. If the channel isn't open for them to express themselves, they get caught up very easily and it just starts to feed on itself."

Halsted's life swung on the arc of a new type of sexuality based on images that had been born of his art. His life and his film typify not only the great experiment of the 1970s but also the wrenching effect of the 1980s, when suddenly a context for living was no longer left for those who had survived AIDS. Through his ability to express his inner life in publicly presented films, Halsted enabled an entire generation to explore images and actions that would create a culture that burned bright for a few years before being extinguished, just as surely as was Halsted himself.

CHAPTER 7

What Might Have Been

Where would the great experiment have ended were it not for AIDS? As Edmund White wrote in his book *The Farewell Symphony*: "I assumed there was going to be a future and that it would get more and more extravagant. We saw gay men as a vanguard that society would inevitably follow. I thought that the couple would disappear and be replaced by new, polyvalent molecules of affection."[1]

There were signs in the late 1970s and early 1980s that gay men were already tiring of a lifestyle that was entirely focused on sex. If we think of the 1970s as adolescence, with all of the exhilaration and pain that adolescence implies, then it would have been natural for most participants to later integrate sexual exploration into more balanced lives. The elders that issued from the scene would have been available to help a younger generation navigate the complexities of sexual experimentation and further the experiment. These elders would have developed a tempered view of the world that they could have shared with new initiates. Only years of experience produce realizations such as the one that Arnie Kantrowitz had regarding the clubs and bars:

> What I concluded after years and years was that it was ultimately a kind of masturbation. These people were my fantasy; there was just a body there. I projected on to them what kind of person I wanted them to be, and that was hot. But I was really having sex with my-

self. Another way to look at it in a positive light is as though it was a communal game. All of us were in this together. We all knew what kinds of things we wanted. We knew how to act the fantasy. By certain clues, either verbal or in body language, you could let your partner know what you wanted. Since we knew our vocabulary together, we could be what our partners wanted us to be.[2]

If the sexual experiment of the 1970s had not been abandoned and was now seen in a positive light rather than carrying the weight of AIDS, a connection between generations of gay men might be easier to achieve. These intergenerational connections between gay men foster the ability to manage shame. An older man who has experienced a period of youthful intensity around sexual experience can tell a young man just entering the scene that it is possible to come out the other side into a balanced life. Just the fact of seeing these older men still alive can be hopeful to a young man whose entire view of sexuality is wrapped up in self-destructive shame and a belief that gay sex must always lead to AIDS. But, as will be discussed later in this book, young gay men often see the older men who did survive as spoilers and predators.

Felice Picano sees the great sexual experiment as being naturally excessive because it was uncharted territory:

When you say you're liberated, you're making a statement. You've got to prove it and, if there are no limits in front of you because there's never been gay liberation before, there's no horizon over there. So you just go wherever you're going. There's nothing to stop you. You were on a constant exploration. Did people abuse it? No question. Did we go too far? I don't know. I don't think so. If AIDS hadn't come along, we'd still be dancing. Who's gonna stop us?[3]

Perhaps the most interesting and open-ended view of the 1970s sexual experiment comes from the "Foucault Live" interviews in *Semiotext(e),* done shortly before Foucault's death, where the philosopher advocates for creative sexual experimentation without a clear political agenda. Foucault's view in the

1980s is remarkably similar to that of Charley Shively's in *Fag Rag* a decade earlier, in that both believe that gay sexual culture has the potential to develop entirely new forms of relationships that can transform and deeply threaten dominant society. Foucault's enthusiasm for the revival of male friendships has echoes of *Fag Rag*'s calls for comradely love. Foucault's view of gay life is active and evolving rather than positioning passive acceptance as the hallmark of a successful civil rights campaign. He exhorts the reader to "understand that with our desires, through our desires, go new forms of relationships, new forms of love, new forms of creation. Sex is not a fatality; it's a possibility for creative life."[4]

Foucault participated in S/M, visited the Mineshaft, and firmly positioned the sexual culture of gay men in the realm of creativity and experimentation:

> What you have, then, is a situation where all the energy and imagination, which in the heterosexual relationship were channeled into courtship, now become devoted to intensifying the act of sex itself. A whole new art of sexual practice develops which tries to explore all the internal possibilities of sexual conduct. You find emerging in places like San Francisco and New York what might be called laboratories of sexual experimentation.[5]

Given that gay sexuality has been examined in medical terms throughout its history, it is perhaps a mistake to look at the 1970s as an experiment. If it was an experiment, though, it was spiritual rather than scientific. But with all experiments, regardless of their realm, one expects a conclusion before moving on to the next stage of exploration. The danger in concluding an experiment early is that the data will be lost or, at best, never analyzed.

The sexual experiment of the 1970s was for gay men to live as sexual artists. Artists are often defined in connection with the high culture of commercial art-making practices. We too often believe that artists are only those who produce paintings, symphonies, films, and dances. It is far more interesting to define artists in terms of culture in its broadest sense. The historian Jacques Barzun writes in his *From Dawn to Decadence*:

Their "culture" consists only of local customs and traditions, individual or institutional habits, class manners and prejudices, language or dialect, upbringing or profession, creed, attitudes, usages, fashions, and superstitions; or, at the narrowest, temperament. If a word is wanted for the various pairings of such elements, there is *ethos.*[6]

Beginning with Stonewall and extending into the early 1980s, when AIDS first began to drain away creative energy, the gay men of the 1970s created a culture, an ethos, that positioned them as some of the greatest artists in history. Their medium was sex and they marshaled all of the creative tools at their disposal to render sex in the most revolutionary way ever seen.

It is so easy to see only the negative aspects of this experiment that was necessarily abandoned before its conclusion. It is so difficult to see how these practices could have grown into a culture that was sustainable and loving. But we must recognize what was created and not look at it only through the scrim of AIDS and shame. How would it have ended? This, of course, is unknowable; but we must remember that what was begun was begun in service of revolution, not self-destruction. Is it too late for us to pick up those threads of revolution and become artists once again?

SECTION II

After

CHAPTER 8

The Rise of the East Village

Returning to the metaphor of a theater, "Before" is the distant past, backstage and obscured behind the scrim. "After" is the immediate past, now playing onstage as we watch from the auditorium of the present. The action onstage stands between us and our legacy. In 1980 the scrim of AIDS began to coalesce, partitioning the lives of gay men into a before and after. While some of the physical locations and acts of the 1970s sexual vanguard would persist for another five years, or even longer, the time of experimentation had ended. America's tolerance for social change in the 1970s had not created the radicalism of gay sexual life but had encouraged it, and in the 1980s the mood of America began to shift to a corporate mentality that embodied all that the radicals of the previous two decades had feared. The American mood in the 1980s was nothing new; the country had seen long stretches of conformity before. In fact, conservative eras like the 1950s had bred the revolts of the 1960s. What was new was the ever-increasing power of the media and its parasitic hunger for novelty. Beginning in the 1980s, the media strip-mined American culture, ripping through the recent past in search of subcultures that might be diluted into commercial content and then abandoned, exhausted.

AIDS also contributed to the loss of balance between the energy of the creative vanguard of gay men and the cynical forces that were ascendant in 1980. Beginning in the 1970s, thousands and thousands of gay men had explored a new way of life, learning lessons and preparing to shape American culture with their experience. Because of AIDS, these men were suddenly gone or incapacitated before their experience could be shared with the larger culture or passed on to a new generation of gay men. The void created when they were lost was easily filled by merchants recycling the vibrancy of the past but unable to create a real future. If the first section of this book was an attempt to look behind the scrim of AIDS and reclaim the gay male experiment, this section is an attempt to examine what replaced 1970s sex art as the creative vanguard of American life.

As the often-told narrative of the unfolding of AIDS makes clear, there was limited reporting even in the gay press of the rapidly expanding circle of men who had fallen ill. However, the social networks that stretched across Fire Island, the Meat District, the Castro, and West Hollywood immediately registered the knowledge that something was very wrong. It is natural to focus on the terrible individual impact of AIDS. But there is another immense area of impact that is societal. As cultural forces began to shift with the arrival of AIDS, the disease immediately cast all that had happened in the 1970s into the self-destructive light of shame. The gay community busily went about convincing straight America that we were "just like them" and, therefore, deserved to live. We began to abandon and erase the radical, isolationist culture of the 1970s. Most of the erasure of gay history was undertaken by the gay community itself, hoping that if we "cleaned up" our image, America would care enough to save our lives and offer us basic civil rights.

Gay culture quickly turned on its heel, walked out of the leather culture of the Meat District, and headed east toward the drag queens of the East Village. I will look at the East Village at length in this book because it was the primary site of progressive gay life in New York in the first decades of the AIDS crisis and presents a useful contrast to the West Village culture that preceded it.

★   ★   ★

Even before AIDS, there were signs that the sexual experiment of the 1970s had, if not failed, at least lost some of its luster. Drug use, originally a tool, had become mundane addiction for many. And some gay men must have been wondering how a social experiment of such extremity could be extended over a lifetime. When AIDS arrived, the great experiment of gay sex was only just completing adolescence. The next stage would hopefully have been to create a life that balanced new social practices with the best of earlier traditions. AIDS destroyed the opportunity to balance rebelliousness with traditionalism and left behind a gay world that was forced to renounce sexual experimentation as self-destructive and uncritically embrace heterosexual models.

In 1987 Frank Rich wrote a long piece for *Esquire* called "The Gay Decades" in which he described the "homosexualization"[1] of American culture. What Rich was describing at the time was the homosexualization of popular culture and the new visibility of mass-media images relating to gay life. And in terms of pop culture images, Rich was correct. But were it not for AIDS, one wonders if, in addition to pop culture images, gay culture would have also been able to have a more significant influence over models of social interaction in American society. In actuality what has succeeded is the commercialization of homosexual style but stripped of the threatening and revolutionary power of gay sexual history. Once the gay community was willing to present itself without the sexual extremity of the 1970s, it was far more palatable to the mass media.

The bastardized influences of undiluted gay culture from the 1970s remain visible today in fashion and advertising. If the link between the Mineshaft and a society woman walking down Madison Avenue in leather and vinyl bondage gear seems obscure, it is because the gay men who created these fashions purposely obscured their sources to achieve commercial success. It is also because the gay community, both necessarily and willfully, disowned the sexual culture that inspired such fashion. The fashion press, also dominated by gay men, opportunistically reproduces explicitly gay images stripped of history and context. In the broader society, the very fact that S/M has become a suburban activity complete with a product line speaks to the pillaging of gay cultural history for profit without any effort to present the depth and importance of our culture. In a capitalist society, it is understandable that the most creative, well-produced, and innovative products would find commercial success. However, the commercial success of gay social models and gay establishments tended to lessen their validity as venues of experimentation. The success of gay discos, bars, baths, and resorts was a testament to the quality of their offerings in the 1970s and early 1980s, as straight people discovered the powerful experiences offered by gay culture. As often happens, however, commercial success brought cultural decline as the original power of these sites, dependent upon participation, was sapped by voyeurism. Certainly this process was accelerated with the rise of a commercial gay press able to slickly package and present gay life as accessible and nonthreatening.

None of this would have been negative had the gay community not faced a health crisis that halted their experiments. Were it not for AIDS, gay men may have continued these sometimes pleasurable, sometimes frightening explorations at a pace that would have kept them safely ahead of media saturation. But with AIDS, gay men entered the 1980s with a weakened subculture listed in tourist guidebooks, stripped of its revolutionary roots and enmeshed in a new destructive tendency in American culture toward ironic dabbling rather than passionate beliefs. As American culture became increasingly media-dominated, the machinery of the media demonstrated an ever-escalating need for new subcultures to discover, recast, and consume.

In the late 1970s, we begin to see a cultural acceleration that was originally generated by the media but has become *the* central force in American cultural life. This tendency is deeply destructive: a kind of addiction to images that requires higher and higher doses but yields ever-decreasing highs. The flipping of subcultures once they have been drained of their novelty has the strange effect of never discarding the past but continuing to recycle it in a parasitic way, leaving just enough blood for the

wasted thing to regenerate a few years later. So one continues to
see punks with Mohawks in the East Village to this day, worn
by children with absolutely no idea what they indicate. Young
straight couples saunter down the streets in full leather regalia
completely denuded of its gay history. While fashion designers
have been particularly guilty in the juicing and rejuicing of fashions from the 1960s and 1970s (fashion has tried to revive the
1980s but seems to find it a greater challenge), they can hardly
be blamed for looking back to a time that was so much more inspiring than the present. What persists from 1960s youth culture
and 1970s sexual explorations are not the ideals but the images—
what the performer Penny Arcade has described as the gentrification of ideas.

Without the AIDS crisis, the first group of gay sex pioneers
might have been viewed by younger generations as a source of
inspiration rather than spoilers or, worse, feared sources of infection. These older men might have maintained an intergenerational bond that would have inspired a new set of participants to
take the great experiment into the larger culture. When one
looks back at the widening circle of eager straight and bisexual
members at the Catacombs in San Francisco, it seems entirely
possible that the group that was exploring sexual cultures in-
vented by gay men might have been converted. By the mid-
1980s, however, the sex pioneers were gone, and their work was
seen through a firmly anchored scrim painted with wasting bodies and secret, shameful deaths.

The enormity of AIDS, especially after two decades, makes
global or even national assessment essentially meaningless. One
can really only look at narrow communities for understandable
indicators of impact and change. For that reason, downtown
New York is essential to viewing the first wave of AIDS. In the
1980s New York was the undisputed center of the cultural
world, with a particular dominance in the visual arts. The city
also demonstrated at that point a unique physical compression of
creativity in downtown Manhattan, literally focusing the atten-

tion of world culture on the area between Fourteenth Street and Canal. New York, because it was so central, had the most to lose in terms of the rich creative culture directed by gay men. For these reasons, downtown (soon to become "Downtown") New York is an ideal case study for cultural change in the context of AIDS. It would be naive to suggest that AIDS was the only cultural change agent at work in downtown New York in the 1980s. But it is certainly possible to look at AIDS as a catalyst that enabled an array of forces destructive to both gay male culture of the 1970s and other vibrant subcultures that coexisted downtown.

To provide a comparison to the 1970s culture of exploration, we can look to the many shortcomings of the culture of irony that followed. The vanguard of the 1970s can be geographically positioned in the Meat District of Manhattan's West Side. If one defines the culture of irony dominating American culture in the 1980s as the cynical recycling of past cultures rather than the development of new, deeply held beliefs, then the Lower East Side of Manhattan was the vanguard of American culture in the 1980s. In other words, the creative vanguard of downtown Manhattan moved east.

This was the world that I arrived into when I reached New York in the early 1980s. For a young gay man in 1984, the "action," such as it was, seemed very much to be in the East Village rather than with the West Village Clones. This dismissive view of my elders derived both from the usual hubris of youth and an unacknowledged fear that AIDS was positioned in the history identified with the West Village.

The use of parallel arcs in history is irresistible but brings with it the danger of warping the shape of those arcs to fit more persuasively together. Still, this danger is worth the risk in understanding the cultural impact of AIDS. One method of understanding is to use geography as an indicator of cultural primacy, with the West Village representing the 1970s and the East Village the 1980s. When I arrived in New York I did not recognize that my chosen identification with the East Village was to be deeply disappointing and that it would take the force of creative radicalism found in ACT UP (AIDS Coalition to Unleash Power) to return me to a view of gay life that included the sexual legacy contained in the West Village.

Every arc must have an apex, indicating the point of greatest influence and conflict as well as inevitable denouement. Anyone who has experienced an orgasm, ridden a roller coaster, or taken a drama class knows the shape of this arc; the long slow build to the crest and then the dramatic, fast drop to resolution. I would position the climax of the 1970s gay male sexual culture at the opening of the Saint in 1981. As the Saint opened, bringing the Clone culture to a new level of visibility and commercialism, AIDS was also attacking the central tenet of gay male culture: sex as creative endeavor and personal rite of passage. If the Meat District was the spiritual center of 1970s sex culture, it is interesting to observe its gradual easterly drift. By the early 1980s, Bruce Mailman's sex emporiums—the Saint and the New St. Marks Baths—marked the forward advance of gay culture. These clubs balanced on the physical and cultural divisions between West and East Villages. If the Bowery is the westernmost border of the East Village, then these two clubs, sited between Second and Third Avenues, barely slipped over the frontier. Mailman himself oversaw the operation from just inside a West Village loft on Lafayette Street.

With the force of sexual culture behind him, Mailman looked eastward into a neighborhood that was, in many ways, more complex than the West Village. The arc of the Lower East Side must be drawn taking into account the cyclical interactions between real estate development, invading bohemians, and poverty. By the time I arrived in New York, the authentic Lower East Side had been shaped into a packaged lifestyle known as the "East Village." The vacuous culture of the East Village rose to media prominence in the form of a busily ironic and corrupt commercial art scene. Although not exclusively gay, the East Village galleries and nightclubs became the primary destination for young gay New Yorkers. In the East Village, radical gay male sexual culture was submerged into a much safer, campy drag culture that harks back to *Queen's Quarterly*.

Bruce Mailman's plan to extend the culture of gay male sex into new territory failed not only because AIDS ripped out the creative engine of the great experiment but also because much of the power of the 1970s sex scene was dependent upon its hidden nature as a subculture. The opening that occurred, as sacred sites like the Mineshaft became tourist destinations, was a rupture through which much of the spiritual energy of the scene escaped. And just as the world of 1970s sex culture was being buffeted by spiritual, medical, and economic winds, a new culture was ascendant in New York.

The writer and editor Richard Goldstein sees the gay life of the 1970s in the West Village as tribal in nature. In opposition to this communal culture of the West Village, Goldstein positions the East Village as an individualistic, but not necessarily negative, society. The East Village pushed sex to the side, rejecting the tribal culture of gay men in the 1970s for a new world of showy outcasts, addicts, and individuals. While individuals in the gay ghettos of the 1970s may have felt isolated or lonely, their impetus for living in the ghettos was to come together, albeit often in an emotionally truncated way. Sex, especially Clone sex that fetishized blue-collar workers, allowed for connections between men of diverse class backgrounds. Disallowing the commercialization of large clubs like the Saint and the exclusivity of resorts like the Pines, men needed few intellectual or economic resources to participate in the most creative parts of gay male sex culture. At the Mineshaft, a mechanic with a beer belly could be the star and, at the baths, a hugely endowed cabdriver was the center of attention—both for a cover charge of less than ten dollars. Whether these blue-collar men looked at their participation as an act of creative exploration or simply an opportunity for a blowjob, they were participating in a social experiment generated by an authentic community.

The culture of the 1970s took the lowest common denominator of sex and elevated it to high culture. Sex was art. In the 1980s, the East Village art perversely inverted this formula. Art was sex. As the East Village gallery scene began to receive the kind of press attention once lavished on the West Village gay scene, it became clear that the Clone was dead, both physically and as an archetype of urban explorer. Artist had replaced Clone. The role of Artist, unlike the Clone, had many prerequisites, including a familiarity with obscure theories that leant meaning to the objects produced and sold in the East Village.

With the easterly movement of gay culture in New York, the gay community was repositioning itself outside the ghetto in a larger constellation of artists, outsiders, and radicals. (Not until the 1990s would the gay community begin to align itself with an Upper West Side lifestyle of children, stability, and consumption.) To the extent that gay people accepted the roles of artist, outsider, and radical that had long figured in the left politics of the Lower East Side, they also accepted responsibility for leadership in those communities and for the histories contained in them. The gays of the East Village in a way fulfilled the early mandate of Gay Liberation Front, insisting on being a part of the larger radical community rather than simply taking on a gay-specific agenda. Unfortunately, participants in this strategy assume huge responsibilities and also stand a chance of losing their identity. The East Village represents a loss of the clear identity gay men enjoyed in the 1970s, a loss of identity that created a significantly weaker American culture.

There were two ways of being in the East Village. One was dependent on a real connection to the history of the Lower East Side and some connection with the political and artistic legacy of the community, while the other can be summarized as slumming. Although a generalization, it might be said that people who moved into the East Village before the rise of the 1980s gallery scene were more likely to have had some lasting connection to the neighborhood rather than simply riding the new trend. Charges of gentrification by artists and gays were certainly understandable as the East Village became a media darling in the 1980s.

Although the Lower East Side has long attracted outcasts, it became increasingly difficult in the 1980s to distinguish between groups of authentic outcasts and those who were posing. The position of gays as outsiders also became more confusing as gays positioned themselves as another component of the glamorous rejected culture of the East Village. Culturally, gays became indistinguishable from artists in the East Village culture. The role of outsider gained another layer of complexity when the East Village gallery scene discovered how to market angst, sometimes real and other times manufactured, as a profitable commodity. Gay artists were well represented within the East Village gallery scene, but even the most politically aware of them such as Keith Haring and David Wojnarowicz seemed to bring only their individual visions to the East Village rather than a political agenda. Perhaps it is unfair to ask gays to be more politically active than straights or to demand that artists maintain an unselfish vision of the world. However, because both groups seemed to move unquestioningly into the East Village in search of opportunities in the commercial galleries, their original intentions are indistinguishable from one another and, in retrospect, easy to condemn. If a politician makes policy thoughtlessly, artists and gays understandably do not excuse the politician's actions as misinformed but, in fact, well intentioned. Yet this seems to be the argument of the artists and gay people who graduated from Ivy League schools, moved into a poor, working-class neighborhood in the 1980s and then attempted to recast themselves as resistant to the forces of gentrification.

The Center for an Urban Future released a groundbreaking report in November of 2002 that, for the first time, illuminated both the positive role of artists in regenerating economically depressed neighborhoods and their negative impact in displacing low-income residents including, ultimately, the gentrifying artists themselves. The report begins with the statement that "no single industry attracts other sectors to the extent that art and culture does."[2] The magnetizing effect of culture, including gay culture, is problematic when it is utilized by larger economic concerns such as government and private developers as the cornerstone of a strategy that has profit as its ultimate and only goal. The center's report is clear-eyed to a remarkable extent in the face of the prevailing view that arts and culture are a panacea for urban problems. The following is a key finding of the report:

> Issues of gentrification and displacement are one of the biggest barriers to cultural development at the neighborhood level.... Issues around the displacement of community residents, local merchants, manufacturers and artists were found to be a major barrier, slowing specific development projects and creating resentment at the local level. These issues play out in particularly unique ways in New York City. Cultural development here is not about regenerating abandoned downtown hubs, as is often the case elsewhere, but about better integrating the creative sector into already dense residential and business communities.[3]

But from this statement, which many in the arts community will likely find sacrilegious, the report veers back to the shockingly traditional statement that "among [the creative economy's] greatest strengths is the ability to attract other businesses and jump-start neighborhood development. Arts and culture do this by giving local economies their 'soul.'" The use of the word *soul* is very troubling in the context of using artistic subcultures as economic accelerants. The poor people who lived in these neighborhoods before artists and gays would surely be surprised to know that they did not already have souls and, walking down Avenue A today, one would be hard-pressed to see the numbing parade of tourist shops as anything approaching the soulful windswept streets of the Meat District in the 1970s.

Many of the artists and intellectuals who moved to the Lower East Side in the 1970s saw it as a desolate wasteland with a rich political and artistic past. These were people who may have been gay or lived as artists but also had a long-standing connection to the neighborhood from growing up in New York. It is important to distinguish between their arrival and that of the gallery scenesters. Sarah Schulman, the writer and activist, moved to Avenue D and Seventh Street in 1979 and then to

Ninth Street between First and Second, where she still lives today. Her view of the neighborhood was not of a thriving environment where artists were displacing locals:

> Artists don't cause gentrification; there have always been artists
> here. Gay people don't cause gentrification. But the argument in
> the day, that gay people were the shock troops, that's bullshit. Gen-
> trification is a systematic policy event that occurred globally in
> every major city in the West. And the argument that gay people
> psychologically opened these spaces, that's false.[4]

In fact, by the time Schulman moved to the Lower East Side,
the area had established itself as a thriving lesbian neighborhood
complete with bars and a lesbian health clinic. Perhaps because
they were not interested in opening large, flashy clubs and were
themselves poor, lesbians had already integrated into the Lower
East Side in a way that no other group had achieved. The lesbian community on the Lower East Side was largely invisible to
outsiders. The lesbian businesses and gathering places were not
intended to bring in thrill seekers and, in fact, their patrons
avoided bringing attention to themselves out of a sense of protection. The fact that some of the women, like Schulman, had
grown up in the area further added to their ability to produc-
tively and ethically mix with Lower East Side residents.

When the Saint opened in 1980 as the largest, most commercial
expression of gay male sexuality ever, it did so on Second Avenue in the center of what was becoming the hottest cultural
scene in New York, perhaps the world. The poet laureate of the
scene was a gay man named Rene Ricard: a nasty, even more
cynical version of Andy Warhol, who enjoyed the power of
making and breaking careers in his East Village empire. Ricard's
"Pledge of Allegiance" appeared in a 1982 issue of *Artforum,* urg-
ing his subjects to tolerate any level of grating obnoxiousness in
hopes of commercial gain:

> In society culture is a matter of individuals. One must never make
> the blunder of mistaking someone at the center for someone at the

periphery. One must have the sense of the moment and the real story. The truth, if you wish, doesn't come pre-wrapped in newsprint. You meet the moment in the form of individuals and you pay attention because the Delphic utterance is often accompanied by loud farts and spoken through rotten teeth.... One acquires a tolerance of ambiguity: the gatecrasher you eject tonight may turn you down for a job tomorrow.[5]

Ricard's manifesto, while sharing some scatological rhetoric with the proclamations of *Fag Rag* a decade earlier, could not have differed more radically in its underlying assumptions. Here, in 1982, was a gay man whose gayness was no longer a point of pride but rather another item, along with (supposed) poverty and addiction, on a list qualifying him as an outsider. And this was not an outsider who wished to stay on the outside. Ricard's outsider prayed for the power bestowed by media attention and the financial clout of the commercial art world. As the world of the Clone came crashing down, Ricard and other gay men jumped ship and turned their attention to the East Village galleries.

The 1980s were generally a time when the popular culture machine thoroughly blended any and all unmined subcultures and regurgitated them in desiccated, digestible consumer bits. The East Village scene in particular was astonishing for its ability to elevate those subcultures directly to the highest levels of power and commerce. Rather than creatively blurring traditionally high and low art forms—or more accurately, blending art produced for the upper middle classes with popular forms intended for the working classes but enjoyed as a guilty pleasure by others—the East Village systematically strip-mined black, Latino, gay, and drug cultures in search of profit. Perhaps it is expecting too much for the East Village artists to have taken on the political struggles of their neighborhood. Writing about the East Village, Walter Robinson takes this view even further: "The avant-garde is not a mystical calling; it is a profession with rules like any other."[6]

The East Village galleries institutionalized the turn-of-the-century practice of bourgeois slumming. They also added shopping to the practice so that collectors could be titillated by their adventure while validating their Sunday afternoon tours as a search for hot new artists. In effect, the canvases and sculptures purchased from the East Village galleries became souvenirs in much the same way that stuffed rhino heads lugged home by earlier generations of rich tourists were tokens of an African safari. When hung on the Park Avenue wall of a rich white collector, a Basquiat canvas and a rhino head become remarkably similar, in that neither indicates an awareness of or commitment to the original environment that produced the object. Only the most powerful (and often gay) of the East Village artists, notably David Wojnarowicz, succeeded in creating work that could survive outside of its original context, and even then it was sometimes in another media, as was the case with the elevation of Wojnarowicz's writing over his visual artworks in the years after his death. Carlo McCormick assessed the real importance of the East Village scene as an indicator of a larger trend in American society: "The tangible importance of the East Village is not that it is something new but that it is a clear articulation of the character of this confusing moment in art history."[7] I would further his thesis by claiming that the East Village art scene typified a confusing moment in American history generally and reflected a culture diminished by AIDS and media saturation.

The East Village was typical of scenes where the participants, as soon as they have secured their reputation as insiders, dismiss the scene as over. In 1982 Ricard was already writing, "The excitement . . . is that we've seen it here before the media killed the fun."[8] The "we" in Ricard's sentence is a vital clue to the heart of the East Village scene. *We* who were on the outside and wanted in. *We* who created a new inside predicated on our earlier rejection. *We* who take immense pleasure in making the former insiders beg for admission. This all sounds remarkably like high school, and like high school, the East Village gallery scene lasted about four years. Participants like Ricard were sure to fetishize the heroic briefness of their glory: "I didn't have time to stop and think whether what I was doing was right; I had to make my history quick because there would be no future, merely a gossamer world blown about on the zeitgeist."

Many of the iconic artists of the East Village such as Wojnarowicz, Jimmy DeSana, Nicholas Moufarrege, Martin Wong, and Greer Lankton, would soon die of AIDS. These artists lost to AIDS are often regarded as some of the most genuine examples of talent from the East Village. This may be due to the fact that their short careers were romanticized, but it is also possible that their connections to gay culture provided a grounding that many of the other artists in the scene lacked. Whereas the emerging artists of the early 1980s East Village were divided into opposing camps of neo-expressionism, neo-conceptualism, and, later, Neo-Geo, many of the artists lost to AIDS did not seem to fit comfortably into any style. Greer Lankton's sculptural puppets, relating to her life as a transgendered woman, were particularly at odds with the canvas-heavy scene. Wong, DeSana, and Wojnarowicz all seemed too genuine for the preening style of the East Village.

As a gossip columnist for the *Village Voice*, Michael Musto was at the center of the East Village nightlife and asserts that: "Gay people were at the forefront of the East Village scene."[9] Musto describes a world in which mainstream publicity and careerism replaced the cultural explorations of the gay nightlife of the 1970s:

> The '80s downtown scene did become too hyped for its own good. By nature a work in progress, it became swarmed on by too many outsiders either ogling with binoculars looking for the next big thing, causing a lot of the Boho types to cash in their chips and try to sell out. It became impossible to top clubs like Palladium or Area, with their gigantic production values, and with the *New York Daily News* covering club characters every day—mentioning them and running their picture—the casual act of going out became a publicity free-for-all, with drag queens knocking each other over to get in the picture.... I was also one of those people angling for

> *Daily News* mentions, which emphasizes the potential absurdity of
> press people writing about other press people. It all exploded when
> downtown became absorbed by the mainstream and a new scene
> had to emerge. By '89, the club kids were prevalent in the club
> scene—they were even younger clubbies with even shorter atten-
> tion spans, even greater willingness to shock, and even larger
> dreams of fame and glory.[10]

As it grew to 450 galleries, the East Village art scene willfully and knowingly hammered the nails in the lid of the Lower
East Side's coffin. From that point on, the Lower East Side became the story of real estate development in which artists were
central players. Ironically, many of these artists then built careers
on the identity of outsider that was represented by their living
on the Lower East Side. The extent to which participants in the
scene were not only oblivious to their effect on the community
but also tried to cast themselves in a heroic light is astonishing.
The writer Gary Indiana was the art critic for the *Village Voice* at
the zenith of the East Village scene. In 1999 he wrote a remembrance of the scene for a special East Village issue of *Artforum:*
"Often these paintings depicted emaciated, punky-looking guys
with their limbs twisted and bleeding from stab wounds, and
when you saw the middle-class white kids making this art,
mostly good-looking boys of about twenty whose parents lived
in Greenwich, you had to laugh."[11] There is no denying that the
East Village was a good time in the 1980s and that many lasting
bonds of affection were formed between the participants. The
issue is the price of the party and its lasting effect on New York
as the former capital of world culture. AIDS is frequently cited
as a key factor in ending that party; but it may be more accurate
to say that AIDS created a cultural vacuum that allowed such a
shallow celebration to begin.

If one is to assign blame for the deterioration of the authentic Lower East Side, it is impossible not to mention New York
University (NYU). Starting at around Third Avenue but eventually penetrating much deeper into what had become the East

Village, NYU radically expanded its student housing eastward. As a corporation, NYU made a savvy investment in the neighborhood by purchasing devalued properties, tearing down the original buildings, and constructing bland dormitories. As a university, NYU was somewhat immune to the sort of criticism that commercial developers faced. To date, NYU has effectively annexed the area around St. Marks Place between Second and Third Avenues as part of its Washington Square campus. NYU provides another opportunity for middle-class, suburban adolescents to insert themselves directly into the subcultural shopping mall of St. Marks Place with no sense of the area's true history.

The East Village was an important testing ground for gay culture because the gay men and artists who comprised the East Village would be the community that would be left to respond as activists to the challenge of AIDS later in the 1980s. Many of the older men in the West Village had already died, were too ill to organize, or were understandably more concerned with creating services for their friends and lovers who were dying. Because the new gay community centered in the East Village was constructed rather than authentic, it would take until ACT UP's formation in 1987 (surprisingly initiated by the firebrand Larry Kramer, who had to realign himself toward the new community rather than his Fire Island friends with whom he had created the Gay Men's Health Crisis) for an effective response from the vanguard. The economic, intellectual, political, and gender divisions of New York's gay community in the 1980s were staggering. When faced with the death of men in their twenties who a few months earlier had been perfectly healthy, when faced with the cultural assaults of a tightly knit, deeply believing Religious Right, this newly constructed gay community would be hard pressed to mount a defense that was not only effective but sustained. By the time that AIDS had been identified, many of the men who had lived in earlier authentic communities rich with a sense of history and shared experience were already dead.

CHAPTER 9

New Role Models

Cookie Mueller and David Wojnarowicz

As in the 1970s, drugs continued to play an important role in gay life. Although a great deal of the East Village culture could be seen as transitory and cynical, drugs formed a common denominator for a stronger element of the culture. Through addiction the Lower East Side had the ability to "bite back" in a unique way through the power of its most enduring authentic culture, the one culture that has had the ability to bring "contact" among all the diverse populations who have arrived to the Lower East Side. This culture of addiction would be tied inextricably to the AIDS crisis both through the sharing of needles and unsafe sex decisions made as a result of drugs. That the Lower East Side has to varying degrees over the years been a drug mart is not unique; many poor communities have been utilized in such a way. However, the Lower East Side has long been fetishized as a site of self-destructive glamour. Beginning in the 1950s, addiction grew into an autonomous cultural force that first inspired and then degraded many artists and intellectuals drawn to the area, as well as those who came to blindly rebel against their backgrounds. Those who participated in the area's drug culture, particularly heroin use, were quickly assimilated with others of all races and classes who physically needed what the neighborhood had to offer and shared a culture that was more powerful than any background. Whether they were the gentlemen of the gilded age, the displaced Beats, the hippies, the punks, or the East Village artists, those who aspired to junkie culture were likely to attain membership. Rick Prol's paintings from the 1980s of an emaciated, black-clad rebel with a spike in his arm, screaming with excitement and horror at having become what he yearned for and feared, are the quintessential expression of the Lower East Side drug culture.

The complexity of addiction, particularly as played out in a self-conscious, theatrical environment such as the East Village, is perhaps best seen in the life of the writer, actress, and character Cookie Mueller. Mueller is a kind of touchstone for the desexualized gay culture of the East Village. Because she had appeared in the gay cult films of John Waters and was an occasional lesbian, Cookie fit easily into the world of gay men. She was also exactly the kind of "messy girl" that gay men idolized in the camp culture of the East Village.

Reading Cookie's work and descriptions of her life, it is as if two parallel worlds existed for Mueller. Her factual existence fits into a depressing narrative well suited to the East Village—one of self-imposed exile, selfishness, and addiction. The other side of Cookie's life, drawn from her writing and descriptions of her from her myriad friends, is dependent upon the same dreary facts but transcendent of them. Whereas Mueller destroyed herself, Cookie lived life as a full-tilt exploration. The opening to her collected writings sadly sums up both parts of her life:

> Fortunately I am not the first person to tell you that you will never die. You simply lose your body. You will be the same except you won't have to worry about rent or mortgages or fashionable clothes. You will be released from sexual obsessions.
> You will not have drug addictions.
> You will not need alcohol.
> You will not have to worry about cellulite or cigarettes or cancer or AIDS or venereal disease.
> You will be free.[1]

Mueller's life seems to have been spent constructing a new family to replace the one that she rejected in suburban Baltimore. Although rigid and cold, her "family of origin" seems not to have been particularly abusive. Their main fault seems to have been their blandness, especially after the death of Mueller's brother at the age of eleven. In reaction to this tragedy, Mueller's mother confided to her daughter the correct response to any difficulty in life—change hair colors. The dutiful daughter noted that from that moment on her closet contained more bottles of hair color than clothing. Including Divine, John Waters, Nan Goldin, and other outcasts, Mueller's later, self-created family could certainly not be described as bland. They flaunted the rebel status Cookie so admired. One sees Cookie most clearly through the eyes of some of these notable friends, such as John Waters, who describes her as "a writer, a mother, an outlaw, an actress, a fashion designer, a go-go dancer, a witch-doctor, an art-hag, and above all, a goddess."[2] Only a goddess in the world of John Waters would be cherished for "her maddening habit of snorting instant coffee before she went out because she 'didn't have time' to make it the normal way."[3]

By the time she arrived in New York, Cookie had already established outsider credentials including life as a hippie in San Francisco and a stay in a mental institution. She also trailed behind her a down-market glamour derived from roles in a number of early Waters films. She had portrayed Divine's daughter in *Multiple Maniacs* (1970), the spy in the crossover cult classic *Pink Flamingos* (1972), a delinquent beautician in *Female Trouble* (1974), Flipper in *Desperate Living* (1977), and Betty Lalinski in *Polyester* (1981). She later had small roles in other underground films—including Eric Mitchell's *Underground USA* (1980), Amos Poe's *Subway Rider* (1981), and Susan Seidelman's *Smithereens* (1982)—though she never really enjoyed the film career she desired.

Mueller seemed more comfortable in the role of white-trash fag hag than that of lesbian, although she enjoyed a long-term relationship with a woman who was described as "her traveling companion." Mueller almost never mentions her life as a lesbian in her own writings but it is discussed in Linda Yablonsky's autobiographical novel, *The History of Junk*, where Cookie appears as a character called Honey Cook:

> Honey was not a pusher. She was another would-be writer and sometimes actress, mother to an eight-year old named Mike. She knew Jayne Mansfield's life story by heart and never went any-where without eyeliner. She worried about her looks, which only fascinated me: a toss of White Minx-tinted hair over blue-flame eyes that winked at the world; whore-pink lips under a Teutonic nose that snubbed it.... She lived in the Village with a blues singer named Lute, a tough, striking blonde out of a film-noir comedy.[4]

Mueller may have been one of the original lipstick lesbians but not everyone appreciated her down-and-out glamour. In his introduction to her collected writings, Waters describes a cab-driver picking up Cookie and remarking, "It's a shame about that hair."[5] Throughout her writing, Mueller seems to see her body as something to experiment with, remaining detached even when she describes stuffing the limp dick of a rapist inside herself to get it over with. There is also a certain sense of won-der about the body. In one essay, Cookie explained, perhaps fac-tually, that human eyes do not grow but remain the same size throughout one's life. And then there is the body as drug recep-tacle. While she was busily drinking, injecting heroin, snorting coke, and gulping pills, Mueller took time out to write a self-help column for the *East Village Eye* in which she both com-posed the readers' questions and provided the answers.

Cookie was a creature of the East Village but she created a world that shared certain characteristics with the Mineshaft era. By erasing any separation between art and life, she operated in a world where self-expression and self-destruction are sometimes indistinguishable during one's immersion in it. In Mueller's world, drugs were art. In *The History of Junk*, Yablonsky's char-acter remarks to Honey Cook, "Art? I don't want to hear about art. The most important thing happening in our culture is drugs, that's what I say."[6] Mueller dressed up addiction in very appeal-ing clothes, snorting and shooting her way through the art world

A-list of the 1980s and traveling all the way to Italy only to find more drugs on the sunlit Amalfi Coast.

If Cookie Mueller's legacy consisted solely of the jaded Cookie who penned an art column for *Details* or the zany Cookie giving advice in the *East Village Eye*, she would be easily dismissed as a colorful but tragic figure whose personal impact was limited to her immediate circle of friends in the closed world of the East Village. However, her collected writings published in 1997 by High Risk/Serpent's Tail show a talented writer who got lost in the indulgences of the East Village. Her early, serious pieces, particularly those about her childhood, reveal a clear-eyed social critic who is anything but oblivious to the chaotic world around her. Also, her astonishing *Fan Mail, Frank Letters, and Crank Calls* (Hanuman, 1988) entirely prefigures the social criticism of Bruce Wagner's hit novel *I'm Losing You.* Mueller weaves the narrative of *Fan Mail* through a series of phone calls, letters, postcards, and telegrams, and demonstrates a sad, compassionate, funny voice that rings clearly beyond the confines of the East Village.

Mueller specialized in life decisions that were both affirming and wildly destructive—choices that were amazingly similar to the gay men of the 1970s whose experiments turned deadly when the stakes were unexpectedly raised. Mueller also tried to have it all by integrating a child and a husband into her life. Her decision to have a child, to stay clean during her pregnancy, to honestly show her child the world she lived in, could be seen as an act of hope. Only her son, having grown up in that world and lost his mother, can say if it actually was. Mueller's further reinvention of herself through marriage to the Italian artist Vittorio Scarpati ended sadly in his death from AIDS, but she wrote that "Vittorio has learned that, like a flood of sunlight, hope can vanquish gloom."[7]

Cookie Mueller's life as a performance had high stakes and her addictions, with their accompanying needles, tipped the scales. The East Village bit her back. When she is seen in the luminous photographs of Nan Goldin or through the wry words of John Waters, it seems worth it. When Cookie described her own life in her own words, it seems far less romantic. In a short story called "Valerie Losing 2," Cookie writes of a woman who wakes up to find that she has lost one of her toes. It is simply gone, used up. One wonders if that toe stands for a life, a soul, hopes and dreams. The story ends with Valerie putting her toe loss in perspective:

> In the last fifteen years, she had lost a lot, beginning with her virginity. She had lost two husbands, countless girlfriends, passports, bankbooks, wallets, one apartment, plants, a car, a dog, valuable jewelry; there were so many things. This was nothing new, only slightly different. She had lost so much it was just something else to mourn over for a bit. She took it in stride. There is a great art to handling loss with nonchalance.[8]

★   ★   ★

How to weave together the threads of the first decade of AIDS; a decade that began with the decline of Clone culture, moved to the hype of the East Village, and ended with the art of ACT UP? As a visual artist, performer, filmmaker, and, especially, a writer, David Wojnarowicz melded the radical nature of gay sexuality, the self-conscious outsider status of the East Village drug culture, and the flash-point politics of the late 1980s. He was steeped in the writers of gay male history—Genet, Rechy, and Burroughs—as well as influenced by the political discourse of ACT UP.

Like most truly radical people I have known, David had a great gentleness to him, which was evident when I first met him at a party in the late 1980s. Only slightly acquainted with the art world at the time, I had no idea who this tall, thin, shy man was, but I remember talking intensely with him for most of the party. A few years later, reading his devastating collection, *Close to the Knives: A Memoir of Disintegration*, I found it hard to reconcile the memory of the person I had met with the terrifying beauty of his writing. *Close to the Knives* remains perhaps the most important work of art to come out of the gay male experience in the twentieth century. David's mature voice as a writer brings to life the full wonder of gay sex, its beauty and loneliness, the endless walking, the search for love in sites of incredible degradation. Such was my admiration for the book that I organized an event at the Drawing Center in New York in 1991, where some of downtown's leading lights read sections of the book as a kind of tribute to its influence. David himself, by then quite ill, attended and read his own work at the end of the event, filling the gallery with his intense rage. It was the second and last time I would meet him before his death in 1992.

A selection of David's journals, edited by Amy Scholder, was published by Grove in 1999 under the title *In the Shadow of the American Dream: The Diaries of David Wojnarowicz*. While much of the later material is reiterated in *Close to the Knives*, the early sections of the diaries are invaluable in providing a glimpse of how hopeful, even naive, David remained through his early twenties despite the experiences of his early life. David's childhood had been marked by periods of abuse from an alcoholic father who was also probably a closeted gay man. His father's death by suicide did not bring a great improvement in David's life, as he continued to be abused by those who bought his body on the streets of New York. The most heart-wrenching aspect of his years living on the streets of New York is not the act of prostitution but that David seemed to be looking for the love of a father in the men to whom he gave his body.

Although he later disavowed most heavy drugs, they were for a time an important part of David's life, integral to many of the horrific visions he would transform into beauty through the power of his writing. By 1980, David writes: "I feel like I've lost my innocence, now that I finally have fucked with needles, the whole romantic attachment to them being blown with the first shot. Now it's just down to the simple level of intake and warmth."[9] David's series of self-portraits wearing a Rimbaud mask from 1978–1979 include an image of David (Rimbaud) slumped against a wall with a needle hanging from his arm.

The fact that David didn't slip into the furthest depths of

heroin addiction, a journey that seemed to appeal to him, can be attributed to a man who would, in fact, function as a father figure in his life, the photographer Peter Hujar. First lovers and then soul mates, David showed Peter his track marks after several weeks of shooting heroin and vomiting constantly. Peter told David that, if he continued to use heroin, their relationship was over. This seemed to have been sufficient to hold David to a course of pot, Ecstasy, and speed.

Speed was a particularly important drug to David's writing during the phase when he would wander the piers on the West Side Highway. David's writing reaches its highest level of beauty when he is consumed by a kind of wanderlust, often fueled by speed. Whether driving with a horny wonder across the harsh flatness of America's deserts or striding through the ruined piers and having sex, the process of mapping and, literally, marking his territory is integral to David's art. Not only did he mark his path through the decaying landmarks of downtown through his writing, David blew smoke from his ever present cigarette out over the Hudson, "spilled his seed" on the dirty floors of the piers, and actually painted some of the walls and windows there. In *Close to the Knives*, he describes the mysterious images with which he and other men adorned the crumbling structures:

> Passing down a long hallway there were glimpses of frescoes, vagrant frescoes painted with rough hands on the peeling walls, huge murals of nude men painted with beige and brown colors coupling several feet above the floorboards. Some of them with half-animal bodies leaning into the room's darkness with large outlined erections poised for penetration. Other walls contain crayoned Buddhas and shining gems floating above their heads in green wax.[10]

His descriptions of the piers and the West Side Highway sex scene evoke the haunted loneliness of anonymous sex. His writing is filled with fellow travelers on the road. Some of David's greatest tenderness and lust is reserved for the long-haul truckers parked along the West Side; the inherent loneliness of their life of travel generating a melancholy sexual charge for him:

> As each cab swung by me there was a video blaze of tiny green and red ornamental cab lights framing the darkened windows containing a momentary fractured bare arm or dim face filled with the stony gaze of road life. In these moments my face travels an elongated neck out my side window and floats up into the shadows of their open windows to place its tongue in between the parted lips of each driver. I could feel their arms reaching through the breeze of our moving vehicles to embrace me from behind.[11]

What fame David achieved during his lifetime was largely a result of his visual artworks, but his relationship with the East Village art scene from which he emerged was troubled. As can be seen in his writing, David's spiritual life was centered in the gay male past of the piers; the beauty of his descriptions of men wandering along the Hudson reaches a nearly religious tone. His odd cadence is filled with descriptions of men as "fellas," street crazies as "characters," and he would surmise that something was "prolly" good. His language clearly identifies him with the waterfront world of Genet, Burroughs, and Fassbinder rather than the theories and ambition of the East Village. David's daily work was in the East Village but the West Village provided the inspiration and emotional foundation for that work.

Still, David lived in the East Village at Thirteenth Street and Avenue A until Peter Hujar died, and then in Peter's loft at Twelfth Street and Second Avenue until his own death. The recognition that he had so long hoped for arrived with the publication of his "Rimbaud" photos in the *SoHo News* in 1980 and shows in the hot East Village galleries Civilian Warfare and Gracie Mansion. The glare of East Village stardom didn't particularly suit someone whose ideology was as serious and personal as David's. In the East Village memorial edition of *Artforum*, Dennis Cooper describes running into a furious, disillusioned Wojnarowicz in the mid-1980s:

> Wojnarowicz sat down with me on a stoop and launched into a tormented, self-righteous, hour-long harangue that has, ever since, struck me as definitive of East Village Art's brief moment, for better or worse. He said that his success was destroying him because

he couldn't reject it in good conscience. He'd dreamed of this kind of recognition and had even fantasized about exactly the kind of black-sheep art world that the East Village scene encompassed in theory.... But this belief had been contingent on the idea that New York was secretly full of artists who had as clamorous a sensibility as his own. Instead, he found himself surrounded by peers whose talent was merely raw, and raw only by virtue of economic hardship, but whose sensibilities were as coddling and self-indulgent as those of the Salles, Fischls, and Longos who populated the official art world.[12]

David's move eastward had been no more successful than that of the larger gay culture. There is a weakening in David's work that coincides with his success in the East Village, a kind of self-righteous political insistence that rings false in the way that his more personal work never does. A hopefulness that David had seen as his redemption in the hard years of his early life was beginning to drain away in the cynicism of the East Village. David's journals are sparse in the mid-1980s: he was dealing with the deaths of friends and began to see writing as his primary artistic practice (although his visual artworks remained the main source of profit) rather than a means of personal reflection. In 1985 David met the last of his lovers, Tom Rauffenbart, who shared the remaining years of David's life and serves as the executor of the Wojnarowicz estate. Rauffenbart describes their meeting:

> We first met in November of '85 but didn't speak. We had sex in the basement of a movie theater on Third Avenue and Thirteenth Street. Then, New Year's Day of '86, I was back there. David was there and we hooked up again. I invited him home that night. When we met, he was on Ecstasy, which was unusual for David. He was worried because somebody told him that, if you fell in love on Ecstasy, you should wait two months to know if it's real.[13]

Rauffenbart is a self-described homebody who was not involved in the art world, and this seemed to be a comfort to David. Rauffenbart says: "David would clean my house. He would never clean his own house. He liked to have somewhere to go where he could settle down and be domestic." At the time, after having had his moment in the sun in the East Village, Wojnarowicz seemed particularly antagonistic toward the art world. Distrustful of its financial promises, David began to hide money in his loft rather than deposit it in a bank or let it remain with his gallery. Rauffenbart describes going with David to a gallery on West Broadway that had damaged one of his paintings and would not fix it. David took a tire iron into the gallery and punched holes into the walls in retaliation. David's dislike of dealers, in particular, fit nicely into the proto-punky profile that the art world so likes to project. On the cover of the East Village memorial issue, *Artforum* uses a disingenuous but funny photograph of David painting a window on Pier 34 with Mike Bidlow. On a filthy window, David has painted a parasitic insect holding out a little picture with the text, "Hi ... My name is Tony Shafrazi ... Hi ... My name is Mary Boone ... Hi ... My name is ... Hi ... Name is ... I am your hope." Above the dealer/insect, David has painted a hangman labeled "Victim of Hype" and the directive, "Artists: stay in control of your work ... hearts+minds."[14]

David did develop many friendships in the East Village scene as well as meeting the leading "characters" of the day. Rauffenbart says that the only time David came home starstruck from a dinner party was the night he met Cookie Mueller, although they did not become friends. The East Village scene was souring both in tone and profitability by the mid-1980s, and David shared its decline even as he had ridden the boom. By the second half of the 1980s, not only was David somewhat stuck in terms of his creativity, AIDS was beginning to rip apart his world and reinforce long-held fears. As Rauffenbart explains: "David was haunted by a whole lot of demons. The fear of being on the streets alone was so pervasive with him. Of course, there was AIDS too. Peter died of AIDS and we were diagnosed."

As David became more ill, he found it increasingly hard to work. Still, some of his most harrowing and beautiful passages of writing come from this period. His illness also motivated him to use film as a new medium for his work. Although they were not shown in the retrospective of Wojnarowicz's work at the New Museum, David's films are as raw, evocative, and poetic as any of his work. The unfinished "Death of Peter Hujar" crystallizes the urban experience of gay men mourning, moving from images of Peter's dead body to shots of a rainy city that are instantly recognizable as David's.

David was peripherally involved in ACT UP, mostly through generous donations of his work to the group. (The reading at the Drawing Center described above was, in fact, a benefit for ACT UP's needle-exchange program.) David's political agenda, while it includes a rage and sexuality that fit well with certain parts of the ACT UP image, was darker. In 1989 and 1990, however, David became a poster boy for the kind of radicalism that ACT UP most lauded during a censorship battle around the exhibition "Witnesses: Against Our Vanishing" at Artists Space in New York. Sadly, David and his work are probably most widely known because of this useless struggle between the National Endowment for the Arts and the nonprofit arts community.

"Witnesses: Against Our Vanishing" was quite a beautiful show before it was overshadowed by controversy. Organized by the photographer Nan Goldin, the power of the show came not so much from the individual works but the fact that those included were actually her friends who were either living with AIDS, had already died, or were at the center of the epidemic. The show included work from Darrel Ellis, Allen Frame, Peter Hujar, Greer Lankton, Mark Morrisroe, Tabboo!, Wojnarowicz, and others. Goldin's show was not so much about AIDS as it was about friendship among outcasts. To her great credit, Goldin saw that sexuality was being repressed because of AIDS and wanted to put the most extreme examples of her circle's sexual lives on view. Looking at the assembled group of artists provides a snapshot of the gay faction of the East Village art community, complete with outsiders, sexual outlaws, transgendered women, drag queens, and, most especially, addicts.

★   ★   ★

David's enduring accomplishment was not political but personal, in creating an inner vision through his early writings that brought to life, once again, the power of gay male culture. The power of these writings has been shown in their growing influence and continued vitality. On the other hand, David's retrospective exhibition at the New Museum in 1998 was a cold, dead affair, demonstrating that the self-referential work created for the art world would inevitably lose some of its intensity when taken out of its original context.

The captivity of illness must have been a terrible burden for David, who so loved to wander and cruise and drive without a destination. His enforced stillness was so strange to him that he almost didn't recognize himself. He wrote in his journal:

> I feel like it's happening to this person called David, but not to me. It's happening to this person who looks exactly like me, is as tall as me, and I can see through his eyes as if I am in his body, but it's still not me. So I go on and occasionally this person called David cries or makes plans for the possibility of death or departure or going to a doctor for checkups or dabbles in underground drugs in hopes for more time, and then eventually I get the body back and that David disappears for a while and I go about my daily business doing what I do, what I need or care to do. I sometimes feel bad for that David and can't believe he is dying.[15]

David was perhaps the only through line connecting the sexual artists of the 1970s with contemporary gay men. By mapping the hallucinatory world of sexual artists created by Genet, Rechy, and Halsted, David ensured that it would survive, at least in the written word. By walking and recording his visions, David insisted that there was beauty to be found among the ruins of the West Village. If anyone had the power to extend the map of that world eastward, it would have been David. But now the western piers are gone, the Saint closed, Times Square sanitized, the Meat District transformed, and David is dead. So much is lost.

CHAPTER 10

The Sexual *Flâneur*

By 1984, AIDS had reached critical mass in New York. It had by then been named, even though all of its underlying pathology was not understood. By the end of 1984, under the old (and narrow) CDC guidelines, five thousand cases of AIDS had been reported in the United States. About half of those cases were in New York City, and they disproportionately affected the sexual pioneers of the 1970s. The first wave of AIDS cases in New York City was particularly visible because it focused on a group of men who were the most privileged tastemakers in American culture. Many of these men fit into the interlocking groups of Clones that gravitated to either Fire Island or the Mineshaft or both. In 1984 AIDS was still new and growing but its influence had reached every aspect of gay life.

Even though the East Village was the new center of gay life in the 1980s, some remnants of the 1970s Clone sexual culture still persisted in New York, concentrated on the West Side, with spotty coverage uptown and eastward. One way to bring the geography of the time back to life is to mentally walk the streets as a sexual *flâneur*, noting the history of gay male Manhattan as it existed in 1984. (A *flâneur* might be described as an informed walker or a tour guide of a sort. Gay men have always excelled at this art, and Edmund White's recent book *The Flâneur* gives one a magnificent view of Paris.) Although gay male sex took place throughout the city, the remnants of Clone sex were very much downtown, with a few spots in Chelsea and an important outpost in Times Square.

In 1984 one could begin a walking tour of gay sex by strolling down Christopher Street, an area shell-shocked but still active. The streets were still full of men frequenting the rather tepid bars near Seventh Avenue and moving slowly toward the headier scene that began at the West Side Highway. At the corner of Christopher and Hudson, the Christopher Street Bookstore functioned as a kind of standing bathhouse, with slamming doors piercing the silence of the men who circled endlessly, peering into booths. The bookstore attracted a mix of neighborhood locals, bridge-and-tunnel types, closet cases and off-duty hustlers who might be had at a reduced rate. Badlands, a leather bar, bordered the West Side Highway and marked the extremity of sexual culture on Christopher Street.

In the 1970s an elevated roadway ran above the West Side Highway, adding a perpetual gloom to the parking and cruising area below. Although the elevated roadway had been torn down by the 1980s, the area bordering the river was still sexually charged. There one encountered an interlocking mix of older Clones, younger queens, hustlers, and teenage gays, usually black or Latino. In the near distance, rotting piers extended into the water itself. Some of the piers remained covered, whereas others were open to the sky, serving as urban beach and outdoor bathhouse. The West Side Highway was as vibrant on a Tuesday night as on a Sunday afternoon. Circling cars usually contained enticing examples of white trash from the outer boroughs and Jersey, stopping for a bit of action before heading home to suburbia and (sometimes) heterosexual lives. Sex in the cars accommodated both hustling and a convenient quickie. To reach the piers that were still covered in the 1980s, one walked a few blocks north to the riverside bordering the Meat District. Two covered piers survived into the 1980s and, with their exposed industrial materials, shattered glass, and gaping holes in the floor, each was a surreal wonderland of decay, gay sex, and drug use.

Turning back toward the city and crossing back over the West Side Highway, one arrived in the Meat District, which in

1984 was still a theatrical, deserted, and somewhat dangerous destination. A few lofts had been converted to residential use, but Restaurant Florent on Gansevoort Street between Green-wich and Washington was the only real sign of the trendiness to come. On most winter nights, garbage cans burned with a few homeless men huddled around them while transgendered hook-ers worked the streets. Cutting through the Meat District at an angle, the abandoned High Line railroad provided a reminder of the area's industrial past. The Meat District would gradually be ruined as a site for gay sex, but it is difficult to describe it as be-ing gentrified in the sense of displacing poor populations. The area had been, for many years, either abandoned or given over to industrial use. Until recently one could go out the front door in the morning and be surrounded by the still shocking sight of huge carcasses being pulled into processing shops. In summer the streets were greasy and stunk of fat.

The Meat District in 1984 still offered the singular pleasure of navigating the maze of parked meat trucks at night to find sex in the narrow corridors or in the open back of one of the vehi-cles. America would be shocked to know how much red meat it has consumed that had been carted around Manhattan in a truck still slick with the previous night's sex. Although the famous Anvil had already closed by 1984, the Meat District was still an-chored by three important historic landmarks of sexual explo-ration, two of which remain open, although in diminished form, today. The Mineshaft, the most extreme of sexual theaters, would operate profitably until 1985, when the New York City Department of Health would close it along with most of the city's bathhouses. If one went to the Mineshaft on a Saturday night in 1984, one would still find some regulars and a steady stream of new converts engaged in the full range of sexual activ-ity for which the club was famous.

Also interesting were the two clubs in the ominous triangu-lar building on the eastern border of the Meat District, where Hudson and Ninth Avenue converge. In the basement, the Hellfire Club provided a reasonable facsimile of Hades as deco-rated by a serial killer. Cold stone walls became slick with sweat as an evening progressed. Tattered sofas sat close by metal cages. The club, which seemed small at first, was mazelike, with a number of interesting hidden nooks and doors that opened into strange, small rooms. In fact the architecture of the club was fluid; a previously open room might be unexplainably closed one weekend but another previously hidden nook opened to reveal a new sexual setting. The space seemed alive. The club hosted alternate nights for straights and gays interested in S/M —an important (albeit isolated) point of contact between the two cultures. Still open today, the club was much discussed in the popular media as a favorite hangout of Andrew Crispo. Crispo, a New York art dealer, was accused of being involved in the S/M murder (the victim's body was found wearing a leather mask) of a male model in 1985. Crispo was never convicted, but his assistant-*cum*-flacky, Bernard LeGeros, took the rap for the crime. David France's *Bay of Toys*, which recounted the murder, provided a lurid, exciting description of a Meat District still re-plete with coke-fueled S/M, snuff films, the Mafia, and male hustlers.

On the other side of the Hellfire building, at street level, another club called J's Hangout provided an after-hours (and of-ten after-work) jerk-off environment that is also still in opera-tion. J's was less picturesque than the Hellfire but provided for an interesting streetscape on an early Monday morning when di-sheveled men emerged into the mix of Wall Streeters on their way downtown to work. The Meat District was also home to a range of other clubs that opened and closed quickly, but the Mineshaft, the Anvil, the Hellfire, and J's had cemented the area's reputation.

If one were to take a swing uptown before turning east, the route would traverse what is now New York's premier gay neighborhood, Chelsea. In 1984 Chelsea had already developed as a gay center but without the commercial strip of restaurants and bars that now extends up Eighth Avenue from Fourteenth Street to Twenty-Third. At the time, Chelsea was home to New York's two most popular leather bars, the Eagle and the Spike. Located on Eleventh Avenue, in the waterfront section of Chelsea, the bars seemed more connected to the Meat District than the residential streets of Chelsea. Indeed, housing projects and industrial warehouses formed a rough buffer zone that one had to cross to reach the bars. Leather men would cruise back and forth between the two bars, only a block apart, looking for action. The art galleries that now line these blocks effectively used the sexual-outlaw profile of the area to establish their cutting-edge status in a manner reminiscent of the Lower East Side's journey from authentic to constructed community.

Twenty blocks uptown in Times Square, the porno theaters provided a somewhat more restrained setting for sexual explorations. The fact that the theaters were open and busy during the workday added to their importance as a sexual setting for closeted gay men who were only in the city during the day and returned to their wives in the evening, perhaps pulling over in their cars on the West Side Highway for one last release before going home. By 1984 and 1985, the Times Square theaters were beginning to succumb to the conveniently parallel forces of public health and "urban renewal" that Samuel Delany so brilliantly details in *Times Square Red, Times Square Blue*, but they would remain active well into the 1990s. Most of the gay sex theaters were located on Eighth Avenue in the few blocks above Forty-second. The theaters, grand movie palaces at one time, were for the most part dirty shells where porn was projected on blurry video rather than film. Few watched the porn in any case, preferring to wander the aisles and drop down into an empty seat for a quick encounter before going back to work. The balconies of the theaters were slightly more restrained than the back rooms in downtown bars and clubs, but held a greater fascination because of the mix that Delany describes. The Times Square theaters were the arena for true interclass "contact," frequented by actual working-class and poor men as opposed to downtown venues where many of the participants only dressed the part.

Finally, returning downtown, one would find a smattering of gay male sexual outlets housed in movie theaters in the East Village. The theaters, most with unmarked doors opening up to stairs leading down to mazelike, filthy, and surprisingly huge basements where booths had been constructed. Unlike Times Square, where the theaters still functioned to an extent *as* theaters, the East Village spots seemed like fronts that hid the main action downstairs. These theaters were clustered in the area between Second and Third Avenues below Fourteenth Street. The theaters, along with street pickups, still provided some interesting moments of interaction between white gay men and Latino men who may or may not have been closeted. This mixing was less prevalent in the bars, clubs, and discos on First and Second Avenues such as the Rock and Roll Fag Bar, Boy Bar, and, of course, the Saint.

This walking tour might seem to present a picture of a still vibrant gay male sexual culture and perhaps it does in terms of opportunities for sex. What had changed, however, was that each sexual encounter was weighed down with a roster of questions about its safety and the nagging aura of self-destruction and shame. Although they may not yet have changed their behavior, gay men did not enter into these encounters in 1984 with the freedom that they had enjoyed a few years earlier. Aside from concerns of actual medical safety (rules for safe sex are still in flux and were very confusing in 1984), the change in emotional health is also important to note. When one's conception of sexual life moves from an arena of creative exploration to that of certain self-destruction, the emotional toll is immense. Young gay men entering urban life in the 1980s saw constant evidence in the form of rapidly wasting elders that sexual exploration was not only wrong but deadly. They joined a community that had turned away from its past and floated amorphously in the cynical mix of the East Village. This atmosphere finally stamped out the last few creative embers of 1970s sexual culture and was the catalyst for gay men to actively repress their sexual heritage.

Carolyn Dinshaw, director of NYU's Center for the Study of Gender and Sexuality, considers the real contribution of gay men in the 1970s as "the creation of a culture of pleasure,"[1] where the taking of pleasure was not only acceptable but expected. That culture of pleasure, perhaps not entirely guiltless but expansive, had disappeared by the mid-1980s. Gay men continued to have sex, but the physical release of sex was a poor substitute for the earlier world of gay men where, as Felice Picano says, "there was no horizon."[2] Gay men in the 1980s faced not only horizons but imposed borders of what was permissible.

One of these borders involved the baths. Because gay baths had grown directly from the steamy camaraderie of earlier straight establishments, they existed as a site of sexual exploration long before clubs and discos appeared. A number of these baths remained open well into the AIDS crisis, creating widespread dissent within the gay community about the validity of such establishments in the face of a sexually transmitted epidemic. Most of the baths were located in lower Manhattan, with the exception of the Mount Morris Baths on upper Madison Avenue, which caters to men of color and is still open today. By 1984, the roster of baths downtown was shrinking. Along with the filthy, exciting Everard Baths at Twenty-eighth and Broadway, the New St. Marks Baths (which had supposedly opened in reaction to the Everard) was still operating and still bringing in a huge profit for the Saint's owner, Bruce Mailman. The baths had always been the financial backbone of Mailman's operation, far more profitable than the Saint, which was open only a few nights a week and depended upon cash-draining extravagance. The baths literally never closed and often had a line of men down the stairs waiting to get in. In 1984 Mailman began to face pressure from highly visible activists such as Larry Kramer to respond to the health crisis by closing St. Marks. Whether he was justifying continued profits or really believed he could educate patrons, Mailman refused to close the St. Marks. Susan Tomkin, Mailman's longtime assistant, recalls:

> They didn't close the baths until December of 1985.... He didn't want to close it. The community didn't want to close it. The clients didn't want it to close. His feeling was that they were going to do it anyway so why not let them do it where we could give them information. When they came to close the baths down, there was no lock for the door. The baths had never been shut since the day they opened.[3]

In 1985 the gay community's internal debate became moot when the Health Department ordered the closure of the baths and most other sexually oriented venues in response to AIDS. Mailman's argument that sex would still go on in private and that the baths were at least a place to reach men with educational material has some credence, given current infection rates. Still, it is difficult to assess Mailman's response given the fact that he was both a gay man, a businessman, and a man who would later die of AIDS. Tomkin believes that Mailman actively ignored the possibility that he might become sick: "He never thought he was going to get sick. Maybe a lot of guys think that way. Makes it easier."

Mailman's response was also complicated because of his unusual role in the world he had created. Although he came to dance at the Saint on a Saturday night and would go to the baths, he was relatively anonymous in that world. He did not socialize with his staff and, for the first few years of the Saint's operation, few people outside the club knew what he looked like. Aside from avoiding harassment as a famous club owner, Mailman was likely aware that it would not have been good business for a short, rather unattractive man to be the figurehead of New York's greatest emporiums of gay male beauty. Although Mailman participated in the sexual free-for-all at the Saint and the baths, he also had a long-term relationship with John Sugg that was to last until the end of his life—the couple would have celebrated thirty years together had Mailman lived a few more days. Yet Mailman's life partner was not interested in the Saint and the baths except as a business. Tomkin estimates that Sugg came to the Saint no more than five times during the years it was open. Mailman's relationship was the norm at the time and he explained to Tomkin that sex outside the relationship was no more than athletics, "sport fucking."

Mailman had obviously planned on the St. Marks Baths becoming a long-term and profitable investment. In 1981 he bought 8 St. Marks Place, next door to the baths, with the idea of expanding into the adjoining building. Mailman found that removing the tenants was far more difficult than he had planned, however, and plans for expansion stalled and were then canceled with the closing of the baths in 1985. Tomkin denies that Mailman had planned to develop the East Village into the city's new gay neighborhood: "He liked the East Village the way it was. He liked the diversity."

Yet the potential existed for Mailman to re-create the West Village on the Lower East Side. He owned several properties including the landmarked Colonnades building on Lafayette and condos elsewhere in the neighborhood that could have provided housing for his loyal customers who moved between the Saint and the baths, stopping for lunch and dinner at Mailman's restaurant on Second Avenue. With the closing of the baths, the key to his cash flow, Mailman was faced with the challenge of increasing the Saint's profits. When he finally opened the Saint to the straight world on Friday nights in 1985, Mailman succeeded in doing just that—at the high cost of further weakening the protected world of gay sexuality. As Tomkin explains:

> Bruce was under a lot of pressure from the straight world to open the Saint to them. They wanted to do parties. We were only open Saturday and Sunday. So we opened on Friday to straight people. It was never the same. A lot of the original members didn't like the fact that it was open to straights. I think it was the worst thing in the world when they opened to the straight world. That place was not created for straight people.

Mailman may have been providing AIDS information and condoms at the Saint, but they were not always well received by the membership, who longed for the days when there were few restraints on their behavior. By 1988 many of the original members of the club had died and those who remained were in mourning. The club developed a haunted feeling. In 1987 the other holdout from the heights of gay disco, Paradise Garage, closed when owner Michael Brody lost the lease on the SoHo garage that housed the club. The lease issue was, however, only one component of the Garage's closing that included the fact that Brody was battling AIDS and the club's star DJ, Larry Levan, faced an escalating drug addiction. The Paradise Garage was remarkable in its longevity (it opened officially in January 1978) as its membership base was black and Latino gays with considerably less spending power than the Saint's membership. The Saint reflected its membership in being nearly too perfect, almost precious, in its perfectly designed alternate universe. The Garage was more about sound and music. Paradise Garage and Larry Levan are widely credited with being the catalysts (along with Frankie Knuckles in Chicago) for the house music scene that became a profitable market for the music industry in the late 1980s and early 1990s. Mailman himself had never cared much about the musical component of the Saint, focusing more on the decor, and indeed many criticized the "Hi-Energy" sound that developed at the Saint as soulless and reflective of the mostly white titans of art, fashion, and advertising that danced there each week. Naturally, there was crossover between the two clubs, but it would probably not be unfair to say that there was an element of unspoken racism at the Saint—white DJs played to white men in a fussy environment with a high membership fee.

But by the second half of the 1980s, the Saint itself no longer had the feeling that Mailman had intended—of a class act, the best. When a developer offered to buy the building in 1988 to build the area's first multiplex theater, Mailman accepted the offer. Tomkin explains:

> He got a good deal for the building in May 1988. He didn't necessarily want to keep going but a lot of people wanted it to go on so we did the Saint-at-Large thing [off-site parties that featured the Saint's DJs and were marketed to the club's old members]. But in order to maintain the certificate of occupancy, the people who bought the building asked us to go back in and do parties in 1990. After that, we left completely. Bruce's interest had waned and, I guess, his health had started to decline.

Mailman's party palace had succeeded beyond anyone's expectations in bringing the Clone lifestyle to a new level of visibility and influence. Yet only a few years later, there were few reminders of Mailman's achievements. The St. Marks Baths would never reopen. The Saint's dome and star machine were sold and the building was eventually torn down after the multiplex development failed. The movement of 1970s' Clone culture eastward had failed and, with the disappearance of the Saint, its last reminders were gone.

Between Stonewall and AIDS, at least two successful models for gay male culture had been developed and were thriving. These were both sexual models that depended upon different standards of beauty and class resources. These models mixed, informing one another, but remained distinct.

In the first instance, the leathersex or S/M world was the furthest from mainstream American culture and, therefore, was the most influential as a vanguard. It had developed specialized theatrical spaces for explorations that were so extreme as to be better related to art than sex. The aesthetics of this world were revolutionary—allowing men who might previously been thought of us as ugly to participate on the basis of their hypermasculinity or muscular bodies. Further, working-class men could not only participate in this world but were lauded as the highest standard in that their masculinity was seen as real. The participation of working-class men might have necessitated them traveling from the suburbs into the center of Manhattan, San Francisco, Chicago, or Los Angeles, but the price of admission to the clubs themselves was not prohibitive. The leathersex world faced challenges, particularly in terms of drug use, but it was still functioning and influential by the early 1980s. The fact that many men participated in this world only in secret, or as a compartmentalized part of their lives, only increased its power as ritualized art.

The second model was a commercialized and social form of gay life that depended upon more traditional beauty or financial resources. It would be somewhat too easy to characterize the Fire Island Clones as typical of this second model because they had, until the late 1970s, allowed for some instances of economic and political diversity. However, as the price of admission rose with the real estate values in the Fire Island Pines, this second group narrowed and slowly became a lifestyle rather than a functioning vanguard. What had been revolutionary only a few years earlier—living an out gay life in an openly gay resort—had become a consumer exercise by the end of the 1970s.

The Fire Island model eventually became the dominant form of gay male life and was opened to a broader public, at least in an aspirational sense, through entrepreneurs like Bruce Mailman. Ironically, the aesthetics of this lifestyle were heavily influenced by the leathersex world but, when these symbols of exploration—wearing leather, fisting, masculine definitions of beauty—were transplanted from the leather world into commercial settings such as the Saint, they wilted.

Why did this second scene, dominated by the beautiful and powerful Clones, triumph over the rawer but more authentic world of leathersex? The easy answer is that AIDS made extreme, raunchy sex seem too frightening. But AIDS ultimately killed just as many of the Fire Island men as the Mineshaft crowd. AIDS was, after all, known at one point as the Saint Disease for the huge percentage of Saint members represented in the early deaths. Later, proponents of S/M sex would be among the most successful in effecting behavioral change and lowering infection rates.

No, the deeper reason for the rapid decline of the leathersex world was perception rather than actual infection rates. This was one of the first examples of how the gay community's responses to the AIDS crisis were determined by nonstatistical, political agendas. This can be seen in Bruce Mailman's purge of the leather sensibility from the Saint in 1984. In a void of factual information, surely it was the dark and dirty that brought death rather than the promiscuous but pretty. As a lifestyle, the idea of financial success and the purchasing power that comes with it were easily more appealing. Although the circumstances were tragic, the demise of a more radical, separatist lifestyle may not have been entirely bad were it not for the fact that the extreme leathersex world still held the seeds of revolutionary change that were so important to American culture and were seen nowhere else in the country at the time—or since.

Gay people were still among the movers and shakers in the East Village, but with a few exceptions their sexuality was no longer a source of power. Gay male sexuality in the East Village was mostly sublimated into drag and other camp forms that were not only palatable but also profitable in the straight world. Boundaries of style and political intent were already beginning to form in the early 1980s that would become important later, particularly with the development of a new gay style around ACT UP. The artist and historian Jonathan Weinberg recalls one such instance of tension between West and East Villages: "From a historian's standpoint, it's interesting to me to read Keith Haring saying that they put up signs that said, 'Clones go home.' That they were very much aware that there was a West Village and there was an East Village."[4]

Like all children, the gays of the East Village tended not to acknowledge their historical debt to the Clones, unaware that in a few years a new type of clone would arise from ACT UP that would be just as rigid in definition as any leather man cruising Christopher Street. Perhaps the relative invisibility of gay men in the East Village art scene derives from the fact that any kind of gay visibility was seen as relating to earlier Clone culture. This willful ignorance of the past and self-imposed invisibility, however, has a demonstrable effect when looking at the published histories of the Lower East Side. While Christopher Mele's *Selling the Lower East Side* acknowledges the presence of gay men throughout the area's history, other more traditional historical overviews such as Janet Abu-Lughod's *From Urban Village to East Village* manage to avoid using the word *gay* entirely.

The development of camp and, in particular, drag as a primary identifier of gay culture centered in the clubs of the East Village and later penetrated pop culture at unprecedented levels through performers such as RuPaul. The marketing skills of drag queens–*cum*-promoters were an estimable force in 1980s American culture; particularly notable was the growing influence of Lady Bunny's "Wigstock." Films, television shows, and plays about gay life now regularly use an East Village–style drag queen to denote their hipness. These current drag queens have an amazingly narrow pedigree that almost always leads back to the Pyramid Club or Boy Bar.

Using drag as a nonthreatening way of indicating gay life in popular culture allows mainstream America to avoid their more difficult feelings about actual gay male sex. I believe that in fifty years' time we will look back at drag and camp as the minstrel shows of gay culture—amusing but ultimately sinister and degrading, an easy way for straight culture to avoid the realities of our sexuality.

As the idea of gay male sex became paired with death during the 1980s, a sort of condescending pity became an easy and acceptable reaction to what had only a few years before been a culture so experimental that it was threatening. When sex is removed from gay culture as happened in the East Village drag scene (backroom gropings aside), the culture opens itself to being co-opted by supposed friends on the left, enemies on the right, and gay men themselves who are uncomfortable with sex. What does it mean that gay men can accept drag queens as an integral part of their culture but still stigmatize transgendered men and women? Drag queens and the desexed gay men of pop culture reassure us by allowing us to avoid the complexities of actual sexual behavior.

CHAPTER 11

ACT UP

I was fairly typical of the generation of young gay men who emerged into adult gay life in New York in the mid-1980s. Selfishly, I saw AIDS as more of a spoiler than a crisis, something affecting older men who were not a part of my life. I remember my lover, Dino Moraitis, and I saying to friends in the mid-1980s that we were lucky that no one we knew was sick. But I would soon bury Dino and participate in a new era of gay creativity as exciting as the sex art of the 1970s.

Arriving in New York, I sought connections to the gay world but could find none. I told Dino one night that I wanted to visit the Mineshaft because I knew it would close soon. Our visits to the Mineshaft, the Saint, and the Times Square theaters were like visits to archaeological sites, places still visible but clearly of the past. We were most comfortable somewhere between the alluring past of the West Village and the hollow future of the East Village, so we settled on University Place, balancing on the border. Our friends tended to be straight women and we were not closeted but disconnected.

It is all the more amazing to me that, out of this rigid and isolated experience, I could have been forever changed by something as simple as a poster. In 1987 I began seeing a remarkable poster on the streets of downtown New York. The poster seemed to resonate with a new kind of energy, with its glossy black field interrupted by a pink triangle and, near the bottom, large letters reading "Silence = Death." In small type at the bottom of the poster, readers were questioned:

> Why is Reagan silent about AIDS? What is really going on at the Centers for Disease Control, the Federal Drug Administration and the Vatican? Gays and lesbians are not expendable ... Use your power ... Vote ... Boycott ... Defend yourselves ... Turn anger, fear, grief into action.

In even smaller type, hiding in the corner of the vast field of black, was a copyright notice reading "1987 AIDS Coalition to Unleash Power." The poster demanded action but refused to name specifics. The designers of the poster (including the brilliant Avram Finklestein, who would later become a member of the groundbreaking design collective Gran Fury) realized that they needed to reach gay men with style as well as substance, using the provocative, teasing methods of advertising. My recognition of the physical beauty and rage contained in the "Silence = Death" posters must have been a similar experience to that of gay men who saw Fred Halsted's *LA Plays Itself* in 1972 and realized that there was an entire, hidden world seething beneath the visible gay scene. Suddenly, though I knew nothing about it, I felt intuitively that there was in fact a gay world that I could not only identify with but also aspire to join. The poster itself, because it was created before ACT UP came into formal existence, lacked a meeting time, contact information, or tangible direction. Although the poster did not act as an advertisement for ACT UP, the designers who created it were involved in organizing ACT UP, and the poster's sensibility was perfectly in tune with the new group.

At the time, I was working at the Kitchen, a center for video and performance art, and a glamorous woman of about my age had recently joined the staff. Maria Maggenti had long blond hair and had already adopted the ACT UP Clone style of black leather jacket, white T-shirt, ragged jeans, and heavy black shoes. As ACT UP's repertoire of buttons and "crack-'n-peel" stickers grew, the leather jacket would become a billboard for slogans and images. The ACT UP Clone drew certain elements from earlier Clone style and updated them with an East Village sensibility; the jeans were battered and worn loose in the style of black youth rather than the tight contours of the West Village. The style suggested an idealized body but was more conducive to a range of body types than the 1970s Clone look, including the female body. The ACT UP Clone could be either male or female, but the look was distinctly sexual. Maria wore it well. The sexualization of lesbians for gay men was a major departure from the 1970s when all female bodies were considered anathema to gay male sexuality. In the world of ACT UP, flirtations, love affairs, and simple fucking were fairly common between gay men and lesbians who had formed new, powerful relationships that came without the rules of precedent.

Maria, who was later to achieve success as a filmmaker and screenwriter, would take me to my first ACT UP meeting. I was immediately enthralled with the left politics espoused by the members, especially the women. There were certainly beautiful men in the room and they were made all the more exotic by the fact that they were blindingly articulate and filled with a focused rage. Although I was enthralled with ACT UP, it was not a particularly welcoming atmosphere. For a young gay man from Iowa who had never done any political work, ACT UP was as intimidating as any gay bar. My experience of ACT UP was that it was about the constant interaction of groups of mostly anonymous individuals. In fact, ACT UP shared many traits with twelve-step meetings including a connection between members that was based on a common experience rather than actual familiarity. While I formed lasting friendships with several people, there were many others whose names I never knew even while I was sitting in jail with them.

The daily culture of ACT UP was filled with the cliques and crazies of gay bars, because that is where many of the gay male members had learned how to interact with other gay men before becoming radicalized by AIDS. When an entity is based upon the loosest definitions of democracy and informed by emotions such as grief and rage, many of the social conventions on which daily interactions are predicated are understandably lost. However, that behavior is not unfamiliar in a leather bar or during a performance piece, and for me it is most productive to understand ACT UP in terms of those unstructured environments. To look at ACT UP as a loose space filled with creative individuals has the added benefit of removing the idea of leaders and stars. In the same way that it would be impossible to assign credit or membership to a free-floating group that came together in a bar, it is fruitless to assign credit or blame to individual members of ACT UP. Those who quietly attended committee meetings or who only marched in demonstrations played just as important a role as those who spoke fiercely from the floor or were quoted in the press. Individuals were relatively unimportant in the larger cultural action that was created by the group. ACT UP outwardly detested the idea of star players, especially if they fit the old model of gay white men. Larry Kramer wisely lowered his profile after his early central involvement. Other high-profile members (such as Peter Staley, who unfurled banners on the facade of the FDA and the floor of the New York Stock Exchange) were admired, but with an undercurrent of resentment for their individual visibility.

I arrived in ACT UP too late to participate in the group's first action, a march on Wall Street on March 24, 1987, to demand access to drugs and a coordinated national response to AIDS. However, I had made it to ACT UP in time for the group's first anniversary march on New York's City Hall in 1988. The group insisted on targeting not only arch-conservatives like Ronald Reagan and Jesse Helms but also liberals such as then mayor Ed Koch, whose closeted fear prevented him from effectively responding as mayor of the American epidemic's center. ACT UP was at its best in the streets, and it was particularly inspiring on that day at City Hall. The mix of blazing graphics, chants, television cameras, police hostility, and deep passion made an easy case for political involvement to a young gay man who had never felt a part of anything. I still have a photo of my

friend Maria, who had taken me to ACT UP, being carted away
in a bus after her arrest; her head sticking out of the window, she
was still screaming slogans. For the first time, I wanted to belong
and to be more than an observer.

Soon after, I was introduced to Donald Moffett and other
members of Gran Fury. As the Kitchen's PR director, I commissioned Gran Fury to produce a poster. Its response cemented my
belief that this was a group with whom I could fully identify.
Gran Fury's design, indicting those who hid behind facile cultural responses to AIDS, perfectly summarized what I felt about
the growing impotence of art in the face of AIDS. Similar to the
"Silence = Death" project, Gran Fury's poster for the Kitchen
was printed on wildly expensive, high-gloss black paper and carried a screaming white text:

WITH 42,000 DEAD

ART IS NOT ENOUGH

TAKE COLLECTIVE DIRECT ACTION
TO END THE AIDS CRISIS

The Kitchen's board of directors was apparently less than
pleased with this message invalidating art's power to respond to
the most pressing social issue of the day. The poster eventually
led to my resignation from the Kitchen. What the poster had
achieved for me personally, however, was my first connection to
the gay community and an overall shape for my central beliefs
about the function of art in American life. Over the course of
the next three years, I would participate in ACT UP in two
ways—one that was constantly fulfilling and the other that was
ultimately destructive.

My fear of being arrested was finally overcome by my need
to participate. I joined what was called an "affinity group" for
ACT UP's national protest at the Federal Drug Administration,
demanding accelerated and compassionate access to HIV drugs.
The purpose of an affinity group is to protect the individual during the arrest process and articulate specific messages within the

larger shape of the demonstration. Each affinity group was assigned a number or "wave" that would be used in coordinating
the flow of the action, and most took on campy names. I can't
recall that my affinity group ever had such a name but we decided on a vivid visual identity in the form of bloody lab coats
that we believed illustrated the culpability of the research bu-
reaucracy in AIDS deaths. The affinity group gleefully painted
our lab coats with splashes of gory red paint, dripping hand-
prints, and slogans such as "The FDA has blood on its hands."
On the day of the demonstration, the police looked particularly
worried as they approached us in our crimson lab coats: forced
to pick us up during the arrest process, they wore thick rubber
gloves.

Although I was arrested only a few times, the arrests remain
my best memories of ACT UP. For most members, including
me, the arrest process was mostly boring and involved sitting in
jail for a few hours waiting for paperwork to be processed after
which one would receive a summons. Most cases were either
dismissed because of technicalities or ended in a warning. However, not all arrests were so predictable, and women, in particular, found that they might be strip-searched or treated in a
threatening manner. Smaller protests without the benefit of television cameras and thousands of participants were sometimes
more dangerous. Although ACT UP encountered violence at
many demonstrations such as the 1992 Republican National
Convention in Houston, the worst injuries ever sustained by an
ACT UP member were suffered by Christopher Hennelly at a
demonstration closer to home. After a Monday night meeting in
February 1991, the membership decided to march on the Mid-
town North Police Precinct to protest the use of excessive force
at an earlier demonstration. I remember that many of the police
were on horseback that evening, which always added to the
sense of danger. Without warning, the police charged the group
and began to pick off marchers, including marshals, without
warning. Hennelly received blows to the head and was taken
into the station house, where the beating continued. The force
of the blows resulted in seizures affecting the right side of his

body and his speech center. Hennelly remarks, "I was lucky I had people from ACT UP over those years baby-sitting me when I couldn't walk and talk right."[1] Hennelly received a modest settlement after fifty-nine depositions, but his case to the Civilian Complaint Review Board would prove more frustrating. In 1997, with a settlement already agreed upon and with extensive videotape of the incident available, the Review Board substantiated the case but declined to act upon it. The case file was also returned from the Review Board with substantial evidence missing. Hennelly continues to have seizures to this day, but he states gamely, "I used to have several dozen a day. Now they only happen a few times a month when I'm fatigued."[2]

Aside from participating in demonstrations, raising money for ACT UP through sales of contemporary art was my other focused activity within the group, and through this work I came to know many wonderful artists, dealers, curators, and collectors. However, ACT UP's "Auction for Action," which I worked on intensely, had unexpected consequences. The event raised more than six hundred thousand dollars for ACT UP, an unprecedented and, ultimately, unhealthy amount of money for a group that often positioned itself in opposition to mainstream AIDS organizations. The sudden flood of money led to several very painful and divisive cases of embezzling, including one that pitted the mostly white gay men of the Fund-raising Committee against a black man who admitted to stealing large amounts of money. Money also created troubling political quandaries such as paying the *New York Times* twelve thousand dollars for a large ad after having earlier marched outside the home of the paper's publisher in protest of inadequate AIDS coverage.

Both conflicts and unity were played out at ACT UP's Monday night meetings. The meetings, famously fiery and long, often started with the group stating the mission statement in unison, "ACT UP, the AIDS Coalition to Unleash Power, is a diverse, nonpartisan group of individuals, united in anger and committed to direct action to end the AIDS crisis." They often ended in exhaustion or hurt feelings. The Monday night meetings functioned on the pragmatic level of organizing actions, disseminating treatment information, and allowing committees to make reports. They also provided a forum for socializing and cruising. But the Monday night meetings also developed the culture of ACT UP itself, a culture that was inclusive but intensely competitive, highly sexual, intelligent, and chaotic. ACT UP provided a forum for many people who might have been shunned in more mainstream gay society to be recognized for the first time. Most of these people were recognized because of their apparent intelligence and hard work. But others found that the Monday night meetings were a forum in which freedom of expression could be stretched to its limit. The group's decentralized leadership structure and focus on consensus decision-making was itself a political statement in response to the hierarchical structure of many AIDS organizations. The revised "ACT UP Working Document" stated this belief up front:

> One fundamental principle has to be emphasized. There is only one body of authority, supreme and unappealable, in ACT UP and that is the general floor at the weekly Monday night meetings. It is the sole legitimating and financial authority. The floor can, by majority vote, decide whatever it wishes.[3]

If there were ACT UP members who were embraced as "stars," they were women. Many of ACT UP's men were enthralled, for the first time in their lives, by women. Older men who had lived through the 1970s gay/lesbian split found themselves working in concert with their female counterparts for the first time in a decade. Younger men who had never taken women seriously were forced to confront their misogyny. Women who had been activists since the 1960s trained younger men who had never been politically involved. And, finally, the men of ACT UP saw that women were actively participating in saving the lives of men when they could have easily remained sympathetic observers.

Whereas ACT UP was dismissive of the contemporary gay male power structure, it was steeped in the history of earlier political struggles. ACT UP sometimes operated at the borders of nonviolence but always remained within them. ACT UP's civil disobedience training was largely based on the guidelines of the War Resisters League. ACT UP's Civil Disobedience Manual opens with a quote from Frederick Douglass:

> Those who profess to favor freedom, yet deprecate agitation, are men who want crops without plowing up the ground. They want rain without thunder and lightning. They want the ocean without the awful roar of its many waters. This struggle may be a moral one; or it may be a physical one; or it may be both moral and physical; but it must be a struggle. Power concedes nothing without a demand. It never did and it never will.[4]

Members of the Left have derided ACT UP as a group of middle-class white gay men, radicalized only when their lives were in jeopardy and grooving to the words of Frederick Douglass. I would maintain, however, that *middle class* is not always a derogatory term and that the civil rights movement, so lionized by these same naysayers, was also filled with middle-class activists who would later return to resolutely traditional lives. It seems to me that Frederick Douglass remains a more laudable role model for gay men than Rene Ricard and Andy Warhol. The influence of left politics in ACT UP was not superficial. In addition to the many female members who had been involved in political struggle for years, the group also included a straight man, Mike Spiegel, who had been the former national secretary of Students for a Democratic Society (SDS).

One of the most inspiring and intelligent speakers at ACT UP meetings was an older lesbian named Maxine Wolfe. Wolfe is testimony to the fact that the group valued people with experience and commitment. In an interview with Laraine Sommella, Wolfe describes her view of the group:

> ACT UP has always been called a gay white male group. But the group of people who started ACT UP initially included women and people of color. There have always been lesbians and gay men of color and straight women. About the only group not really rep-

> resented in ACT UP were straight men, and there have been a couple of those too. Even though the Lesbians were a small group, we were the people who had done politics. We were the people who did the civil disobedience training. We have always been the marshals.... The men have always been the graphic artists and we do the xeroxing and typesetting. There are things that everyone has access to. Gay men have access to graphics; we have access to reproduction.[5]

ACT UP achieved many tangible victories, particularly in forcing the American medical establishment to respond more compassionately to those with life-threatening diseases. Another great achievement of ACT UP was empowerment of those who had previously played the role of passive patient. In 1988 ACT UP's Treatment and Data Committee held a teach-in for the group. Its essential lesson, as stated in a handbook for the session, was, "Know your shit. Knowledge is power. Every significant gain won by ACT UP has flowed from our unassailable command of the issue."[6] This knowledge, when paired with direct action, was an intimidating force for pharmaceutical companies and researchers accustomed to unquestioned authority. Activists were told, "Any scientist is influenced by received dogma and industry alliances. Challenge them to make sure that these things are not biasing their research."[7] When still confronted with an unyielding system, the committee suggested:

> Most rewarding of all is the well-orchestrated drug company action. For the most part, pharmaceuticals are much more worried about their public image than monolithic government bureaucracies. Make sure the action plan is well designed and that you have what you need for a successful action. Sometimes this includes handcuffs or electric power drills.[8]

ACT UP single-handedly created an awareness of the greed of pharmaceutical companies and continues to keep this issue in the spotlight. ACT UP thanklessly provided mainstream AIDS organizations with the "bad cop" pressure that allowed others to work within the system utilizing a "good cop" persona. But some of these achievements have since been questioned even by those involved in ACT UP. Drugs did reach people with AIDS, but many were ineffective or toxic. Pharmaceuticals have lowered prices in some cases but still hide effectively behind arguments of inflated development costs and copyright protections. And many of us went to work in those very institutions we criticized.

To my view, the great and enduring achievement of ACT UP was less directly related to AIDS research. ACT UP provided a forum where gay men and lesbians could at least provisionally trust one another after the divisiveness of the 1970s and where men were forced to acknowledge the skills and power of women, both personally and in political struggle. The women who came to ACT UP did so out of complex reasons. Many of them had a long history of political involvement but had never found an organization that was open to both feminist and gay concerns.

Ann Northrup was perhaps the most visible woman in ACT UP. Northrup had left CBS News to work as an AIDS educator at the Hetrick Martin Institute and had a background in civil rights and feminism. Northrup had not faced the homophobia that many lesbians had found so prevalent in feminism: "I was part of the *Ms. Magazine* faction that was very lesbian friendly. I made my own choices about stepping away to concentrate on news."[9] Having come from a background in television news and growing up with four brothers, she was comfortable working with men, but found that there was a significant "difference between being appreciated for who you were and being appreciated despite of who you were." Northrup was admired in ACT UP because of her commitment and her central role as one of the group's Monday night meeting facilitators. But her relationship with gay men in the group was also based on other factors:

> I felt I was made into sort of a mother figure in ACT UP because of my age. My attitude played a part too—I have a smart mouth. I'm not one of those who describes herself as a gay man but I know that I'm not the traditional granola lesbian. Maybe because I'm too

much of a news junkie, a pop culture person. When I was helping run the meetings at ACT UP, I stood up there with a large sense of entitlement and self-respect. That attitude of "Fuck You" to the world was an attractive quality at that point to people who were feeling threatened and vulnerable. I had people tell me they were empowered by that.

Sarah Schulman suggests that the socialization of women as caretakers played out very strongly in ACT UP. As a writer, Schulman's involvement was further complicated, as she had a particular presence in the group and a connection to gay men. She is pragmatic about the relationship, though:

> Gay men were treating us with respect and that was very intoxicating. Now I realize that the reason that happened was that they were desperate.... So many men died that there were so many gaps, places where women would usually be excluded—and I mean that personally and professionally—so if your boyfriend died or your best friend died and you needed a new friend and the person you were dealing with every day was a woman who knew how to be a friend, then all of a sudden she had a value she would have never gotten in your life if all the men hadn't died.... There was also a space for me professionally that was created by people dying. For me personally, this weird coincidence happened because I was writing about AIDS. I didn't realize that men would then be interested in me and take me seriously because I was writing about them. If you're ambitious and you want to have a real career, you have to hook up with men. Suddenly I had these opportunities because I was reflecting men.[10]

Despite the relatively positive experience of Schulman and Northrup, there were deep difficulties in the political relationship between men and women around AIDS. Women were certainly involved in ACT UP because they loved particular gay men who were dying of AIDS and were compassionate, but I also believe that many women in ACT UP tended to embrace a broader political agenda, using AIDS as a focal point. The women of ACT UP were understandably concerned with women being enrolled in drug trials and receiving care. It was natural that lesbians in ACT UP believed that HIV would become a major risk not only for straight women but for lesbians as well. It is only from a contemporary perspective that we can see that straight women have become an important if statistically small segment of AIDS cases in America and that the threat to lesbians never materialized.

The larger political goals of ACT UP necessitated moving AIDS beyond the gay community, first through projections based on small statistical samples and later through actively warping the demographics of the disease. ACT UP actively participated in the campaign, discussed later in this book, to reframe AIDS as a disease that would eventually touch all segments of the American population. As Ann Northrup explains, this strategy was understandable in the late 1980s:

> The idea of saying AIDS is not a gay disease to some extent was adopted as a prevention tool to convince the entire population that they were at risk because AIDS had been portrayed by the media as a gay disease. There was so much misinformation that the concept of "AIDS is not a gay disease" was in part invented to deal with that and also to attempt to situate the disease in a way that would make people more sympathetic. I think the prevention idea was certainly laudable. The plea for sympathy was missing the point because it would have been better to say these are people worth saving and caring about no matter what your rotten bigoted ideas are. It was self-defeating in the end, of course, and what it eventually did was to destroy credibility and undermine support for AIDS. I think the heterosexual population didn't have widespread infection because they don't have sex! But when it became clear to them that they were not going to die in droves ... it undermined everyone's credibility. They said "you lied to us." ... It would have always been better to pursue a strategy of self-respect and dignity ... but it's complicated and there were both good and bad reasons for it.

The broadening of ACT UP's agenda and the supposed changes in the demographics of the disease led to a fundamental disagreement about the future of the movement that would eventually lead to a splintering of ACT UP. Though ACT UP New York received much of the attention, ACT UP was an international movement. Other ACT UP groups in America were also bringing together gay men and lesbians for the first time in many years and faced similar challenges in framing a long-term agenda. Ferd Eggan was living in Chicago when ACT UP formed there:

> ACT UP Chicago was formed by a tight-knit group of lesbians and two or three gay men.... They were seven or eight longtime gay and lesbian activists who had very left politics and they became the leadership body of ACT UP Chicago.... Gay white men whose main radicalization was that they had HIV went along with that broader agenda for the first couple years but then started to assert that they had special needs that were more urgent than building a movement. They were the same people who, once AZT began to be distributed, left because they'd gotten what they wanted.[11]

In addition to bringing together gay men and lesbians, ACT UP played a pioneering role in developing media as an activist tool. James Wenzy was one of the pioneering video activists to emerge from ACT UP. Wenzy now maintains the ACT UP New York Web site (www.actupny.org)—the source for many of the historic ACT UP documents cited in this text. Like every other ACT UP member, Wenzy had to find his way in the group: "I was never one to walk in circles or chant slogans so I thought my contribution could be to tape the actions."[12] Wenzy and collectives such as DIVA-TV (Damn Interfering Video Activists) short-circuited the belief that people with AIDS were dependent upon the mass media to validate and educate. (Nearly one thousand hours of videotape created by Wenzy, DIVA-TV, and other video activists has been preserved by the Estate Project and resides in perpetuity as the Royal S. Marks Collection of AIDS Activist Video at the New York Public Library. These tapes are a prime example of the Estate Project's work with material outside the context of traditional art forms. The tapes are seminal documents of the time in which they were created. In

2000 the Estate Project collaborated with the Guggenheim Museum to present a survey of the videos, curated by Jim Hubbard. The presentation, which garnered major media attention, served to alert historians that the tapes existed as a resource.) The work of these activists was often self-distributed, much of it aimed internally at the AIDS community. However, it did have a larger influence. For example, Wenzy produced an influential Manhattan Cable Public Access show called *AIDS Community TV* for a number of years, regularly screening footage from ACT UP protests as well as completed activist tapes:

> It took me three years to get my own weekly public-access show on Manhattan Cable. I noticed that the mainstream media would sometimes cover an issue a week or so after I did a show on it. I have a feeling that there were some mainstream media people watching it.

While the AIDS activist videos created by ACT UP members formed an alternative to mainstream media coverage of AIDS, the organization itself was very much part of the media culture and utilized it brilliantly. ACT UP was truly revolutionary in terms of harnessing press coverage and educating and manipulating the media. The group's success in this area was due in large part to well-designed graphics, articulate spokespeople, and carefully staged demonstrations. But equally as important was the fact that key ACT UP members were themselves from the world of media. In addition to Ann Northrup, who had come from CBS News, Vito Russo and Larry Kramer had an early grounding in media; other members such as Bob Rafsky worked at huge PR firms such as Howard J. Rubenstein Associates. Michelangelo Signorile would later become editor-at-large of the *Advocate,* and a columnist for *OUT* magazine and author of several best-selling books on gay issues. At the time he came to ACT UP, he was not politicized but very familiar with the workings of the mainstream media:

> I came to ACT UP in 1988 as a freelance writer covering entertainment and parties for magazines like *People* and *New York*

Nightlife. Before that I had worked for an entertainment publicist. I went to ACT UP with Michael Musto because we knew that really cute boys went there. I grooved on it immediately and went to the Media Committee, where I thought I could contribute something.[13]

Signorile soon became the coordinator of ACT UP's Media Committee, convinced that ACT UP could actively engage the media using the tools that he and other professionals had learned in their previous work:

Certainly, creating new forms of media was great, and critiquing the media was terrific. But it was important to use the existing mainstream media to bring attention to the epidemic. That meant using a lot of the PR tools that we were taught. ACT UP understood that almost immediately. It was such a great theatrical group that it was easy to publicize. After a while, all you had to do was call the Associated Press and they would be there. The larger challenge for us beyond publicizing protests was affecting the media by planting stories about the government. That took cultivating relationships in the way that really high-powered PR people do.

As ACT UP began appearing regularly on the national news, the group became accustomed to using the media to promote its agenda. Politicians responded to ACT UP's media access, the legal tender of any political career, as they had never responded to any other type of pressure. ACT UP seemed to have successfully conquered the heart of American culture via the mass-media feeding tube. However, America's short attention span applied as much to ACT UP as any other news story. Media coverage became harder to maintain after a few years, as Signorile explains:

In a way, ACT UP like any successful group became a victim of its own success. The shock tactics after a while are not a big deal. Your strategy becomes absorbed and at the end of the day, the media is providing a product and it wants new shtick. It's difficult to reinvent yourself when you're a grassroots organization and not Madonna. It started to become clear to the media that AIDS was going to be contained, so to speak, to certain demographic groups and that made a lot of people less interested.

The media itself became the focus of one component of ACT UP's greatest demonstrations, Day of Desperation. In January 1991 ACT UP mounted a series of disruptions in the life of New York City (other groups also mounted actions in other cities) to illustrate the disruption AIDS had created in our lives. Since New York is the country's media capital, a group of activists decided to invade the studios of major television networks during the evening national news. Activists successfully penetrated the *CBS Evening News* with Dan Rather and the *MacNeil/Lehrer NewsHour* in an unprecedented breach of America's sacred evening news, which had increasingly been ignoring AIDS as its novelty waned. While the CBS audience only saw a brief image of a protester on camera, the disruption of the *MacNeil/Lehrer NewsHour* on PBS was much more successful. When protesters entered the studio, Robin MacNeil was forced to announce to viewers: "There's been a demonstration in our studio; it was a group of nonviolent demonstrators from ACT UP who complained that we and the media are spending too much time and attention on the war in the Middle East, which they say will never kill as many people as are dying of AIDS, and I told them that this program has spent a lot of time on the AIDS matter and will be covering it more in the future."[14] Not only had ACT UP managed to intercede directly into the netherworld of talking heads that controlled the media, the group had placed exactly the right words into the mouths of those talking heads.

I view ACT UP's actions as a kind of performance in the same way that 1970s sex crossed a boundary between life and art. But I believe that ACT UP was much more influenced by feminist art than the theatricality of 1970s leathersex. The power of ACT UP actions came from integrating the theatricality of the demonstration itself into a holistic process of behind-the-scenes preparations. The groundedness of the holistic process, related to earlier political movements and feminist art, could be attributed indirectly to the female-directed sensibility of ACT UP. Feminism produced a number of widely influential performance artists such as Suzanne Lacy, Judy Chicago, and Carolee Schnee-

man. As described by Jeff Kelley in the anthology *But Is It Art?*,
the performances of these women included a range of actions
similar to ACT UP demonstrations. These performances were

> experiences that some of them—and especially Lacy—extended as
> art works on a social scale in the forms of visual images, press re-
> leases, community meetings, letters to police chiefs, ritual per-
> formances, self-defense classes for women, public spectacles, media
> events, videotapes, networking among social-service agencies, and
> as curricula for inner-city teenagers on how to critically evaluate
> the mass media. These forms of social extension seldom come from
> art; they come instead from experiences and professions beyond
> the arts.[15]

Lacy's work, which took place largely in California, included blood as a central metaphor and medium that would be
echoed in ACT UP actions a decade later. Her work around
rape, in which she would outline women's bodies with chalk
and write on the sidewalk, "A woman was raped near here,"
forms a direct antecedent for ACT UP's frequent "die-ins,"
where members fell to the ground while others outlined their
bodies in chalk and wrote slogans such as "One AIDS death
every ten minutes." Even ACT UP's political funerals had a theatrical precedent in a performance by Lacy in 1977, in which a
funeral motorcade followed a hearse from the Women's Building in Los Angeles to City Hall, "at which point nine seven-
foot-tall veiled women ... emerged from the hearse"[16] to bring
attention to women raped and strangled in the city. A photo of
this beautiful action shows the shrouded figures standing on the
steps of City Hall in front of a banner that reads "In Memory of
Our Sisters. Women Fight Back."

As Ann Northrup says, "There is very little new in the
world." Did the politically experienced women of ACT UP,
who would have been familiar with feminist performance, con-
sciously bring these methods to the group? Probably not; they
certainly never explicitly spoke of them to the membership. But
it is important, particularly for those of us whose first activist

work took place in ACT UP, to recognize that we did not invent the world (as many of us believed at the time). Beyond that humility, it is also vital to know that ACT UP occurred in a continuum of political action in America and that history suggests that the excitement of ACT UP can happen again. Even the parts of ACT UP that seemed so specific to its time, such as the manipulation of the media, had been explored before. Kelley describes how Lacy had focused on the press during the performance of "In Mourning and in Rage":

> Rather than depending upon the press to report on the performance per se, the performance was itself a kid of ritualistic press conference designed to capture and fix media attention by anticipating and appealing to its journalistic conventions, including the need for bold, simple images ... concise statements ... a familiar dramatic narrative ... the repetition of images over and over for maximum press consumption.[17]

One wonders at the fact that Lacy's actions were not able to achieve widespread penetration of the media in the 1970s. Certainly the media itself was markedly different in the 1970s, and Lacy was operating more or less in isolation, but the difference in public response might also be related to the fact that ACT UP took the methods of feminist performance and made them look heroic by transferring them onto the bodies of beautiful dying young men. In the American cultural equivalency table, the death of a young man, even a homosexual, probably still outweighs the death of a woman.

Some members of ACT UP did in fact think of demonstrations in terms of art. Jon Greenberg, who had been involved in the *MacNeil/Lehrer NewsHour* portion of Day of Desperation, described such actions as theater:

> ACT UP demonstrations are theatre outside the bounds of the physical theatrical space. They are theatre in the world, and accomplish the types of reactions, actions and catharsis that all people in the "conventional theatre" only dream about. We use the same tools, however. Research, intensive pre-production planning,

bringing together the actors (demonstrators), rehearsing them and getting to their motivating emotions (anger, fear, loss, love for each other), sets, props, fundraising, publicity—all this for the single goal of creating a spectacle that will change people's lives and change the world.[18]

Greenberg, who was a member of ACT UP's Alternative and Holistic Treatment Committee, believed so deeply in the theatrical validity of activism that he even requested a political funeral, famously proclaiming in crowded elevators, "I don't want an angry political funeral. I just want you to burn me in the street and eat my flesh."[19] Greenberg was not just reactive. He had a deep sense, perhaps informed by his involvement in holistic treatments for AIDS, of the proactive importance of ACT UP actions. His writings about ACT UP echo those of Rechy and Foucault on 1970s gay male sexuality:

I believe that every action we do has significance and meaning on as many levels and layers of the infinite experience as we are able to comprehend. Sometimes we are not able to see how completely meaning infuses our daily activities but that doesn't mean that the meaning is not there. It simply means that we have not yet been awakened to the meaning.[20]

In December of 1989, ACT UP staged a demonstration that moved it into a new realm of radicalism that was described by some as warranted and by others as having gone much too far. In response to the continued interference of the Catholic Church (particularly in New York under the leadership of Cardinal O'Connor) in presenting sexually explicit HIV-prevention campaigns, ACT UP decided to mount a public protest in front of St. Patrick's Cathedral during Sunday mass. ACT UP was aware that a second, supposedly covert action planned for inside the cathedral, had been leaked to the police and media long before. However, the general membership of ACT UP was not aware that individuals within the group intended to go much further than the agreed-upon action of standing up in the pews to disrupt the mass. As a legal observer (dressed in my Sunday best) inside the church, I can say that the reaction of the church-goers to those of us who stood up in the pews to chant or hold signs was already visceral. The reaction to those who walked to the front of the cathedral to take Communion and then dropped, threw, or spit out the consecrated host indicated that those activists were participating in an act that, for Catholics, bordered on violence. In the aftermath of the action, ACT UP as a whole was divided as to whether the actions of individuals were warranted and whether the group as a whole should have endorsed those actions rather than simply being blamed for them after the fact.

ACT UP staged another protest two years later that also provoked rage. Although ACT UP's disruption of mass at St. Patrick's Cathedral was perhaps our most aggressive action, the most theatrical and, to my mind, most beautiful of our demon-strations was the culmination of Day of Desperation. On Jan-uary 23, 1991, the day after the evening news disruptions and following a morning of protests in the streets of downtown Manhattan, ACT UP entered Grand Central Terminal at rush hour. Grand Central is an ideal space for a demonstration be-cause, short of closing down the station, it is nearly impossible for authorities to control the traffic flow through multiple door-ways to the street and access tunnels from the subway. By 5:00 P.M., there were hundreds of ACT UP members moving casu-ally through the crowded space. Commuters were rushing into the terminal, intent on reaching trains that would take them to the untroubled idyll of suburbia.

At precisely 5:00 P.M., ACT UP members pulled out air horns, and shrill sirens echoed through the incredible space of Grand Central's main hall. One member clambered up onto the arrivals/departure board and placed an AIDS banner over the train schedule. Another group had entered the hall and reached the center of the space, carrying what appeared to be shopping bags with helium balloons floating above them. As the bags were opened, a huge banner rose slowly toward the ceiling, stating

"Money for AIDS, Not for War." Although the sign over the departure board was quickly removed, the huge banner floated out of reach in the center of the immense space.

As a cheer rose up from the activists, panicked commuters rushed toward their waiting trains. Hundreds of ACT UP members revealed their presence in the hall by sitting down and blocking access to the trains. While this was intended as a nonviolent action, the violence and hatred of the commuters was of a level that I had never seen. Those of us sitting on the floor were kicked as the commuters, like a stream of ants, began to literally climb over our bodies. ACT UP had created the perfect metaphor for AIDS in this country—normal Americas were willing to literally walk over our bodies while ignoring AIDS.

Like any great work of art, Day of Desperation raised troubling issues. A woman screamed at me, "I have a sick child at home." I screamed back, "I have a sick lover at home." ACT UP definitely alienated many people on that day in January, some of whom were probably sympathetic to AIDS. However, ACT UP at that moment had crossed into the realm of art. Day of Desperation had ceased to be about tangible activist goals: it had become a huge performance, a theatrical event designed to express desperation and rage. It will remain emblazoned in the memories of all those who participated. It was the moment when my generation was able to live fully as artists and achieve something as transcendent as the Mineshaft or feminist performance. It was the moment when we created something more beautiful than the starlit sky of the Saint. It was, in fact, the first moment in my life when I felt pride rather than shame.

Day of Desperation was a climax for ACT UP, marking the group's greatest achievement and also the beginning of its decline. Although ACT UP continues to meet and work on important issues, active membership has shrunk from hundreds on a Monday night in New York to a dozen. Ann Northrup continues to attend meetings, although she now reads the *New York Times* sports section during the meeting as a sort of psychic protection: "Someone once said to me that the natural life of any volunteer activist organization is about three years. So I think the biggest factor of all was that it had run its course. People could sustain their interest in something like that for only a finite amount of time."

ACT UP had run its course, but there were other factors that accelerated the group's decline. Most notably, many of the early members were dead or very ill. Clinton had been elected president, and it was difficult to fight someone who was at least sympathetic even if he achieved nothing. The division in the group between those who wanted to save their lives and those who wanted to build a movement became more visible as somewhat promising treatments appeared. Some of ACT UP New York's most influential male members split from the group to form Treatment Action Group (TAG), which worked more closely with researchers and government agencies. As Schulman describes:

> The split in ACT UP was ultimately about access. Do we do everything we can to make everything available to everyone or do we get involved on an elite level and stay alive? The people who supported access are dead and the people who went for the elite, insider thing are alive. They left and took all their power. The current global condition, even the New York City condition, where there is no access to treatment, is the consequence of the movement changing in midstream. And I understand why those people changed it. I mean, they're alive.

In the intervening years, ACT UP has developed as an important player in the fight for international treatment access. During the 2001 presidential election, a small group of about twenty ACT UP members staged successful demonstrations, bringing to light then vice president Al Gore's pressure on South Africa to uphold the copyrights of the pharmaceutical industry rather than producing cheaper, generic versions of HIV drugs (as allowed under World Trade Organization rules in a health emergency). Through relentlessly chasing Gore during his campaign with chants of "Gore's Greed Kills," ACT UP found a new issue that Northrop articulates:

> We finally had some drugs that might make a difference and people [outside the United States] had no access to them. We were right back to all the class issues. And if anyone cared we could be giving drugs to people outside of America and saving lives like we were doing here.

With a new focus on the destructive power of international corporations to affect government policy, ACT UP fit nicely within the agenda of the new antiglobalization movement that was gaining attention for dramatic protests in Genoa and Seattle. Such an alliance could effectively position AIDS within a broader agenda, where some ACT UP members had always believed it belonged. This positioning is effective in using AIDS as a catalyst for a discussion of issues around access to health care, but one wonders if the gay and lesbian civil rights component of AIDS will fit as comfortably within the antiglobalization movement. In the 1980s gay and lesbian issues had become synonymous with AIDS and, once AIDS had been de-gayed, gay and lesbian activists were left without much of an engine. Michelangelo Signorile has noted a shift in tone from some activists involved in the new movement:

> I'm not really sure yet where gay people fit in the antiglobalization movement. I know gay people who are involved in it and they say that gays can now be part of the larger Left, that they don't want their politics to be about just one issue. But that kind of reminds me of what lesbians were told in the feminist movement, what gays were told in the antiwar movement. Queerness will always be marginalized and will always need its own movement because it goes against the larger heterosexual system. People on the Left may have a focus on race or class or homophobia. But they focus mostly on the thing that affects them personally. So it worries me that people don't feel that we need a gay movement anymore.

There is no doubt that ACT UP remains a central player in AIDS activism today. During the International AIDS Conference held in Barcelona in July 2002, ACT UP members stormed the stage shouting "Shame!" as U.S. Health and Human Services Secretary Tommy Thompson tried to deliver a speech describing the U.S. contributions to the global effort to stop AIDS. ACT UP again successfully focused world media attention on the failure of government to adequately address AIDS (in this case the U.S. contribution to the Global AIDS Fund). ACT UP now operates on a global level that, because of its awesome scope, makes the crisis in the United States seem insignificant.

ACT UP's achievements in bringing gay men and lesbians together have been lasting, albeit around a narrow range of issues. Because gay men have become so radically desexualized, their alliance with lesbians around the struggle for gay marriage and adoption rights feels more comfortable now than it did in the 1980s. Yet this work, which is unquestionably important, naturally lacks the life-and-death urgency felt during the first years of AIDS. Looking at the lives of gay men and lesbians who went through ACT UP together, one can at least say that we came to know one another.

As for me, I will always have at least one memory, filled with pride, that will counteract whatever shame I might still feel about my history as a gay man. I will always remember sitting on the floor of Grand Central Station. My arms were linked with gay men and lesbians who were, for a moment, one. I felt, for that moment, a connection that I pray will be felt by younger generations one day when they too discover the power of living as artists.

Lost

CHAPTER 12

Owning AIDS

After looking backstage at the sexual creativity of the 1970s and then watching the narrative of AIDS unfold in front of the foot-lights, it is time to bring up the houselights and consider those of us who remain in the audience. What is our relationship to the dramas of "before" and "after"? What are our feelings to-ward a legacy that contains both radical sexuality and a deadly disease that is sexually transmitted? The answers to these ques-tions are deeply troubling. We have allowed the history of radi-cal gay sex to become intermingled with AIDS, and then thrown them both away as relics of a painful past. Because of this, the gay community continues to pay a huge price measured in the physical and spiritual deaths of young gay men whose lives are ruled by shame and ignorance of the past. I can see no other explanation for the fact that young gay men remain, after decades of death, the largest statistical group of new HIV infec-tions in America. The young men now becoming infected with HIV are not connected to a gay history that includes AIDS as well as the sexual experimentation of the 1970s. They do not know the radical excitement of the Mineshaft. They do not know the joy of dancing under the stars at the Saint. They do not know the pride of marching under the ACT UP banner. And they do not know the grief of losing absolutely everything. If they do not know these things, it is because we, the gay com-munity, have abandoned our history in favor of the empty promises of assimilation.

★   ★   ★

The gay community cannot so easily give up ownership of the AIDS crisis in America. In America, AIDS was and is a gay disease. Like all intentionally inflammatory statements, these depend upon definitions of terms. First, we must define *gay* as it relates to AIDS demographics. In 1981, *gay* could easily have meant middle-class gay white men living in a major urban center. Twenty years later, *gay*, a politically charged word denoting community, has been recast in the clinical demographic of "men who have sex with men." This new definition was created in response to the increasing racial and economic diversity of gay men contracting AIDS and the levels of homophobia in some communities of color. "Men who have sex with men" are shamed, isolated individuals far more likely to remain closeted and comfortably invisible than *gay* men.

The word *ownership* also needs definition and clarification. When AIDS first hit the gay community it traveled quickly through a relatively small, close-knit group of men. HIV's ease of transmission through this network of social and sexual connections during the first wave of the crisis reflected the narrowness of the population it was affecting. The homogeneity of the infected population intensified the emotional devastation and created a new sense of community. As sex had in the 1970s, illness became the organizing principle to gay men (and many concerned lesbians) in the 1980s. When anything—be it sex, death, ethnicity, or religion—becomes a central determinant of community membership, it cannot simply be discarded later. Ownership in this context implies a continued study of how AIDS affected the sexual culture of gay men and how it continues to weigh upon the most central decisions and behavior of gay men. As gay men, we must reclaim our history, troubled or not, rather than abandon it or let it be co-opted.

Statistics from the Centers for Disease Control (CDC) have been questioned since AIDS appeared. However, no other comprehensive national picture of infection rates and AIDS cases has been developed. CDC definitions of AIDS have been criticized on a number of valid levels, including their use as the basis for a diagnosis. In 1993 the CDC expanded the surveillance case definition of AIDS. (Official definitions of AIDS have changed several times since the beginning of the epidemic—testament to the status of HIV/AIDS as a socially constructed phenomenon, a biological reality mediated by science, politics, and mechanisms of public health.) Perhaps the most generic working definition of AIDS at present provides a group of clinical conditions or laboratory markers that are indicative of severe immunosuppression due to HIV infection.

The definition of AIDS was expanded in 1985 and again in 1987, after an international group of scientists reached a consensus on the causal role of HIV in the development of AIDS. The 1987 definition of AIDS was based on a constellation of twenty-three opportunistic infections. It soon became clear, however, that this definition did not accommodate all of the populations presenting with HIV disease. Although the CDC definition of AIDS was never intended to fulfill a role beyond epidemiological surveillance, public health authorities and governmental agencies utilized this definition in the allocation of services. Thus, it was possible for a seropositive individual with almost no T-cells, someone who was visibly sick on a micro- and macroscopic level, to be denied services—financial assistance, health care, or a hospital bed for the poor or homeless—because he or she did not technically have AIDS. In response to intense lobbying (particularly among activists representing women, communities of color, and the poor), the CDC expanded the definition in 1993 to include laboratory markers of severe HIV disease and other clinical conditions that cause severe illness and death. Under the new definition a person officially had AIDS if he or she had severe immunodepression—a CD4+ cell count below 200 or when CD4+ cells represent less than 14 percent of all lymphocytes. In addition, pulmonary tuberculosis, recurrent pneumonia, and invasive cervical cancer were added to the list of opportunistic infections and conditions that described the onslaught of AIDS in an HIV-infected body.

The expanded definition had significant statistical results.

The first quarter of 1993 witnessed a 204 percent increase in the number of new AIDS cases reported over the same period in 1992. However, the proportion of infected groups (heterosexual and lesbian transmission as opposed to homosexual male transmission) to one another within this increased number of cases did not change radically.

If we look at ownership as not only emotionally important but as a key factor in allocation of resources and development of effective prevention campaigns, it becomes increasingly clear that we cannot afford to assign ownership of AIDS in America for rhetorical reasons. This is, however, exactly what happened, and the gay community itself initiated it. For very different reasons, groups as diverse as ACT UP, Gay Men's Health Crisis (GMHC), and the American Foundation for AIDS Research began in the late 1980s to put forward the message that "AIDS is not a gay disease." For ACT UP, the message was predicated on a larger set of political beliefs about accessibility of health care and a suspicion that official statistics were wildly undercounting women and minority populations. Many ACT UP members who had long-term political interests viewed AIDS as the stepping-off point for building a movement rather than simply advocating for treatment. For service providers such as GMHC and research institutions like the American Foundation for AIDS Research, one could cynically say that this "de-gaying" was a strategy to increase funding through validating the importance of AIDS, but more likely, these organizations were trying to make sense of shifting demographics that were far less clear at the time. On a personal level, perhaps many of us were hoping that by telling straight people that *their* lives mattered, they might say that *our* lives mattered too. Unfortunately, that was not the result.

The result of recasting the epidemic was a skewing of prevention efforts toward a heterosexual message, particularly in communities of color where even the mention of the word *gay* was enough to derail the process. (Also, one cannot overlook the work of Senator Jesse Helms in making sure that federal dollars could not be used for the kind of prevention that would actually help gay men change their sexual behavior. His recent "conversion" on the AIDS issue during retirement does not even really warrant discussion.) In the end, all of the communities affected by AIDS have been left with failed prevention models that are simply not based on the realities of the disease or the kind of sexual transmission that is actually occurring.

Whether one agrees with the CDC numbers or not, there should have been a huge percentage change in the demographics between 1990 and 1994 if a large segment of women were being missed in the earlier definition. However, in 1990, under the old definition of AIDS diagnosis, 89 percent of the reported AIDS cases were male and 11 percent were female. In 1994, with the new definitions in place, 83 percent were male and 17 percent female. This is not to discount the population of women (13,287 in absolute numbers) with AIDS at the time. However, was the move to present AIDS as no longer a gay disease based on these numbers, a funding strategy, a political belief, homophobia, or some combination of the above?

Because the American public hears almost exclusively about the heterosexual impact of the global AIDS epidemic, one might be forgiven for believing that the situation in the United States is the same. Yet at the International AIDS Conference held in the summer of 2002, the CDC presented the results of a new study summarized by the *New York Times* as follows: "Gay men account for the largest proportion of new HIV infections, or 43 percent."[1] If men who openly identify as gay are already the largest new infection group, it is not a great leap to suspect that there is a much larger group that includes men not willing to reveal gay sex as the source of their infection. Because these unaffiliated men do not recognize AIDS as a central part of their culture, many do not even know that they are infected. Another study presented by the CDC at the 2002 AIDS Conference reported that among those found to have HIV, 90 percent of blacks did not even know they were infected. Why? Duncan MacKellar, a CDC epidemiologist, explained that these men perceived themselves to be at low risk of being infected despite having engaged in high-risk sex like unprotected anal intercourse.[2]

Is this a development that occurred only in the past few years, a fluke that the United States has not yet had the opportunity to respond to? Hardly. Let us look back at the statistics within the male AIDS population and see how it has changed over the course of the crisis. If we look at the totality of the crisis up until the year 2000 (the most recent summary of the crisis available at this moment) the male demographics break down to the following:

Men Having Sex with Men   57.9%
IV Drug Users   21.2%
Men Having Sex with Men and Using IV Drugs   7.6%
Hemophiliacs   0.8%
Heterosexual Contact   5.4
Transfusions   0.8%
Undetermined Cause   7.6%[3]

Even if we do not add in gay men who also use IV drugs or some number of the undetermined-cause cases, we still have an overwhelming majority of the cases among gay men. Even in years with the most cases of heterosexual transmission for males, the ratio of gay to straight AIDS cases was at least 2:1. Were the funding structures and prevention campaigns for AIDS reconfigured based on the 5.4 percent of the population being infected through heterosexual transmission? If there was another group that demanded attention, it was IV drug users. However, prevention campaigns that explained to them how they could clean their works to avoid HIV infection through shared needles were viciously suppressed through enforcement of statutes restricting the sale of syringes without a doctor's permission. Needle-exchange programs still remain, at best, underground, or more commonly, illegal and subject to harassment in most American cities. Reinforcing the confusion about reaching IV drug users is the deeply held belief that gay men are white and IV drug users are straight blacks. In terms of AIDS, gay men and

IV drug users were sacrificed on the unlikely twin altars of progressive politics from the Left and homophobia from the Right.

Let us take one last step in terms of statistics. Among male AIDS cases, there has been one significant shift over the course of the epidemic. In terms of race, black non-Hispanic men (using CDC terms) have overtaken white non-Hispanic men over the course of the crisis, and AIDS cases in Hispanic men have risen exponentially. (Native Americans and Asian/Pacific Islanders remain a small but significant percentage of total cases.) Again, the perception has been that cases within communities of color must be among heterosexuals infected through IV drug use. Many who have worked closely with communities of color dispute this notion, however. The Van Ness Recovery House in Los Angeles has become involved in research that is not only scientifically rigorous but also unafraid to look at issues of sexuality. Kathy Watt, the executive director, says:

> Other than hemophilia and IV drug use, the straight people who have been infected, for the most part, were infected by someone who, in a world where it was okay to be gay, would be gay. Most of the black and Hispanic men who have infected their wives and girlfriends, if there weren't taboos and shame in their communities, they would be living gay lives.[4]

Watt's view of infection rates brings us, once again, back to the idea of ownership. From the point of view of the gay community, funding for services is plummeting both because the crisis is perceived to be over and because so much funding has become focused on the "AIDS is no longer a gay disease" model. Given the current skyrocketing infection rates among young gay men of all colors, this model clearly does not serve the gay community. Less than 13 percent of HIV-prevention efforts are directed at gay men, even though gay men still represent the majority of AIDS cases and remain the largest at-risk population.[5]

HIV prevention in the United States under the "AIDS is not a gay disease" model has failed. While the United States publicly scolds China and Africa for ineffective prevention campaigns, Dr. Helene Gayle, who directs the CDC's HIV program, says, "We tend to think about our rates in the United States being so much less than what we are seeing in other countries, and that is true if we look at it overall but [the findings] show that there may be populations in this country that have rates and potential for explosion analogous to what we have seen in other parts of the world."[6]

When three in ten black gay men in America are infected with HIV,[7] it is clear that we must refocus our efforts on reaching this population. Unfortunately, this is the most difficult of tasks, asking two beleaguered and suspicious groups—blacks and gays—to work together on an issue that triggers complex defense mechanisms. There are scholars and activists better qualified than I to develop ways for these communities to work together, but I think it might be useful to note that both groups share an investment in "respectability" that makes it difficult for them to come together to save lives. (The role of respectability in relationship to the black community's response to AIDS is brilliantly discussed in Cathy Cohen's *The Boundaries of Blackness: AIDS and the Breakdown of Black Politics*.) In the gay community, a self-conscious respectability actively puts forward a positive image of a racially and economically diverse gay world that is mostly proven false in gay ghettos from Greenwich Village and Dupont Circle to West Hollywood and the Castro, where young gay men of color face terrible discrimination and objectification. In the black community, the investment in respectability means avoiding any action that might bring public attention to the fact that AIDS is disproportionately affecting black gay men and IV drug users: to acknowledge these AIDS cases means acknowledging that black gays and addicts exist. Self-policing in marginalized communities indicates an internalized self-hatred that manifests itself in a paranoia that the dominant culture is constantly watching, waiting for breaches of the carefully constructed respectability. Self-policing also denies basic problems in a way that ensures that they will never be dealt with because the underlying issues (be they selfishness and racism among privileged gay men or homophobia in struggling black populations). One might say that self-policing to maintain respectability (be it gay or black) is an attempt to create a revisionist culture that is more palatable to the larger world than the authentic culture that reflects the messiness of deep history.

The current infection rates among young black gay men have coincided with American activists turning their attention to the global AIDS crisis. Phill Wilson is currently executive director of the African American AIDS Policy and Training Institute at the University of Southern California. He is the founder of the National Black Lesbian and Gay Leadership Forum and cofounder of the National Task Force on AIDS Prevention. In a 2002 interview with David Mixner on the Web site gay.com, Wilson points to the painful consequences of focusing globally on AIDS: "Right now, the wider AIDS/HIV community is more interested in Africans living in Soweto, Kampala and Harare than black gay men in Los Angeles, New York or Chicago. I find it mind-boggling. How can you be so concerned about black people in Africa and not give a damn about black people you see every day?"[8]

Colin Robinson, director of the New York State Black Gay Network, would frame the issue in another way. "My concern is not that we care too much for the black community in Africa but, that when we show concern for HIV-infected black men in the U.S., it is because we fear that they are bi-sexual and might spread the disease into the straight community."[9] Robinson's organization represents a network of seventeen groups serving black gay men in New York State and he believes that the problem has not been the use or misuse of terms like "men who have sex with men" or "same-gender-loving men" but in how these men are reached. Robinson has pioneered the establishment of a black gay church and works with women—such as girlfriends or female relatives—who are significant in the lives of the men at risk. "The real work is not to choose but to broaden. It's not the term that's so important but how we reach them."

If one looks at white gay men who grew up in the Midwest, the typical course for these men is to make the only empowered choice that they have—to leave their rural homes for the gay ghettos of urban America where they will find acceptance. To present a "respectable" public image of gays as reflective of heterosexual norms and worthy of basic human rights, gay leaders have erased the sexual revolution of the 1970s and have, in fact, erased gay male sexuality altogether in favor of a two-child, Ford Explorer, Home Depot kind of existence that is completely disconnected from the gay heritage. While this kind of existence may indeed be deeply comforting to those who have faced decades of death and mourning, the price of forgetting our heritage in favor of an outside normalcy is too high, because it leaves behind so many. For the fact is that not every gay man is capable of meeting aspirations dependent upon middle-class economic and educational tools. Furthermore, not every gay man, regardless of race and class, aspires to these values.

We must insist on ownership of AIDS as a disease that, in America, affects primarily *gay* men, not *men who have sex with men.* This will not be easy and it cannot be accomplished by only the most at-risk groups of gay men. We face a future where the youngest, most isolated gay men with the fewest resources are left to respond to a crisis that decimated powerful, connected gay men twenty years ago.

As a person living with AIDS who has been actively involved with gay life for more than thirty years, Ferd Eggan talks about this issue of ownership:

> I miss the camaraderie of being an AIDS activist and being a PWA [Person with AIDS] with a certain mystic bond and connection with other PWAs. In some ways, the interactions we had with people we loved who had AIDS or were AIDS activists gave us something to own that was really necessary. It's just that I'm not sure if we're entitled to it, if we were entitled to it then or if we're entitled to it anymore.[10]

I do believe that we are entitled to it, if for no other reason than because the gay community's current relationship to AIDS is allowing young gay men in America to become infected at rates as high as those seen in the developing world. The groups of people living as self-identified gay men must, unfortunately, reclaim AIDS in hopes that we will form an identifiable community of support for the "men who have sex with men." It seems to me that there is no way to fight AIDS without owning it.

CHAPTER 13

Hope and Caution

Assotto Saint and Felix Gonzalez-Torres

Identity politics was the touchstone of gay life in the 1990s, and I believe it's both instructive, and interesting, to consider two gay men, both lost to AIDS, who struggled with issues of identity in both their work and their lives. Both of their lives illustrate, in complex ways, the issues of ownership and abandonment of multiple identities.

The members of the black gay writers collective Other Countries comprised a group that seemed on the verge of bridging the gap between black and gay identities until nearly all of them were lost to AIDS. Assotto Saint was a member of Other Countries who was blindingly articulate and uncompromising in his criticism of the challenges facing gay black men. Like Marlon Riggs, Essex Hemphill, and other black gay artists in the 1980s, Assotto Saint insisted on adding gay black men to the pantheon of heroic figures usually presented to the larger black community and was unafraid of presenting the downtrodden glory of the gay life he witnessed.

Assotto Saint was born Yves Lubin in Haiti in 1957 and his pen name reflected his basic strategy in life—take something big and make it bigger. As Yves Lubin, the man, he was already exotic and dramatic, but vulnerable. As Assotto Saint, he became an iconic voodoo priestess and an organizing force in the emerging world of New York identity politics. When Yves took on the public name of Assotto Saint in 1980, he was casting off the weight of his out-of-wedlock birth in a small Haitian town. Yves said of the name Assotto Saint, "By using the *nom de guerre* of Saint, I also wanted to add a sacrilegious twist to my life by grandly sanctifying the loud low-life bitch that I am."[1]

Yves's love of the dramatic was rooted in his Haitian childhood and the rituals of the Catholic Church. "The Catholic Mass, especially High Mass on Sundays and holy days, with its colorful pageantry, trance-inducing liturgy, and theatrical ceremony, spellbound me. And that incense—that incense took me heaven-high each time. I was addicted and I attended mass every day."[2] But his love of tradition and ceremony was juxtaposed with the shame of being the boy who "got straight As, ran like a girl, cute powdered face, silky eyebrows—I was the kind of child folks saw and thought quick something didn't click."[3]

Marie Lubin, Yves's mother, left Haiti in 1965 for Switzerland, entrusting her son to the care of an aunt. When she later moved to New York, she formed the bridge that would lead her son to an unlikely new life in the United States. When Yves visited Marie in 1970 in New York, he had already had secret gay experiences in Haiti but he had never experienced open gay life. On his visit, his mother took him on a trip to Coney Island:

> Two effeminate guys in outrageous short shorts and high heels walked onto the train and sat in front of us. Noticing that I kept looking at them, my mother said to me that this was the way it was here. People could say and do whatever they wanted.... I kept fantasizing that there was a homosexual world out there that I knew nothing of. I remember looking up in amazement as we walked beneath the elevated train, then telling mother I didn't want to go back to Haiti.[4]

In the ten years between his move to the United States and his reinvention as Assotto Saint, Yves explored the new and wondrous gay world of New York in the 1970s. He was fascinated and inspired by the outer edges of New York gay life. The images he collected during these years would later form the basis of many of his poems and the characters that inhabited his theater pieces. He chose for his African-American heroes the souls that had to struggle most courageously. He was particularly drawn to the tawdry glory of Marcia P. "Pay It No Mind" Johnson, who had helped form STAR (Street Transvestite Action Revolutionaries) and was later a well-known transsexual hustler in the West Village in the 1970s and 1980s. I came to know Johnson during her time in ACT UP and, along with many, mourned her loss when she was found dead, floating in the Hudson River in an unsolved murder. Johnson is immediately recognizable in Yves's short story, "Miss Thing/for Marcia Johnson":

> had you been driving on the west side highway by 10th Street last thursday, you would have seen miss thing turning it out at 4:00am/long blond tresses sprigged with gold, plucked eyebrows, purple mascara around the eyes to make them look large & luminous, cheekbones that won't quit, thick green flutters, chain-shaped silver pendants framing her coffee-colored full face, ruby reds & loads of rouge to hide the shaving marks, reeking of avon, she was bad/the way she carried on waiting for a john, everyone could tell that she was a he/[5]

Yves's stomping grounds included the Mineshaft, where he witnessed many amazing and horrifying images. He loved to recount stories to friends like the poet Walter Holland, who recalls that when Yves would reminisce, he would talk playfully: "He found it all wonderfully amusing and outrageous."[6] Yves may have made light of the scenes played out at the Mineshaft, but he was more than an observer. Yves used the rituals of the place to deal with the shame he felt about being a black man. In his play "Black Fag" he writes,

> last night
> in that tub at the mineshaft
> bare
> i stared
> beyond the still thick smoke

beyond the bulged crotches
beyond the milling flies
beyond the blessed beauties: statues posed against the walls
beyond those boys bent for joy
beyond the dreams of bathing in a thousand white dudes' cum
to wash a dark shade off my skin
beyond the dreams of their fingers grasping my head still
to wave the wooliness out of my hair
beyond the dreams of their golden showers
a' falling
a' streaming hot over my face
to melt the imperfect
beyond . . .
beyond . . .
i shut my eyes for an instant
to forget the hurt
in never loved
been loved as I needed/[7]

In fact, Yves did find his great love in 1980 in the form of Jan Urban Holmgren. When they met, Holmgren was a Swedish flight attendant with American Airlines. Holmgren was also a musician, and the couple began to collaborate on theatrical events and records. Yves was criticized by some of his more political friends for having a white boyfriend, but the two lovers developed an intense relationship that would last the next thirteen years, until Holmgren died of AIDS. The 1980s was a wonderful decade for Yves; he was in love, he was included in the first volume of *Other Countries: Black Gay Voices,* and he established his own press, Galiens (a contraction of "gay aliens"). But by the time I met Yves in 1991, his life had become entirely focused personally, politically, and artistically on AIDS. Both he and Jan had found out that they were infected in 1987, and by 1990 Yves was caring for a very ill Jan while burying scores of friends and watching his own health deteriorate.

As with so many gay writers, Yves's voice became marked by intertwined veins of rage and sorrow. The rage was directed equally at the neglectful U.S. government and the black community that he felt had betrayed him. (Both Yves and Essex Hemphill had begun to speak out after watching the seminal writer Joseph Beam die alone and destitute, abandoned by the black community because he had AIDS.) Walter Holland recalls Yves as being "angry and tremendously upset with the African-American churches, the culture of denial. He bemoaned the fact that many African-American men did not even seek medical attention because they were so ashamed. Yves really felt that his way of combating that was identifying himself as HIV-positive. He would talk to anyone and everyone about AIDS."

My impression of Yves when I first met him was, strangely enough, that he was motherly. There was something about his presence that was reassuring even in an apartment taken over by signs of Jan's illness. The apartment, like Yves, was a study in contradictions, such as the leather cap that perched on a shelf alongside a feather boa. When I would ask him questions he deemed shocking, his hands would lift up from where they were primly positioned in his lap to frame his face as he would chortle, "Oh, my *deeeear*." His hands in fact were his most striking feature. They were often in motion and their preferred level was above shoulder height. As part of his drag act, Yves had taken to wearing long gloves to accentuate the expressive qualities of his hands, or as he told Walter Holland, because "everyone's gotta have a gimmick."

Above all, even after we became friends, Yves was polite. Of course, his patience with me might have reflected our shared concern with preservation of his work. This was a long-standing issue of importance to him, as he was also the executor of the estates of three other writers and he knew that his illness imperiled not only his own legacy but also theirs. He knew that words had the power to change and that the preservation of his artistic legacy was vital. He hoped "that the writings of our experiences serve as testaments to those who passed along this way, testimonies to our times, and legacies to future generations. . . . Our words indeed do triumph over silence, despair and death."[8] Happily, Yves found the respected literary publicist Michele

Karlsberg to serve as his literary executor, and his fears of his mother's posthumous suppression of his work have proved unfounded.

Walter Holland says that Yves had a very balanced world-view; that he was willing to look at the world in shades of gray rather than black and white. And it is true that his fierceness was refreshingly directed at all of his enemies, not just the enemies who were politically useful. When one reads many of his political statements, it is impossible to tell whether he is speaking as a gay man, a black man, a man with AIDS, or some ultimate amalgam of all those who had been repressed in the world. "We must become whistle-blowers," he wrote. "We must become mutha-fuckers with messages and a mission. We must become powerful enough to stand tall and not fall, thrive and not just survive. A tremendous amount of common sense, arrogance, and defiance will get us through."[9]

★   ★   ★

Felix Gonzalez-Torres was the prototype for the era that began in the early 1990s, a time marked by its shimmering lack of a fixed identity. Gonzalez-Torres was, on one hand, an openly gay man with deeply held political and intellectual beliefs. However, he was also capable of willfully buying into an art market that could strip his work of its meaning. His dealer, Andrea Rosen of the Andrea Rosen Gallery, quotes Gonzalez-Torres as saying, "The more someone pays for something the more value it has."[10]

Gonzalez-Torres made some of the most achingly sad visual artworks ever created about AIDS, but he was also capable of giving extensive, personal interviews without mentioning that he was dying of AIDS. A stunningly handsome man who preferred not to be photographed, Gonzalez-Torres believed that "there is no afterlife. . . . If you fuck it up this time, you've fucked up forever and ever."[11] It's anyone's guess what he would have made of his strange legacy.

By the time he died in 1996, Gonzalez-Torres had reached

the starry heights of the contemporary art world and was anything but naive about the realities of the market. While his stacks of offset prints meant to be taken by visitors and piles of sparkling hard candy installed as sculptures and intended to be eaten might have seemed a gesture against commercialism, Gonzalez-Torres made certain that he was represented by professionals who carefully assigned certificates of authenticity for the *one* stack of prints to be re-created in the home of a wealthy collector and the *one* pile of candy to be endlessly replenished in the finest museum collection.

Like many other gay male artists of his generation, Gonzalez-Torres sometimes demonstrated a rather disingenuous offhandedness to the commercial aspects of the art market and a casual personal style that belied a complex and cold understanding of how access to power is a fascinating artistic undertaking itself. The act of ownership was central to the work of Gonzalez-Torres, as Andrea Rosen explains: "Felix loved to be a trusting person. The role of owning his work is a huge responsibility. He wasn't trying to trick the people who bought his work about who he was. He thought of ownership in a really idealistic way as a partnership. Ownership is what makes the work exist."

Although Rosen says that Felix was forthright about who he was and the associations of his work, he could also be intentionally obscure in print. In an astonishing interview with fellow artist Tim Rollins in 1993, Gonzalez-Torres runs through the range of his maddening contradictions. Throughout the interview, he refers in the past tense to a man named Ross: "I used to go to movies with Ross mostly."[12] This is evidently the handsome dark-haired man who appears in the artist's photographs or in the titles of some of his work. Although he makes a point of referring to this man by name, Gonzalez-Torres never explains his importance. Unless the reader was an art-world insider or a confidant of the artist, one would never know that Ross was Ross Laycock, the great love of Felix's life, lost to AIDS in the late 1980s. Also, Rollins repeatedly questions Gonzalez-Torres about the shade of blue that appears in so many of his pieces; the artist evades the question even though he had told close friends that the blue was the blue of Ross's hospital gown. The artist tells Rollins that weights and numbers in his pieces are arbitrary, but he also told friends that the weight of one of the candy-pile pieces was the combined weight of his and Ross's bodies, slowly disappearing, being consumed.

Because many critics, collectors, and dealers have insisted that the work of Gonzalez-Torres is not *only* about his being gay and dying of AIDS, there has been a persistent tension between the commercial art world and gay people who want to claim Felix's work as emblematic of their experience. Rosen explicates this view: "The most powerful part of Felix's work is that he left it open to interpretation. He felt that the only thing permanent was change." The artist himself created the problem, though, by sometimes insisting in print and in conversations with friends that his work was meant to have very literal associations. In an interview with Robert Storr commissioned by the organization Creative Time, Gonzalez-Torres is more forthcoming in describing the relationship of certain work to personal experience: "I made '*Untitled*' *(Placebo)* because I needed to make it. There was no other consideration involved except that I wanted to make art work that could disappear, that never existed, and it was a metaphor for when Ross was dying."[13]

Like many other artists with AIDS, Gonzalez-Torres struggled with his work being constricted by the literal facts of his life, and this probably accounts for the varying ways he described his art to others. This strategy had considerable power. I remember sitting in my office on Forty-second Street staring for weeks at a billboard consisting of a washed-out photograph of an empty, unmade bed, not knowing its maker or intention. I remember thinking it looked like the unmade and newly empty bed that I had shared with my lover, recently lost to AIDS. Had I known that the billboard was a public artwork by Gonzalez-Torres of the bed he had shared with Ross, would it have been a less effective work of art? It certainly would have been less interesting. More troubling is Rosen's assertion that Gonzalez-Torres "never told anyone he had AIDS because he did not want his work to be only about death." If true, this seems like less an artistic necessity than a consequence of shame and fear.

Jim Hodges is a respected artist who was a close friend to Felix and their work shares an openness to interpretation. Hodges strongly suggests that Felix did not want his work to be tied to only one interpretation: "Felix was about inclusion in the most open and free way, not limiting himself. He tried for an experience that was open across the board. The lightness of his nature, his robust life energy is what I get from his work. At every opportunity, Felix would want to avoid being tied into something."[14] However, Hodges acknowledges that it is only natural that the work would always be at least partially tied to AIDS: "As a person living with an inevitable end and watching friends and lovers come to that same end, these were realities that were impacting the creative process. It was Felix's moment. His loss was always at the forefront of his work but it was also about moving forward."

However effective his strategy of making opaque, distanced work in the face of the AIDS crisis might have been, it creates posthumous complications that are troubling in the face of the artist's assertion that he made art because "it leaves a mark. It leaves a statement that you were here, that perhaps it is possible to have a different view of life."[15] Yet what seemed so revolutionary when being made by a living, Cuban, gay, political artist seems remarkably empty of personal legacy now. Was it only cold theories and stark, formal beauty that Gonzalez-Torres intended for his legacy, a sort of Arte Povera minimalism? Or is it that his strategy backfired, that he miscalculated the effect of time as a vital component of his artworks in which not only the stacks of paper and piles of candy but the real person who created them would disappear, lost in the commercial success of the work?

One would like to think that Gonzalez-Torres was incredibly clever in making the dispute over his legacy a continuation of his artistic practice. But it seems more likely that he unwittingly became part of a system that has diluted his memory. Although the idea of continuing change is put forward as a hallmark of Felix's work, there was a concerted effort after his death to authorize and limit his body of work; the most basic strategy for creating a commercially viable artistic estate. In a move unusual for any artist, let alone one of Felix's youth, a catalogue raisonné of his work was rushed into production soon after his death. Rosen says that this was solely due to an offer from a museum to produce and print the catalogue raisonné as its contribution to a posthumous exhibition. However, one wonders why, for an estate generating such high income, an offer of free printing would have more appeal than a course of action that allowed for the compilation of a more definitive (and less politically charged) overview of the artist's legacy.

There have been other criticisms of the Gonzalez–Torres estate, including the will naming his dealer Andrea Rosen not only as executor but beneficiary—a situation generally discouraged by estate planners as having a high potential for conflict of interest. But then Rosen correctly states, "It's a huge sacrifice to be an executor"; she makes the valid point that Felix "groomed her for the job."

The most contentious part of the Gonzalez–Torres estate has always been a list that identifies the work that the artist wanted to "authorize" as part of his official oeuvre. Friends of the artist say that the list was made while he was very ill, but Rosen says that the list was developed through an ongoing process during the entire time that Felix showed with her gallery. She explains that Felix "always reserved the right to take a piece out of his oeuvre." Felix was generous in giving artworks to friends. but unfortunately many of these pieces were exactly the ones missing from his final "authorized" checklist. The list also omitted some of the artist's most overtly political pieces, seemingly tipping his legacy toward more conceptual, some might say decorative, work.

The list, while perhaps rather callous, was not out of character with the statements of the artist, who said in his interview with Storr, "I'm not afraid of making mistakes, I'm afraid of keeping them. I have destroyed a lot of pieces."[16] For an artist whose work was so ephemeral, it is easy to see that snapshots and postcards sent to friends might easily be interpreted as part of his formal body of work, not only diluting his vision but also weakening the commercial value of the work with a glut of questionable pieces. Bill Bartman, director of Art Resources Transfer in New York, was a close friend of Felix's and received gifts of both "authorized" work (Felix warned Bartman not to tell Rosen that he had been given the pieces) and a series of photographs with text written on their backs.

Bartman and other recipients of the "unauthorized" photographs, such as the artist Julie Ault, have struggled to have these pieces shown and published, without the support of Andrea Rosen. The photographs, which have been shown at Bard College and a gallery in Chicago, are unquestionably beautiful and related to the artist's larger body of work. Images of gloomy skies with a single, silhouetted bird in flight are especially familiar to anyone with even a passing familiarity with the artist's work. More important, though, is the text on the back of the photographs. One particularly beautiful text reads:

> Can we take a second for granted? Never. Never. A second is all it takes for life to dissipate. And what do you see? An empty room. But not really. We see history: light, noise, smell, beginnings, dinners, soft long mornings, play, laughter, phone rings, some tears, hope, sex and love, excitement, sadness, history history history.[17]

These pieces, whether intended to be a part of the commercial art world or not, are important in understanding the commitment that Gonzalez-Torres had to the concept of legacy. They do not evoke an artist who wanted his life as a gay man to be forgotten or his life as a gay man to be a private matter:

> ... when the urgency of time becomes so solid, and a whole generation becomes a flock of birds, flying away, traveling, going to an unexplained place. And we, in shock, watching from down here.[18]

Because work by Gonzalez-Torres has posthumously become extremely valuable, one might suspect a profit motive on
behalf of friends who received these more casual, personal
pieces. However, the artist's gallery has also been unsupportive
of the work even being shown, let alone published as a personal
tribute to Gonzalez-Torres. Rosen would probably see publication and exhibition of "unauthorized" work as contradictory to
the very clear instructions from the artist as to what he considered actual artworks. But, as Bartman asks: "Is an unsigned
drawing given by Picasso to one of his friends not his work?"[19]

Bartman's larger point is that "the history of late-twentieth-
century art would not be the same if you took out the gay
artists," and he fears that the contributions of artists such as
Gonzalez-Torres, Jimmy DeSana, and Mark Morrisroe as openly
gay men are being systematically erased, particularly in relationship to the commercial art market. There are some indicators
that Bartman's fears might be warranted. I have long heard reports that one of the most important collectors of Felix's work
has said that the artist was not really gay. Rosen says that such
statements have not been made, but if they were, the collector
probably meant that Felix's *work* was not about being gay. But
even this less outrageous statement seems not only wrong but
unnecessary. If Gonzalez-Torres was forming a partnership with
his collectors, surely they would have been aware of his statement, "[My work] is all my personal history, all that stuff ...
gender and sexual preference.... I can't separate my art from my
life."[20] Therefore, any attempt to distance the artist's life from
his work does a disservice to the original intention of the art.

As with all contentious estates, the love that people felt for
Felix has tended to turn to claims of ownership, rife with both
good intentions and self-interest. As Jim Hodges points out, Felix himself stands behind much of the current contention about
his work. Hodges believes that the artist would have "enjoyed
the controversy but not taken it too seriously." Hodges presents
an image of the artist as a prankster who would probably have
considered the current struggle over his work as an art piece in

and of itself: "Felix was a rascal. He was the cat that ate the canary. You can see the feathers coming out of his mouth. This need to categorize and tie it all up was the model he was working against."

Rosen claims that Felix's work has a limited, specific market. But looking at the pile of blue candy that forms his *"Untitled" (Blue-Placebo)* on the cover of the fall 2001 Christie's catalogue, it is hard to believe that the artist's market is limited. The crisp, perfectly reproduced image on the catalogue elicits a certain sadness. Estimated at $600,000 to $800,000, the image seems far too fragile for the world it has entered. How many of those who bid on the work knew that Felix, Ross, and countless other gay men had bravely swallowed sparkling blue pills hoping to ward off the death that would come to erase their history? Although Gonzalez-Torres was interested in how objects become commodities, Bartman takes a dim view of the individual collectors now buying his work: "Museums are buying it because it's important, but the individuals who are buying it now are buying it as an investment." The sadness of seeing these artworks at the center of empty commercialism comes through the sure knowledge that such high stakes bring with them a warped interpretation of the pieces themselves. The work has become detached from the artist, floating without meaning in a smothering blanket of luxury.

If the art of Felix Gonzalez-Torres is truly meant to be open to interpretation, then I propose one such interpretation. I propose claiming Felix as a gay man who died of AIDS and relating his legacy to that powerful experience. The entirety of the "authorized" body of work by Gonzalez-Torres was created while he watched his lover die and discovered that he too was dying. The work is not about formal concerns; these are only the medium in which they were created. The work speaks of trying to grieve for another person even as you watch your own death approaching. *"Untitled" (Lover Boy)*, a sheer blue curtain hanging on a shimmering window, evokes the memory of the artist's lover; the memory is beautiful in its transparent light but heart-breaking in its inability to provide any real warmth or comfort. The disappearing sheets of the stack pieces are a melancholy statement of life slipping away, contained only in a few words and images that will persist but continually diminish. The twin clocks of *"Untitled" (Perfect Lovers)* are bodies in tune even as they are dying. Dealers, collectors, and critics, many of whom are by their very nature profit-minded, cannot be given the sole power to interpret the legacy of this artist. If he had lived for another fifty years, he would surely have gone on to create a more diverse body of work with a variety of themes. But as the wealthy collectors gather in the auction rooms of the world to buy this work, they are buying the memories of *two men* sucking and eating, laying in bed together, holding one another in the hospital, loving each other as best they can until the batteries in their clocks run down and the hands stop moving.

"Contact" and the Dangers of Assimilation

There is a way for the gay male community to continue the healthy aspects of assimilation without abandoning our history. If we stop being ashamed of places like the Mineshaft, the Catacombs, and the baths, we might once again become a community rich with history rather than a shallow consumer demographic. Instead of abandoning these historic sites as centers of our downfall, we should consider them as historic landmarks of gay liberation. This act of reclaiming might yield an intergenerational connection that, with more effective prevention campaigns, could give gay youth some hope of survival. At the very least, it will allow us to see honestly how we arrived at our current situation.

AIDS impacted American culture not only because so many influential artists were lost to the disease; AIDS also destroyed the gay male sexual culture that gave birth and creative enrichment to these artists. The gay male sexual culture of the 1970s can be seen in the work of a wide range of artists: writers such as Reinaldo Arenas, Howard Brookner, and Michel Foucault; performers such as Leigh Bowery and Ron Vawter; directors like Reza Abdoh, Michael Bennett, and Charles Ludlam; designers such as Perry Ellis and Halston; filmmakers such as Derek Jarman and Marlon Riggs; choreographers like Ulysses Dove and Rudolf Nureyev; and visual artists like Scott Burton, Robert Mapplethorpe, and David Wojnarowicz. Not only were these artists lost; the world in which they developed their creative talents was lost with them. We need to remember that world and how it was lost. As Fran Lebowitz wrote in her 1987 "The Impact of AIDS on the Artistic Community" in the *New York Times*:

> The Impact of AIDS on the Artistic Community is that when a 36-year-old writer is asked on a network news show about the Impact of AIDS on the Artistic Community particularly in regard to the Well-Known Preponderance of Homosexuals in the Arts she replies that if you removed all of the homosexuals and homosexual influence from what is generally regarded as American culture you would be pretty much left with "Let's Make a Deal." The interviewer's lack of response compels her to conclude that he has no idea what she is talking about and she realizes that soon many of those who do know what she is talking about will be what is generally regarded as dead.[1]

One way to understand the importance of the gay sexual culture of the 1970s and what was lost when AIDS interrupted it is to look at the concept of contact. In 1961 the activist and writer Jane Jacobs published a seminal analysis of urban culture—*The Death and Life of Great American Cities*. Jacobs is most widely known for spearheading the campaign to stop the voracious public works official Robert Moses from running an expressway through SoHo and Greenwich Village in the 1950s, but she was at least as much a thinker as an activist and was, for the first time, able to accurately articulate the qualities that made urban life appealing. Jacobs was a great believer in the messy, seemingly unstructured life of a city that was in fact an intricate, delicate web of interconnectedness among urban people. She might well have been describing the impulse to sanitize gay life when she wrote of urban existence, "There is a quality even meaner than outright ugliness or disorder, and this meaner quality is the dishonest mask of pretended order, achieved by ignoring or suppressing the real order that is struggling to exist and to be served."[2]

For reasons to be discussed later, it is ironic to use Jacobs's theories to make the case for the importance of gay sexual life in the 1970s. But still her theory of contact, again and again, echoes gay male sexuality. When Jacobs describes city streets, she says, "They bring together people who do not know each other in an intimate, private social fashion and in most cases do not care to know each other in that fashion."[3] In other words, *contact* might be defined as the bringing together of people from different classes and backgrounds for a shared, vital, albeit temporary, activity. This might be the housewives, merchants, and businesspeople on a healthy city block unconsciously policing their own street, keeping one another informed, and performing small services for one another that add up to an interconnected, kind community. This might also be the men in tearooms accommodating one another sexually, keeping an eye out for the police, and physically maintaining the bathroom in which they gather for sex. Neither the first group nor the second is likely to go to dinner parties with one another, because they are of different classes and backgrounds. But both groups show kindness for one another.

Jacobs sometimes described contact in artistic terms that might equally apply to gay male sexual culture. John Rechy, the great novelist of the gay sexual scene, described the sexual hunt in terms of artistic beauty:

> For me there is a beautiful abstract choreography in the sexual hunt. I know ... that the beauty of the promiscuous sex hunt is almost balletic, symphonic; it is choreographed, it is tremendously beautiful. And I'm going to move it into the area of the art to be produced. Nevertheless, I have a love/hate relationship for the promiscuous hunt. Sometimes after a night of hustling and then moving to dark cruising alleyways, I come home and literally think of nothing but suicide. Other times, when I'm caught in it, I think: "Jesus, God this is the most exciting thing in the world."[4]

Compare Rechy's description of the search for anonymous sex with Jacobs's following description of a healthy city:

> This order is all composed of movement and change, and although it is life, not art, we may fancifully call it the art form of the city and liken it to the dance ... an intricate ballet in which the individual

> dancers and ensembles all have distinctive parts which miraculously reinforce each other and compose an orderly whole. The ballet of the good city sidewalk never repeats itself from place to place, and in any one place is always replete with new improvisations.[5]

It is the diversity and chance of urban life that maintains it as a system. If we look at gay urban life in the 1970s in the same way, the Fire Island set mixed with and was influenced by the Mineshaft men, all the while gaining and losing men from the larger gay population who were making only occasional forays from more traditional lives. There was a ballet and a balance between these groups that was disrupted by AIDS.

There was also a privacy available to the gay sex art participants. Jacobs describes privacy as "a gift of great city life deeply cherished and jealously guarded."[6] Although sex had never been as visible as it was in the 1970s, one no longer had to have sex in public after the rise of safe, specialized sex clubs. The number of participants in these clubs, oddly, allowed for privacy. For men who were not interested in the process of dating or whose sexual tastes were considered extreme, the clubs made privacy possible.

The transitory nature of sex allowed for relationships that might never have existed. Although Jacobs was thinking of, say, the relationship between the Chinese laundress and the socialite, she may as well have been describing the stock trader from the Upper East Side being fisted by the mechanic from New Jersey when she writes:

> It is possible to be on excellent sidewalk terms with people who are very different from oneself, and even, as time passes, on familiar public terms with them. Such relationships can, and do, endure for many years, for decades; they could never have formed with that line, much less endured. They form precisely because they are by-the-way to people's normal public sorties.[7]

In a chapter titled "The Need for Aged Buildings," Jacobs puts forward an argument for both the rehabilitation of old buildings and the continued use of them in their dilapidated state. Gay bars, clubs, and discos have been at the forefront of this activity in that they usually maintain the basic physicality of a building in a rundown area and, sometimes, even fetishize that decay. Gay men were willing to travel into the Meat District to a club with an unmarked door and grimy facade when the neighborhood was still forbidding, even dangerous. Not only were they willing, they appreciated the setting for its vitality.

The retrospective concurrency of thought between the contact that Jacobs proposes in the 1960s and the sweaty contact of gay men in the 1970s would probably not have been welcomed by Jacobs herself, as her writing often includes homophobic statements. The extraordinary writer Samuel Delany pioneered the use of "contact" as a way to describe the importance of gay sexual culture. In *Times Square Red, Times Square Blue*, Delany examines contact through the lens of his experiences in New York City's porn theaters (especially in and around Times Square) from 1957 through the present. Times Square presents an ideal laboratory for examination of contact because of the extraordinary changes that have occurred in the area, many ostensibly because of AIDS and public safety. In reality, many of these changes are based on a viewpoint even less exalted than that of Robert Moses when he proposed ramming an expressway through Lower Manhattan; less exalted because they are based solely on the greed of real estate speculation covered in the shiny wrapper of urban renewal that Jacobs so hated. In 1985 AIDS presented New York with the legal excuse it had so long sought in overriding civil liberties and shutting down the gay and straight porn theaters that lined Forty-second Street and extended up Eighth Avenue, with a sprinkling on the area's side streets. Far beyond the concerns of gay sexual culture, the unique qualities that differentiated New York from Omaha are being systematically eliminated in the name of public safety, transforming Times Square, as described by Delany, "from a highly diversified neighborhood with working-class residences and small human services ... into what will soon be a ring of upper-middle-class luxury apartments around a ring of tourist hotels clustering about a series of theaters and restaurants, in the center of which a large mall and a cluster of office towers are slowly but inexorably coming into being."[8] The Forty-second Street Redevelopment Corporation has either made a horrible miscalculation about the character of New York or, more likely, has chosen to disregard character in favor of profits.

In the traditional view, urban blight spreads, but in reality it is fear that spreads and redevelopment brilliantly uses fear to manipulate public opinion. Having worked in the area for more than a decade, I can attest to the fact that the prostitution and drug use that New York State has conveniently put forward as the grounds for redevelopment of Times Square must be quite rare; I have rarely seen an instance of either. Could it be that New York City will be the first city in history to exist without a single block of a red-light district? How will diverse sexual needs, which have not disappeared from the populace, be fulfilled? If such a district has been demanded in urban environments for thousands of years, can New York be the first city not in need of such an outlet?

It is important to talk about New York in relationship to the cultural changes effected in America by AIDS because areas such as Times Square, the Lower East Side, and Greenwich Village so clearly illustrate what has been lost in terms of the creative energy that flowed from the gay culture of the 1970s. It is very difficult to imagine a rationale that would justify replacing the Saint with an anonymous apartment building flanked by a Starbucks, and transforming Times Square from a true "crossroads of the world" into a heartless strip mall where the only prostitution is that of the few arts groups brought in to signal urban life.

One hates to denigrate New York—a city that has been so victimized already—but it is impossible not to see the relationship between the loss of gay culture and the creeping blandness that has spread over the city, inexorably eating away its creative character until it is much the same as the rest of monochromatic America. Delany's world of contact in the Times Square movie theaters is largely gone now. Culturally, New York as a whole has become retrogressive, although it maintains cultural organizations that will always assure it some degree of centrality. In terms of a culture rich with sexual contact, New York now lags far behind the West Coast. In San Francisco, sex clubs operate without harassment. In Los Angeles, the LAPD drives prospective sex club owners around the city, helping them to select appropriate venues for their businesses. It is interesting that even an architect who enjoys as much success in the *new* New York as Rem Koolhaas would publicly bemoan the decline of New York's contemporary culture. Koolhaas clearly relates this deterioration to a weakening sexual culture. In the journal *Grand Street*, Koolhaas wrote:

> It would have been less ambiguous if Times Square had died a "natural" death, if it had fallen victim to some other necessary expansion—but the leap from sick but energetic authenticity straight into the embalmed cheer of Disney has an intolerable perversity. It is as if the transition from the harmful to the innocent offends a sense of urban dramaturgy, as shocking as a movie suddenly played backward. A coalition of moralists, planners, and a nostalgia-driven entertainment giant expelling, as if in some Biblical scene, the unwanted from the city.... It hardly seems a good omen for Manhattan's continuing relevance in the twenty-first century.[9]

What is lost to AIDS and so well illustrated in Times Square comes back again to the idea of contact and a broader view of safety, relationships, and diversity. The fear used to appeal to notions of public safety in repressing sites of gay sex such as Times Square is not based on actual physical jeopardy from crime or even so much on actual risk of HIV infection. The fear is based on homophobia and intended to shame sexual people into withdrawing from view. As Delany describes it:

> As, in the name of "safety," society dismantles the various institutions that promote interclass communications, attempts to critique the way such institutions functioned in the past to promote their happier sides are often seen as, at best, nostalgia for an outmoded past and, at worst, a pernicious glorification of everything dangerous: unsafe sex, neighborhoods filled with undesirables (read "unsafe characters"), promiscuity, an attack on the family and the stable social structure, and dangerous, non-committed, "un-

safe" relationships—that is, psychologically "dangerous" relations, though the danger is rarely specified in any way other than to suggest its failure to conform to the ideal bourgeois marriage.[10]

It is fascinating to hear the echoes of Charley Shively's provocative call to promiscuous arms in *Fag Rag* reframed by Delany decades later. Shively was keenly aware of the revolutionary fear that gay people could invoke in straight society, and Delany cautions against the fear that we evoke in ourselves when we accept, without question, views of gay life generated by the straight world. Delany rejects the idea that his connections with men in the porno theaters were shameful gropings. Rather, he updates the notion of contact to explain that much is shared in these connections and that they are, in fact, relationships:

> Most were affable but brief because, beyond pleasure, these were people you had little in common with. Yet what greater field and force than pleasure can human beings share? More than half were single encounters. But some lasted over weeks; others for months; still others went on a couple of years. And enough endured a decade or more to give them their own flavor, form, and characteristic aspects. You learned something about these people (though not necessarily their name, or where they lived, or what their job or income was); and they learned something about you.[11]

Shame derives from an awareness of one's difference. That difference was cultivated and transformed by gay men in the 1970s into a creative response. The secrecy that Kantrowitz describes as being vital to the unselfconscious participation in the baths, bars, and clubs of the 1970s began as a response to hostility from a homophobic society, and only when the secrecy was lost was it recognized as a key component to creative identities. The presence of outsiders, of nonparticipants, in the environment fractured the fragile aura necessary for creative sexual exploration and meaningful contact between strangers who would ordinarily not intermingle, let alone reveal their deepest fantasies and fears to one another. Kantrowitz writes about the steep price of acceptance for the gay community:

> The gay world is succumbing to its own revolution. Once invisible, it is now being publicly examined as a curiosity. But the more it shows itself, the less reason it has to exist, because it was the creation of a people in hiding, a people who had to develop a private language and secret rituals and obscure places to survive.... Hiding together in the confines of the gay world, these people convinced each other that they were not "queer" but "special," which served as compensation for having been excluded from the rest of the human race.[12]

What Kantrowitz describes as secrecy and seclusion could also be termed shame. However, shame existed as a compelling force for gay men before the 1980s. For those lucky enough to enter the "special" world that Kantrowitz remembers, shame was accompanied by a clear sense of a gay culture that was distinct and revolutionary. When that revolution ended prematurely because of AIDS, and the very acts of revolution were disowned by the gay community, the shame persisted but without a creative response.

With no hook to hang its hat on, shame manifests itself very differently among young gay men who meet in cyber-chat rooms, disconnected from the immediacy of touch. These young gay men (and, indeed, anyone younger than forty whose entire adult sexual life has been seen through the scrim of AIDS and death) approach sexual encounters full of a dread derived from the certainty that sex is a self-destructive action rather than a revolutionary one. At least two generations of gay men have seen themselves reflected in the mass media as wraiths marching toward death or participants in gay minstrel sitcoms; the first signaling no future and the second no respect. Both reflections are full of the shame that comes with no sense of identity; and young gay men are left to play out that shame in isolation without knowing that there was ever a different world. In the earlier era, shame was transformed into a cherished, creative gay identity; now shame is simply a risk factor.

In the sexual experiment of the 1970s, visual artists, writers, choreographers, composers, and filmmakers were a vital part of contact as defined by both Jacobs and Delany. Artists fulfill two unique functions in society—to document and to transcend borders. The function of documentation is easily seen in the work of someone like Robert Mapplethorpe. Mapplethorpe's most important work was to take the participants of the 1970s S/M world, transpose them within a neutral studio environment, and capture the intensity of their lives. As a photographer, Mapplethorpe did not take his camera to the clubs as a voyeuristic gesture. Rather, he participated fully and then brought his fellow participants home with him. What he documented was not so much the environment of sex as the emotional journey that can be seen in the eyes and bodies of those involved in the great experiment.

Similarly, we can look to the work of the filmmaker Curt McDowell in San Francisco. McDowell was a typically horny young explorer in the wide-open arena of sexual San Francisco in the 1970s. McDowell's films, such as *Loads,* document the physical act of man after man coming. Ultimately, the film is not about the physical act but the emotional underpinnings of that act repeated again and again. In more abstracted forms of art such as choreography and musical composition, this documentation is less visible. Can the abandon with which Nureyev leapt across the stage be traced back to his trips to the playground of the Everard Baths? It is, of course, a matter of interpretation. The interesting aspect is that this interpretation is forbidden because of societal homophobia. Would anyone question a critic who discussed the influence of Nureyev's Russian heritage? Why then is the impact of his life as a gay man living in the 1970s considered an extraneous aspect of his life as an artist?

If artists document their world, using the emotional terrain of their world as the raw material of artistic exploration, what happens if that world becomes dead and one-dimensional? This question brings us to another important role that artists play in society—that of border crossers who transport ideas from one world to another. While there were certain class boundaries that divided the Mineshaft world from that of the Fire Island Pines, artists were citizens of both as well as token members of straight society. Again, Mapplethorpe is one of the clearest examples of an artist who was able to take an extreme vision built upon his emotional and physical explorations of the S/M world and transfer that vision to other worlds. A first step in his influence can be seen through his friendship with Bruce Mailman. It would be hard to deny Mapplethorpe's visual influence on Mailman and his clubs. The matte black surfaces and hard steel angles transposed with the elegance and drama of the natural world as represented by a single orchid define both Mapplethorpe and the Saint. Mapplethorpe then took another, more important, step. Because his work was physically beautiful, it was easy to turn it into a commodity. Therefore, people of wealth and social standing were encouraged not only to acquire the work but also to explore its source material. Far beyond the actual pictures, Mapplethorpe's true act of artistry was to entice wealthy, powerful straight people into looking at, buying, and in some cases participating in acts that were at the extreme end of the gay sex world. It limits the work of an artist to see their talent only in the objects they produce. It is far more interesting to look at their entire lives as part of an artistic practice that can cross boundaries and effect social change at the deepest levels.

And in so many of these seemingly gritty, cold lives, a common characteristic was kindness. Before sexual encounters became wrapped in shame, the men participating showed kindness to one another. Delany's people of the movie theaters cared for one another in many small ways; the men Kantrowitz describes in the bathhouses demonstrated gestures of tenderness; Nurse Peters genuinely cared for his charges at the Saint; the fisters of the Catacombs were involved in rituals of trust; and even the seemingly cruel theater of the Mineshaft involved a small group of men who knew and trusted one another sufficiently to move toward the unseen horizon. If we recast those physical locations, described with such precision and love by those who frequented them, as places of emotional wonder, surely we would arrive at a healthier, less disconnected present life for gay men.

But, again, if the work of artists is to document their world and to transmit that vision across class boundaries, what happens if the world becomes less interesting than it once was? Surely the preoccupation of 1980s art with irony and commodity is no co-incidence in a world where AIDS suddenly halted one of the world's great social experiments. In the current moment, the creative inspiration of gay artists in New York and so many other cities is based not on a city filled with contact but rather the American mass media. Many say that at least today's young gay people can see themselves reflected in the media. One television show in particular is endlessly cited as evidence that gays (if not lesbians) have achieved unprecedented visibility and, therefore, acceptance in mainstream America. NBC's *Will & Grace* is an unqualified hit, reaching a broad audience on a major network (as opposed to more targeted programs such as Showtime's *Queer as Folk*). *Will & Grace* is undeniably funny and brilliantly written, but I asked Michelangelo Signorile if he sees it as the step forward that it is often said to represent:

> I enjoy *Will & Grace* ... they're getting stuff out there that's inter-esting. At the same time, like everything else on television, it's ster-eotypes. It reminds me of *The Jeffersons*—these people who don't really struggle with anything. I understand that it's a sitcom but no-body ever talks about AIDS, drug regimens, and medical problems. This community is putting up a little circus for the larger world. Does it really challenge people to rethink their views or does it just put on a show for them to laugh at? My mother said to me, "I re-ally love Will and Grace. They're such a beautiful couple."[13]

Signorile's comparison of the reception of *Will & Grace* to the upper-middle-class acceptance of black "folks" in a predom-inantly white Manhattan apartment building in *The Jeffersons* in the 1970s seems particularly apt. It is an acceptance, in both cases, based on economics rather than culture. Only the flaming queen Jack, who aspires to be a salesperson at Barney's or the maid, Flo, on *The Jeffersons* retain any of the bite of their origi-nal culture.

How does a young gay man reconcile the sanitized images of

gay life presented in the mass media with his actual sexual urges? The new view of gay life depends upon the belief that uncontrolled sex, particularly gay sex, is inherently wrong and must be either punished or hidden from view for the greater good of society. As outlets for gay sex become increasingly rare, it becomes proportionately more difficult to reach gay men with safe-sex information. In a study from 2000, D. W. Seal and others report that young gay men "feel pessimistic about aging as gay men and may view HIV as a way of escaping a dreaded future."[14]

The dread that these young gay men feel is, in part, related to a lack of generational connection that provides a positive view of gay life. Part of the kindness that existed in the past was demonstrated by the "elders" of the sexual community through intergenerational mentoring. Far from being merely tolerated by the younger men, the elders were the driving force of the community, providing guidance and continuity to what could be a confusing journey. Although his experience is specific to the leather scene, the therapist Guy Baldwin's description of mentoring could be applied to the clubs, bathhouses, and theaters where older men provided examples and guidance for younger men in a sexual environment before AIDS:

> There was a fairly orderly way by which leather elders undertook the socialization and integration of newcomers. This was called the old guard system. But when HIV hit, since this was such a small cultural organism, it had a vastly more shattering impact than it did on the mainstream gay world, because the elders became preoccupied with taking care of one another and the children became irrelevant in that emergency context. And, whenever children become irrelevant, they find their own way. HIV caused younger guys to look on older guys with deep suspicion and fear rather than as mentors. There was a huge generation gap created. Young people began going down some horrible blind alleys that the older system would have prevented.[15]

Carolyn Dinshaw of NYU's Center for the Study of Gender and Sexuality describes the experience of teaching Delany's

Times Square Red, Times Square Blue in one of her classes. The students, far from seeing the benefits of "contact" in the Times Square sex scene, viewed the older gay men described in the book as predators preying on younger, powerless gay men. Some of the suspicion that young gay men feel toward older generations might derive from actual experience. As middle-aged and older gay men trying to continue their sexual lives while dealing with bereavement and their own health challenges, they often make choices that may be seen as destructive to themselves or others. The Van Ness House provides counseling for a large number of gay men and often sees this dynamic. Kathy Watt describes it:

> I think that gay men thirty-five and over don't necessarily put a value on growing older. There aren't enough examples of life in retirement, life in one's forties and fifties. I think that there is a lot of untreated grief. So I don't think human life has a lot of value so there is tolerance of selfish behavior that puts the next generation at risk. We are living in a totally detached, shut-down world where people use sex to fix themselves. It makes them feel better.[16]

It is vital that we rebuild our history and begin to form intergenerational connections. Seal and his colleagues state that, in relationship to young gay men at risk for HIV, "only societal interventions aimed at reducing homophobia and promoting healthy and dynamic gay role models will help reduce fatalistic thinking in this group."[17] If young gay men associate the history of gay culture with shame, there is little reason for them to feel entitled to a full, healthy life as they embark on their own explorations. The abstinence message for HIV has shown dismal results in all populations at risk and is particularly ineffective for young gay men. (Even the surgeon general of the United States has admitted that there is no research to support the effectiveness of abstinence campaigns for any teenager, gay or straight.)[18] These gay men need to be educated about what works in terms of harm reduction in a world where condoms are not used every time and monogamy is not the solution for everyone. Dr. Lynn

Ponton, a psychotherapist specializing in adolescence, a professor at the University of California in San Francisco, claims, "a vibrant sexual culture stimulates other types of creativity."[19] In other words, "just saying no" may mean just saying no to a rich American culture in the future.

The gay community cannot afford to let government control prevention campaigns that are supposed to prevent HIV infection (and address a recent resurgence in other sexually transmitted diseases such as syphilis, gonorrhea, and hepatitis) in young gay men. Title V prevention programs are required by law to include messages that teach adolescents "that sexual activity outside of the context of marriage is likely to have harmful psychological and physical effects."[20] For gay youth, sexual activity in the context of marriage is going to be a long time coming in the United States. It is absolutely vital that the gay community, not an amorphous group of individuals labeled "men who have sex with men," reclaim our sexual history, including AIDS, and refuse to let another generation be lost.

In late January 2003, President Bush announced that he would seek $16 billion to address the AIDS epidemic in the United States and another $15 billion for an international AIDS initiative. *If* this funding is approved, the question remains as to whether the money can be spent wisely enough to make a difference. On the global level, the project will extend well beyond just paying for drugs and must include provisions for basic medical care and potable water. In the United States, the challenge will be to develop prevention programs and treatments that are useful to those actually at risk of contracting HIV or currently living with AIDS. If the plan is to use billions of dollars to promote abstinence until marriage, the domestic funds would be better thrown in with the international pool of money in hopes of developing a truly effective vaccine that could help both Americans and the rest of the world.

Interestingly, another of the president's proposed domestic initiatives has been to develop serious treatment programs for drug addiction. As gay men experience an epidemic of crystal methamphetamine addiction that often has a destructive and deadly effect on their sexual choices, the gay community finds itself in the startling position of having its most serious problems discussed without the word *gay* ever being uttered.

Now that significant money is potentially available, the stakes are higher for the gay community. Will we still be content to say that "AIDS is no longer a gay disease" if it means that billions of dollars will not be used to prevent the deaths of young gay men? Despite our shame, will we be willing to insist that the United States hear that gay men of all colors are still having sex and having sex in ways that leave them open to infection from HIV as well as a range of other diseases?

I propose what might seem a circuitous approach to addressing two related crises—AIDS and addiction—in hopes of arriving at a healthy future. To move forward, we must look back. When we become integrated with our past, we are more able to deal with the problems at hand, because we approach them not as a band of lost boys or isolated "men who have sex with men" but as a community joined together by a common heritage. As gay people, we are the leaders in any effort in this country to deal with AIDS, because we have the longest experience.

We know the history of AIDS and it is our history. AIDS has changed the ethos of a culture that was, in the 1970s, exploring sex as a revolutionary act. With gay men in the vanguard of that revolution, America was able to produce cities like New York, where sexual activity was a sign of vitality rather than blight. AIDS not only killed sexual artists, it also provided conservative, corporate voices with a convenient link between sex and societal disarray that could be used in redevelopment efforts such as the one that turned Forty-second Street from a unique urban environment into another bland mall. In the face of emotional devastation and the need to command additional resources, the gay community understandably abandoned its own sexual history, including AIDS as a grim but central component of that history.

As a gay community, our triumphs and our sorrows have become mixed together; because they are so intertwined, we cannot abandon either our sexual history or AIDS without throwing away both. In discarding our history, we condemn new generations to float without the anchor of a past. In discarding our history, we also deny America the rich, transformative artistry of our experience.

There is a theater where a constantly evolving play is being staged. We are the audience and we are the players. Let not the theater go dark.

The Estate Project for Artists with AIDS

This book was commissioned by the Estate Project for Artists with AIDS (a project of the Alliance for the Arts), and many of the ideas contained in the book grew directly out of my experiences over ten years as director of the Estate Project. I think it is appropriate to end this book with a description of the Estate Project, not only as an honorific gesture but also as an action plan for future projects concerned with preserving cultural history.

How can a work of contemporary art, literature, media, or performance be viewed as an artifact of a certain era? How can one be a historian and an activist at once? How can one turn the attention of major institutions to work that is considered marginal? Most importantly, what role do artists play in a society in crisis?

My colleague Randy Bourscheidt (president of the Alliance for the Arts) and I asked these questions of many informed professionals and ourselves for the ten years, 1991–2001, that I was the director of the Estate Project. We asked the executors, lovers, families, and friends who came to us looking to protect the estates with which they had been entrusted. We also asked artists themselves what they want and need in lives consumed by two things: their work and the struggle of living with HIV/AIDS.

Although the Estate Project began life as a research and advocacy effort, it learned through doing. We dove into the worlds of film preservation, digital imaging, dance documentation, and publishing with the help of the best professionals we could find. After ten years, the Estate Project is still asking these questions but it brings to the discussion the experience of having preserved an immense and diverse group of artworks in every artistic discipline. In an era where AIDS is dropping out of public discourse, the Estate Project presents exhibitions, publishes books, convenes academics, and continues the difficult work of making sure that lifetimes of inspiration are not lost for future generations.

Most directly in relationship to this book, the Estate Project always had a special interest in cultural artifacts of historic importance to the gay community. This manifested itself in a willingness to blur the lines of what is traditionally considered art. Hence, we were able to preserve objects such as videotapes made by AIDS activists that capture the singular achievement of ACT UP and document how political action can reach the level of artistic expression. While the explorations of this particular book have focused more on the cultural explorations of gay men as innovators of social practices, I remain convinced that more traditional artworks such as paintings, drawings, films, dances, and musical compositions will be used by future generations to understand the enormity of AIDS and the unique sensibility that gay men brought to American culture.

The Estate Project's continued preservation work is paired with the need to interpret and present the work saved. We believe that an artwork only lives when it is seen, and our work as preservationists, historians, and curators extends well into the future. And through the continued life of these works of art, we retain not only the memory of the artists who created them but of a way of life that was radical, hopeful, and transformative.

Aside from commissioning this book, the Estate Project made a great contribution to it in helping me to assemble the following list of artists lost to AIDS. The power of names can be felt in two great public monuments of our time—the National Vietnam Veterans Memorial and the NAMES Project AIDS Memorial

Quilt. These monuments function in seemingly different ways —one static and hard, resounding with a quiet power, and the other ephemeral and exuberant with emotion. One was created through the vision of the architect Maya Lin, while the other was a loose framework constructed to hold the work of thousands of anonymous participants. Both have at their heart a list of names and the idea that the accumulation of these names bestows importance on the lost lives they represent.

It would certainly be arrogant to think that the process of compiling the following list of names of American artists lost to AIDS could be compared with the act of creating something like the AIDS Memorial Quilt. Still, it does represent a first step toward recognizing the enormity of the impact of AIDS on the American creative community.

There are many problems inherent in compiling such a list and they are reflective of the AIDS crisis. First, and most sadly, there are many names that should be on this list that are not for fear of legal action or creating more discord in an already tragic situation. The following names are drawn from the records of trusted organizations that have carefully vetted the lists in advance. These organizations include Broadway Cares, the Design Industries Foundation for AIDS, Visual AIDS, Visual Aid, the New York Public Library for the Performing Arts, and, of course, the Estate Project for Artists with AIDS. In addition, we have utilized the extensive research of the dance scholar David Gere, the list compiled by Patrick Merla for his anthology *Boys Like Us*,[1] lists published by *Entertainment Weekly* in the 1990s, and a list from Jay Critchley of Provincetown artists lost to AIDS.

Additionally, placement of the names is difficult because artists work in so many different disciplines. Therefore you will find the name of a writer also listed as a visual artist and a director. We also struggled to find the correct placement for such singular creative creatures as Wayland Flowers and Liberace. Although we have focused on American artists, we could not bear to exclude names such as Michel Foucault and Derek Jarman.

Finally, having gone to such lengths to redefine the word *artist* to include the people who created the sex art culture of the 1970s, I feel frustrated at the fact that there is no organized way to compile their names. Bruce Mailman, who was a businessman, should also be included here as an artist along with the scores of men who created the sex clubs, discos, and baths as well as the men who explored them. However, many of the artists on this list frequented these establishments and their work was informed by the brilliance of the 1970s culture, so in a small way, the accomplishments of those sex artists is still represented in this list.

This is by no means a comprehensive list but I can say with complete assurance that it is the most complete such list ever assembled. Each year at around the time of World AIDS Day and Day without Art, the Estate Project would receive calls from journalists, curators, and administrators asking for a list of artists lost to AIDS. Given the many other pressing matters at hand, we could only give them a small sampling. I hope that this list will be used as a tool for their projects of remembrance as well as further research into the work of these artists.

In his *Ambition and Love in Modern American Art*, Jonathan Weinberg utilizes the following quote from Ecclesiasticus: "And some there be which have no memorial; who are perished, as though they had never been, and are become as though they had never been born."[2] This list is in honor of those creative people lost to AIDS who have no memorial of their own but influenced American life through their lives as well as their art.

WRITERS

Steve Abbott
Hugh Allen
Frank Arcuri
Reinaldo Arenas
Abel Rios Arias
Howard Ashman

James Assatly
David Craig Austin
John A. Avant
Brett Averill
Stuart Baker-Bergen
Charles Barber
Allen Barnett
Joseph Beam

John Beaird

John Terry Bell

Robert Bendorff

Kenton J. Benedict

Richard Benner

Marc Berman

John Bernd

Jack Bissell

Jerry Blatt

Walta Borawski

William Bory

John Boswell

Alan Bowne

Richard C. Bowne

Joe Brainard

Arthur J. Bressan Jr.

Donald Britten

Harold Brodkey

Howard Brookner

Chris Brownlie

Anthony Bruno

Peter Buckley

Walter Rico Burrell

Michael Callen

Bruce Calnan

Fred Cantaloupe

Warren Casey

Tim Cassidy

Robert Chesley

Panos Christi

Brian Cleere

Marvin Coble

Charlie Coco

Christopher Coe

Cyril Collard

Frederick Combs

Copi (aka Raul Demonte)

Steve Corbett

Steven Corbin

Christopher Cox

Gil Cuadros

Sam DíAllessandro

Nicholas Dante

Serge Daney

Iris Delacruz

Americo DeZarte

John Di Carlo

William Dickey

Victor D'Lugin

Tim Dlugos

Terry Dolan

John Dorr

Clifton Dowell

Emmanuel Dreuilhe

Donald Driver

Peter Dvarackas

Robert Edmonds

Bill Elverman

Rob Elwood

James Evangelista

Tom Eyen

Nathan Fain

David B. Feinberg

Robert Ferro

Gary Fisher

Michel Foucault

John Fox

David Frechette

William Franklin

Dexter Freeman

Richard Friedel

Philip Galas

Christopher Gerard
Scott Giantvalley
Benjamin P. Gilbert
David Gilmore
Art Goldsher
Roy Gonsalves
Wayne Gordy
Sam Greenbaum
Howard Greenfield
Stuart Greenspan
Morgan Grey
Michael Grumley
Hervé Guibert
Jeff Hagedorn
Richard Hall
Tony Hancock
Sam Hardison
Mark Hardwick
Craig G. Harris
Stephen Harvey
Terry Helbing
Essex Hemphill
Bill Hennessy
Scott Heumann
Colin Higgins
Leland Hickman
Paul Hidalgo-Duran
Mike Hippler
Leon Hirszman
Charles Horne
Richard Horn
Dumont Howard
Jackson Hughes
Bo Huston
Richard Irizarry
Arturo Islas

Paul Jabara
Robert Jacobson
Clifford Jahr
Michael Jay
Michael Johnson ("Mijo")
David Kalstone
Wayne Karr
Michael M. Katz
Karl Keller
Oleg Kerensky
Kenneth Ketwig
Leland Kichman
James Kirkwood
Gregory Kolovakos
Bernard-Marie Kotlès
Harry Kondoleon
Mark Kostopoulos
Glenn Kramer
Robert Krueger
Barry Laine
Garey Lambert
Robert Larkin
Brian Lasser
Jay B. Laws
Craig Lee
Larry Lee
Stan Leventhal
Michael C. Lipton
Ezra Litwak
Peter Wendell Livingston
Richard Locke
Paul Michael Lombardi
David Londahl
Robert Lord
Stephen Lott
Charles Ludlam

Michael Lynch
Fred Maddux
John Mangano
Kiki Mason
Robert Massa
Gerald Mast
Michael Matthews
Peter McGehee
David McIntosh
Scott McPherson
Timothy Meyers
Ernest Matthew Mickler
Michael Miller
Terry Miller
Andy Milligan
J.J. Mitchell
Lionel Mitchell
Paul Monette
Paul Morse
Cookie Mueller
Armando Nevarez
Ross Lee Neidorf
Jean-Baptiste Niel
Maurice Noel
Mark Oates
William Olander
George Osterman
Craig Owen
Paul Panfiglio
Kevin Patterson
Al Parker
Robert Parola
David Pasko
John Pearson Perry
Glenn Person
Bruce Peyton

Richard Picchiarini
James Carroll Pickett
Henry Post
Tim Powers
John Preston
Leslie Raddatz
Bob Randall
Samuel D. Ratcliffe
John Read
Joel Redon
Robert Allen Reed
James Revson
Marlon Riggs
David Scott Richardson
Larry Riley
Darrell Yates Rist
Will Roberson
David Rodale
Craig Rowland
Gregory Rozakis
John Russell
Vito Russo
Assotto Saint
Rick Sandford
Carl Sautter
David Sawn
Martin M. Schaeffer
Nicholas Schaffner
Jeffrey Schmalz
Harry Seaberly
Paul A. Sergios
Michael Seyfrit
Howard Shapiro
Michael Stuart Shere
Bill Sherwood
Randy Shilts

Paul Shyre
Jack Smith
Justin Smith
Kevin Smith
David Spencer
Duncan Stalker
George Stambolian
Thomas Stehling
Stephen Steinberg
Dudley Stevens
Mark Stevenson
Edward Stone
Otis Stuart
Paul Stubenrauch
Jack R. Sturdy
Alfred Sturtevant
Jeremiah Sullivan
David Summers
Charles Suppon
Milton Tatelman
Paul Taylor
Carl Tierney
Art Tomaszewski
Neil Tucker
Alan Turcotte
Richard Umans
Ron Vawter
BIll Vehr
Joseph Vigil
Paul Walker
Matthew Ward
Jerry B. Wheeler
G. Luther Whitington
George Whitmore
Mason Wiley
Frank Wilson

Jack Winkler
Ron Wise
Ronald Wiseman
T. R. Witomski
David Wojnarowicz
Donald W. Woods
Sidney Wordell
Paul Wychules
Thomas Yingling
Phil Zwickler

ACTORS/PERFORMERS—
THEATER, FILM,
TELEVISION, AND MUSIC

David Abercrombie
Vince Acosta
Mart Aldre
LeWan Alexander
Tom Alexander
Peter Allen
Randy Allen
Seth Allen
John Allison
Lem Amero
Gordon Richard Anderson
Norman Andersson
Keith Arendt
Arnie Armquist
Philip Astor
John C. Attle
Michael Austin
Tony Azito
Adam Corey Balzano
Frank Banks
Chris Barbick

Alan Barwiolek

Mark Bason

Fausto Bara

John Terry Bell

Steve Bellin

Kenton J. Benedict

Stuart Baker-Bergen

Barry Bernal

Bill Beyers

Mel Black

Amanda Blake

Rand Bohn

Richard Charles Bollig

Tim Bowman

Leigh Bowery

Warren Neal Boxer

William Bourne

William V. Boyd Jr.

Thomas Francis Briggs

John Brockmeyer

Bill Brown

Frank Brown

Bob Brubach

Gary Brubach

Howard Brunner

Cisco Bruton

Ken Bryan

Robert Bucholtz

Dan Buelow

Jim Burgess

Stephan Burns

Geoffrey Burridge

Tom Butters

Merritt Butrick

David Cahn

Len Calder

Don Caldwell

Michael Calkins

Bobbie Callicaotte

Edward Campbell

Jack Carlson

David James Carroll

Lynne Carter

Warren Casey

Richard Casper

Dalton Cathey

Ian Charleson

Lee Chastain

Panos Christi

Robert Christian

Dale Christopher

Keith Christopher

Sandie Church

Paul Cira

Jerry Clark

Raymond Clarke

Charlie Coco

Dwain Cole

Cyril Collard

Charles Collins

Frederick Combs

Byron Connor

David Corey-Vernon

Lauro Corona

Danny Corcoran

Dorian Corey

Nicholas Cortland

Ken Cory

Howard Crabtree

Joey Cuevas

John Curry

John D'Agnese

Jack Damlos
Kaipo Daniels
Bowlin Davis
Brad Davis
Palmer Deane
William DeAcutis
Robert Deangelis
David DeBerry
Richard DeFabees
Doug Delauder
Jose De Vega
Bruce Demarest
John Di Carlo
John Dolf
Richard Doran
Mark Dovey
Don Draper
Max Drew
Robert Drivas
Donald Driver
Edward Duke
John J. Dunbar
Edward L. Dwornek Jr.
Dickey Wayne Eddington
Robert Edmonds
Ethyl Eichelberger
Karl Joseph Ellis
Denholm Elliott
Robert Elston
Bill Elverman
Don England
Billy Errigo
Christopher Esposito
Peter Evans
Scott Everhart
Roderick Ewing

Stephen J. Falat
Bruce Falco
Rick Farwick
Thomas Lindsay Fleming
Wayland Flowers
Michael Forella
Dennis Fox
Richard Edward Frank
Dexter Freeman
Leonard Frey
Mark Fotopolous
Tom Fuccello
Tim Fuji
Jay Kevin Funk
Philip Dimitris Galas
David Gallegly
John Ganzer
Kevin Gee
Steven Gelfer
Frank Geraci
Scott Giantvalley
Dieudonne Gignac
Ray Gill
Roscoe Gilliam
Phillip F. Gilmore
Peter Alan Gloo
Miguel Godreau
Chuck Gollnick
El Tal Gomezbeck
Sam Greenbaum
Martin Gregg
Michael Scott Gregory
Morgan Grey
Bob Ground
Howard Gruber
Michael Hagerty

Michael Haimson
Antony Hamilton
Thomas A. Hannan
Larry Hansen
Mark Hardwick
Christian Haren
Gregg Harlan
Charles Harper
Mark Hayden
William S. Hayes
Alan Heer
Terry John Helbing
Essex Hemphill
John S. Heppenstahl
Bill Herndon
Christian Hesler
Peter Heuchling
Hibiscus
Bob Higgins
J. Allen Highfill
Bruce Hilbok
Ken Hill
Bob Hines
Michael Hirsch
Sebastian Hobart
Anthony Holland
Jesse Hollis
John C. Holmes
Jason Holt
Craig Horrall
David Horowitz
Andy Hostettler
Rock Hudson
Richard Hunt
Joel Imbody
Bradley Yoshio Inouye

James B. Isgro
Donald Ives
Paul Jabara
Paul Jacobs
Gerald E. Jacobson
   (aka Jake Everett)
Scott Jarvis
Denny Jerecki
Jerriese D. Johnson
Michael Johnson ("Mijo")
Mark Jollie
Duane Jones
Keith R. Jones
Reed Jones
Robert Jordan
   (aka Leslie London)
Tom Joyce
Raul Julia
Lars Kampmann
Michael M. Katz
Brian Kaufman
Keith Keen
Paul Keenan
Larry Kert
Tom Kindle
Casey Kizziah
John Kobel
Glenn Kolb
Greg Kollenborn
Dennis Kotecki
Tim Kramer
Danny Kreitzberg
George Kretchman
Robert J. Kunar
Gordon Kurtie
Jim Lamb

Douglas Lambert
David Landis
James Langrall
Tom Lantzy
Robert LaOrince
Paul Latchaw
Robert LaTourneaux
Gary Lawrence
Mark Lazore
Bobby Lee
Donald Lee
Irving Allen Lee
William Patrick Leonard
Ernest Lewis
Liberace
Tony Lillo
Mark Lincoln
Mark Linton
Michael C. Lipton
Keith Locke
Roger Locke
J. Victor Lopez
Luis Lopez-Cepero
Larry Lott
Cary Scott Lowenstein
Alan Lozito
Charles Ludlam
Joe Lyn
Larry Lynd
Fred Maddux
Don Maderich
Tom Major
Mark Maples
Vinnie Mancuso
James H. Martin
Gene Masoner

Frank Massey
Lee Mathis
Beau Matthews
Wayne Mattson
David Mattias (Rodriguez)
Luis Maura
Winston May
Joe Mays
Thomas McBride
Dan McCoy
James McCrum
Michael A. McDonald
Aldyn McKean
Kenneth J. McLaughlin
William McLinn
Scott McPherson
Derek Meader
James Medina
John Megna
Pierre Menard
George Metcalfe
Timothy Meyers
Steven Milbank
Court Miller
Wayne Miller
Prentiss "Mitch" Mitchell
Jeff Mitchellcraft
Jack Moran
Paul Morse
Timothy Patrick Murphy
Michael Navarre
Ross Lee Neidorf
Kenneth Nelson
Armando Nevarez
Gerald Nobles
Don Nute

Mark Oates

Michael O'Boyll

Christopher J. O'Brien

Tom Offt

Michael O'Gorman

Brad O'Hare

David Oliver

Bradford O'Neil

George Osterman

Austin O'Toole

Dennis Ott

John Outlaw

Louis Padilla

John Palomino

Paul Panfiglio

Al Parker

William Parker

Robert Parola

Bill Partlow

Ilka Payan

Lenny Pass

Ricardo José Peinado

Gene Pelligrini

Stephen Pender

Paul Penfield

Anthony Perkins

Donald Phelps

Robert Phillips

Richard Picchiarini

Michael Pierce

Clark Piper

Nick Pippin

Joseph Porrello

Joseph Portello

Kurt Raab

Rex Rabold

R. Rhael Rafik

Dack Rambo

Samuel D. Ratcliff

Robert Reed

Scott Reeve

Orrin Reilly

John Remme

Felix Rice

Jess Richards

Ron Richardson

Larry Riley

Brennan Roberts

Dennis Roberts

Meghan Robinson

Tom Rolfing

Howard Rollins

Richard Rorke

Adrian Rosario

Richard Rothenstein

David Rounds

Glenn Rowen

Gregory Rozakis

Ariel Rubstein

Craig Russell

John C. Russell

Keith Ryan

Richard Ryder

Kenny Sacha

Scotty Sachs

Fred Sadoff

Assotto Saint

Robert Salvio

Jim Samuels

Rick Sandford

Stephen Sapuppo

Ken Sasha

Schorling Schneider

Stu Scott

Timothy Scott

Franklyn Seales

Jim Secreast

Craig Seeley

David Serko

John Sex

Ray Sharkey

Paul Shenar

Paul Shyre

David Silber

Mario Siletti

Ken Simmons

Tom Singer

James E. Skinner Jr.

Michael Sklar

Patrick Scott Slater

Larry Sloan

Bebe Smith

Jack Smith

Justin Smith

Martin Smith

Allan Sobek

Dennis Soens

David Spencer

Vernon Spencer

Ron Stafford

David Ross Stenstrom

Dudley Stevens

Mark Stevenson

Larry Stewart

Michael St. Laurent

Danny Strayhorn

Bill Strouse

Donald Struthers

Christopher Stryker

David Ross Stump

Jeremiah Sullivan

Tim Sullivan

David Summers

Mark Sundstrom

Swen Swenson

Paul Swift

Robert E. Tannis

John Tate

Robin Tate

Jason Taylor

Leon Taylor

Martin Teitel

Donny Thibodeaux

Toney Thompkins

Ian Thompson

Joel Thompson

Mark G. Thompson

Dan Thor

Christopher Todd

Dennis Torza

Steve Tracy

Daniel Trent

Joel Tropper

Ted Trowbridge

B.J. Turner

Vanilla

Ron Vawter

Bill Vehr

David Vendetti

Axel Vera

Buddy Vest

Joseph Vigil

Mark Villa

Tom Villard

Clyde M. Vinson
Paul Walker
Martin J. Walsh
Charles Ward
Robert Warners
David Warrilow
Drexel Wassen
Carl Earl Weaver
Byron Webster
Steven Boone Webster
Karl Wendelin
Larry White
Ken Whitehead
   (aka Tiffany Jones)
Jeff Wilkins
Frank Wilson
Nephi Jay Wimmer
Ronald Wiseman
Dan Witt
Raymond Wood
Martin Worman
William W. Wright
Martin Xero
Joseph Yale

DIRECTORS—
THEATER, OPERA, FILM,
AND TELEVISION

Reza Abdoh
Ross Allen
Seth Allen
John Allison
Lem Amero
Robert Anton
A. J. Antoon

Charles Barber
Gary Barker
Richard Barr
Sam Barton
John Terry Bell
Richard Benner
Michael Bennett
Richard Casper
Panos Christi
Jacques Chusat
Raymond Clarke
Cyril Collard
Frederick Combs
David Corey-Vernon
Mark Cullingham
Edmund De Stasi
Americo DeZarte
Harding Dorn
Clifton Dowell
Robert Drivas
Donald Driver
Robert Elston
Ron Field
Nigel Finch
Stefan Fitterman
Ward Fleming
John Galway
Thomas Kahn Gardner
Carlos Gimenez
El Tal Gomezbeck
Gerald Grant
Sal Grasso
Michael Scott Gregory
Jerry Haislmaier
Terry John Helbing
Bill Herndon

Ken Hill
John Hirsch
Stephen Hults
James B. Isgro
Derek Anson Jones
Duane Jones
Michael M. Katz
Casey Kizziah
Jack Krevoy
Wilford Leach
Irving Allen Lee
David Lemos
William Patrick Leonard
Roy London
Luis Lopez-Cepero
Charles Ludlam
Gene Masoner
Michael Matthews
Timothy Meyers
Andy Milligan
Robert Moore
Leland Moss
Gustavo A. Motta
Robert Nigro
Al Parker
Bill Partlow
Michael Peters
Robert Ponce
J. P. Powell
Michael Prevulsky
Sebastian Priest
Peter S. Reed
Norman Rene
Tony Richardson
Will Roberson
Craig Sandquist
David Sawn

Peter Mark Schifter
Paul Shyre
Mario Siletti
Justin Smith
Kenneth Stein
Eric Steiner
Jay N. Stephens
Dudley Stevens
Edward Stone
Martin Teitel
Victor Valentine
Ron Vawter
Paul Walker
Stuart White
Derek Wolshonak
Joseph Yale

DESIGNERS (INCLUDES
COSTUME, LIGHTING
AND SCENIC DESIGNERS,
FASHION DESIGNERS,
AND ART DIRECTORS)

Michael Abbott
Vince Acosta
Daniel Adams
Mart Aldre
Brigham Auld
Ralph Bisdale
Dennis Blaine
Gary Nolan Boatman
Leigh Bowery
Joe Brainard
Jack Brusca
Gene Davis Buck
Chris Butler
Bettina Louise Chow

Howard Crabtree
Robert Currie
Jeffrey Dallas
Timothy D'Arcy
Robert DiNiro
John P. Dodd
Richard Dulong
Perry Ellis
John Falabella
Chet Ferris
Robert E. Franklin
Philip A. Gilliam
Juan Gonzalez
Bill Goodwin
Halston
Tom Hansen
David Harnish
J. Allen Highfill
Ken Holamon
Robert Hoppe
Richard Hornung
C. L. Huntley
Bradley Yoshio Inouye
Jayson Jefferys
Bernard Johnson
Steven Jones
Phillip Jung
Eric Kendricks
Ron Kron
Bill Leach
Ed Massoni
Jerry Maston
Vito MastroGiovanni
Norman Maxon
Michael Minor
Bill Moorehouse
Tom Morano

Patrick D. Moreton
Michael Muller
Geroge R. Nelson
Daniel Paredes
Fleming Pederson
Lewis Rampino
Dean Reiter
Paul Richard
Michael Robinson
Stephen Romano
Richard Rorke
Clovis Ruffin
Anthony Sabatino
Don Schefield
Jeffrey Schissler
Michael Stuart Shere
Henry Lee Sigler
Huck Snyder
David Spada
Greg Tice
Ben Wackerman
Norman West
R. Chris Westlund
Larry White
Jim Willard
Carl Wilson
Kaisik Wong
Greg York
Kenneth M. Yount
Robert Zentis

MUSICIANS—COMPOSERS

Kristopher Jon Anthony
Martin Bartlett
Peter Lake Bellinger
Robert Bendorff

John Bobanick

Anthony Bowles

Jack Briece

Robert Buchholz

Charles Buel

Duncan Campbell

Warren Casey

Robert Chesley

Charles Choset

Jonathan D. Cole

Glen Cummings

Chris DeBlasio

Richard P. DeLong

Robert Durr

Julius Eastman

William Elliott

Dan Erkkila

Humphrey Evans III

Ludar Felsenstein

Jerry Frankel

Lewis M. Friedman

Lee Gannon

Adam Geiger

Carter "Toby" Hall

Calvin Hampton

Eugene Hancock

Phil Harmonic
   (Kenneth Werner)

Peter Hartman

William Hibbard

James Holmes

Jan J. Holmgren

Deolus Husband

Tim Isbell

Richard Jetter

Dean X Johnson

Jerriese D. Johnson

Don Jones

Jeff Jones

Jeff Katz

Keeler

Gregory Kosteck

Mark Kyrkostas

Brian Lasser

Dennis Lindholm

Alan Lloyd

Wayne Love

Michael McCandless

Phillip B. McIntyre

Yvar Mikhashoff

Paul Morse

Gustavo A. Motta

Lance Mulcahy

Jackson Kevin Myars

Donald Wayne Nobles

Robert Nofsinger

Kevin Oldham

Stephen Oliver

Fred Palmisano

Rodger Pettyjohn

William Pflugradt

Paul Pretkel

Mark Riese

Dennis Riley

Ronald Roxbury

Arthur Russell

Frank Santo

Robert Savage

Michael Seyfrit

John M. Shepherd

Brian Shucker

Terry Snowden

Jonathan Spanierman
Marc Allen Trujillo
William Turner
Paul Joe Vest
Louis Weingarden
John Wilson
Harold Zabrack

SINGERS/SONGWRITERS

Travis John Alford
Peter Allen
Keith Barrow
Kerrigan Black
Bobby Blume
Joe Bracco
Tom Brown
Michael Callen
Dave Catney
Cazuza
Keith Christopher
Patrick Cowley
Clyde Criner
David Diebold
Eazy-E
Esquerita
Sky Evergreen
Tom Fogerty
Ray Gillen
Howard Greenfield
Steven Grossman
Don Hall
Dan Hartman
Paul Jabara
Fela Anikulapo Kuti
Freddie Mercury

Jacques Morali
Klaus Nomi
John Outlaw
John Kuhner Ponyman
Larry Riley
Nicholas Schaffner
Jermaine Stewart
Dan Turner
Matt Vernon
Don Yow

MUSICAL PERFORMERS
(INCLUDES VOCALISTS,
INSTRUMENTALISTS,
AND CONDUCTORS)

Edwin Alexander,
    bassoonist
Ross Allen, musical director
William Alvis, pianist
Norman Andersson,
    bass-baritone
Fortunato Arico, cellist
Clinton Arrowood, flutist
John Balka, organist
Frank Banks, musician
Buddy Barnes, musical
    director, vocalist
Randy Barnett, pianist,
    accompanist
Charles Robert Benbow,
    organist, choirmaster
Laurence N. Berry, organist,
    choirmaster
Marty Blecman,
    rock musician, DJ

Richard Charles Bollig,
pianist, choral singer

Louis A. Botto, tenor
(Chanticleer)

Jorge Bolet, pianist

Jerry Brainard, organist

Robert Briggs, bass

Thomas Francis Briggs, jazz
vocalist

David Britton, organist

David M. Brown, violinist

Gary Brubach, singer

Jim Burgess, tenor

Elena Burke, Cuban singer

Brock Burroughs, organist

Douglas Butler, organist

Stuart Challender, conductor

Marc Connors, vocalist
(The Nylons)

Wayne Cooper, funk-rock
singer (Cameo)

Barry Cormack, organist

Robbin Crosby, heavy-metal
guitarist (Ratt)

Frederick Jennings Dare,
organist, choirmaster

Michael Dash, countertenor,
baritone

Charles H. Davidson,
organist, choirmaster

Stephen Davis, organist,
pianist

Ken Dawson, pop singer

Bobby DeBarge, rock/soul
singer (DeBarge, Switch)

Richard P. DeLong, organist,
choirmaster

Andrew De Masi,
harpsichordist

Joseph De Rugeriis,
conductor

Stephen Dickson, baritone

Don F. Dingler, organist

Wayne Preston Drake,
organist, choirmaster

Bill Durham, accompanist

Richard Allen Durio,
organist, choirmaster

Youri Egorov, pianist

David Eisler, tenor

John Charles Ellis,
harpsichordist, organist

David F. Eplee, organist

Christopher Esposito,
musician

Michael Farris, organist

Bruce Ferden, conductor

John Ferranta, violist

James Festa, choral singer

Frankie Fix, punk rock
guitarist (Crime)

Edwin E. Flath, organist,
choirmaster

Kevin Freeman, singer
(Chanticleer)

Craig Robert Fritsche,
organist

John Galway, musician

Douglas Gibson, organist

Steve Gilden, singer

Peter Alan Gloo, pianist,
singer

Jorge Gonzalez, conductor,

pianist, singer
Bill Graham, conductor
Sam Gray, singer
Kenny Greene, vocalist
("G-Love" of Intro)
Kerry Grippe, pianist
Steven P. Grunewald, tenor
Calvin Hampton, organist
Eugene Hancock, organist
Tom Hancock, conductor
David Hart, flutist
Sean Hayes, rock musician
Ofra Haza, pop vocalist
(Israel)
Russell Hellekson, organist
Rand J. Hix, organist,
choirmaster
Howard Hoyt, organist,
harpsichordist
Bradley Yoshio Inouye, violist
Paul Jacobs, pianist
(New York Philharmonic)
Jobriath, glam rock singer
Alex Johnson, organist,
choirmaster
Dean X Johnson, accompanist
Glynnis Johnson, bass
guitarist (Red Red Meat)
Jeff Jones, organist
Keith Jones, singer and actor
Kent E. Jones, oboist
Alex Johnson, organist
Michael Johnson, musician
Bernard Kabanda, singer
(Uganda)
Shakespeare Kangwena,
guitarist, bassist (The

Bhunda Boys, Zimbabwe)
Christopher Keene,
conductor
Anthony King, organist,
choirmaster
Michael Vern Knowles,
organist
Samuel Henry Koontz,
organist
Michael Korn, organist,
choirmaster
Richard Hudson Ladd,
organist
Aldis Lagdzins, organist
Brian Lasser, accompanist
Nicholas Stern Leiser,
violinist
Ernest Lewis, singer
Liberace, pianist, entertainer
Mark Linton, musician
Matthew J. Loden, organist,
choirmaster
Thomas Lorango, pianist
Cary Lowenstein, dancer,
singer, and actor
Billy Lyall, rock keyboardist
(Pilot, Scotland)
David Mankaba, bassist (The
Bhunda Boys, Zimbabwe)
Sean Mayes, rock musician
Norman McBeth, organist
Thomas Joseph McBeth,
organist
Tony McDowell, musician
Phillip B. McIntyre, organist,
choirmaster
Jimmy McShane, rock singer

(Baltimora)
James Meade, baritone
Pierre Menard, violinist
Yvar Mikhashoff, pianist
Steven Milbank, conductor,
    pianist
Gary Lewis Miles, organist,
    choirmaster
Robert R. Miller, organist
John Gordon Morris,
    organist, choirmaster
Gerald Woods Morton,
    organist, choirmaster
Sheperd Munyama, bassist
    (The Bhunda Boys,
    Zimbabwe)
Alan Murphy, rock guitarist
    (Level 42)
Alec Murphy,
    punk rock guitarist
T. J. Myers, singer
    (The Flirtations)
Mark Nathan, musician
Klaus Nomi,
    rock/disco singer
Kevin F. O'Connor, organist
Lucy Offerall, rock singer
    ("Miss Lucy" of The
    G.T.O.'s)
Mickey Ortiz, rock drummer
    (Noise R Us)
Bert Ottley, singer,
    choral conductor
Christopher Palmer,
    musical director and
    orchestrator for films

David Papp, organist
Dennis Parker,
    country/western singer
Glenn Parker, pianist
William Parker, baritone
Evan Paris, violinist
Wayne Parrish, bassoonist
    (San Francisco Symphony)
Bruce Jay Paskow, folk singer
    (Washington Squares)
Walter Pate, pianist
Jeff Pawlak, singer and
    guitarist
Thomas Peck, choral
    conductor
Eddie Peters, singer
Terry Peterson, pianist
William Pflugradt, conductor
Robert Phillips, pianist
Charles Pilling, organist
Lonnie Pitchford, blues
    guitarist
Diet Popstitute
    (Michael Joseph Collins),
    singer/performance artist
    (The Popstitutes)
Joseph Porrello, tenor
Paul Pretkel, conductor
Scott Thomas Prince,
    organist, choirmaster
James Raitt, musical director
Jim Ramseth, organist,
    choirmaster
Black Randy (John Morris),
    punk rock singer
Neil M. Ratliff, pianist,

harpsichordist
Leonard Raver, organist
Edgar Rebich, harpsichordist
Rex Alan Rector, organist,
    choirmaster
Sharon Redd, R & B vocalist
Franco Renzulli, pianist
Paul Riedo, organist (Dallas
    Symphony Orchestra)
Jon Rollins, tenor
Gregg Romatowski,
    organist, choirmaster
Scott Ross, harpsichordist
James A. Roth, organist
Glenn Rowen, choral singer
Ariel Rubstein, soprano
Ron Rusthoven, singer
Craig Seeley, cabaret
    performer
Charles F. A. Senor III,
    organist
Sugar Shaft (Anthony
    Hardin), rapper (X-Clan)
D Sharpe, jazz drummer
Sheldon Shkolnik, pianist
Mark Duane Sick, pianist
Charles L. Silcox, organist
Jon Reed Sims, French
    hornist, band leader
Richad W. Slater,
    organist, choirmaster
Eric Sorensen, tenor
Sid Spencer,
    country/western singer
Benjamin Smith,
    conductor

Fred Stahl, singer
Douglas Stewart Stanton,
    pianist, conductor
James Starkey, baritone
Douglas Steinke, oboist
Conrad Strasser,
    music director
David Summers, singer
Boyd R. Swain, organist
Samuel Swartz, organist
Sylvester, rock singer
Tommy Tadlock, punk singer
Goetz Tangerding,
    jazz pianist
Lawrence Jay Taylor, singer
Emile Tchakarov, conductor
Christopher Teal,
    cabaret singer
Joseph D. Tonti,
    cabaret performer
William Eric Torain, baritone
Vaughan Toulouse, rock
    singer (Department S)
Wayne Turnage, baritone
James Ty Jr., organist
James Tyeska, bass-baritone
Lesesne Van Antwerp,
    cellist, conductor
Joseph Villa, pianist
Paul G. Votta, organist
Bruce Wade, violinist
    (Baltimore Symphony
    Orchestra)
Jack Waldman, rock
    keyboardist
Stephen Boone Webster,

musician
Ricky Wilson, rock guitarist
    (The B-52s)
Bill Wright, cabaret singer
Don Paul Yowell, singer
Harold Zabrack, pianist
Jerry Zimmerman, pianist
Armand Zone, rock singer,
    keyboardist (Fast, Ozone)
Miki Zone, rock singer,
    guitarist (Fast, Man2Man)

VISUAL ARTISTS

Kevin Adams
Carlos Alfonzo
Mark Allen
Sam Allen
Carlos Almaraz
Carl Apfelschnitt
Aaron Apgar
Chuck Arnett
Steven Arnold
Ed Aulerich
Cory Roberts Auli
Sugai Hasan Baharin
Osvaldo Barrocal
Crawford Barton
Charles Bell
Eric Bemisderfer
Wendy Bennet-Adler
Copy Berg
Robert Blanchon
Christopher Boccadori
John Bommer
Richard Booton

Angel Borrero
Juan Suarez Botas
Bern Boyle
Kenneth Bowman
E. John Bragg
Joe Brainard
William J. Branton
Thomas Francis Briggs
Richard Brintzenhofe
Jon Fernando Brito
Wilfredo Brito
John Eric Broaddus
Roger Brown
Jack Brusca
Brian Buczak
Wayne Buidens
Robert Bullinger
Mark Bulman
Abbot Burns
Scott Burton
Jerome Caja
Brian Campbell
Jack Carroll
Patti Chastain Haag
George Choy
Craig Coleman
Michael Colgan
Tim Collins
Walter Compton
Ruffin Cooper
Harold Cortes
Vincent Cosby
Max Coyer
Bruce Cratsley
Lucretia Crichlow
Jackie Curtis

Fidel Danieli
David Cannon Dashiell
Richard Davenport
John B. Davis
Peter Deatt
Guy De Cointet
Jimmy DeSana
Porfirio DiDonna
Humberto Dionisio
Kenneth Donohue
Juan Downey
Kevin Driscoll
Mario Dubsky
Carrie Duran
Sean Earley
Stephen Edlich
Michael Eisenman
Garland Eliason-French
Darrel Ellis
Terry Ellis
Pepe Espaliu
Michael Everett
Roderick Ewing
Gary Falk
Robert Farber
Arnold Fern
Miguel Ferrando
Robert Flack
Edward C. Flood
Bruno Fonseca
Billy Forlenza
Hollis Frampton
Luis Frangella
Barry Frederick
Sam Frinzi
Paul Gannon

Fernando Garcia
Dana Garrett
William Gatewood
Bubba Geiger
Michael Goepferd
Roy Gonsalves
Juan Gonzalez
Felix Gonzalez-Torres
Ken Goodman
Robert Gordy
Tim Goslin
Sylvia Granewista
Tim Greathouse
Michael Green
Tony Greene
Alex Greenfield
Michael Gruenwald
William R. Haines
James Hansen
Russ Hansen
Terry Hanson
Keith Haring
Joseph C. Hartney Jr.
Craig M. Hawley
Paul Hayes
Doug Haynes
Don Hill
Frank Hill
Kent Hines
Rodney Hines
Richard Hoffman
Will Horwitt
Michael Hosner
Peter Hujar
W. Benjamin Incerti
Frank Israel

Eric Jazman
Tim Jocelyn
Leslie Kaliades
Adrian L. Kellard Jr.
Peter Kelloran
Douglas Kenney
Ray Keyton
David Knudsvig
Ken Kostovny
Alan Krause
John Henry Larabee
Julian Latrobe
Thomas P. Licari
Marc Lida
Gin Louie
Steven Lott
Sheldon Lurie
Donald R. Lynn
Dell Madill
Daniel Mahoney
Jay Manning
Robert Mapplethorpe
Rick Marek
David A. Martin
Galen Martinez
Thomas McBride
Gerrard McCarthy
James Ray McCleskey
Kenneth McGowan
Daniel Melgarejo
Steven Terman Mendelson
Mundo Meza
Karl Michalak
Blaine Mitchell
Ronald Bruce Monroe
Frank Moore
Leonard Moore

Rob Moore
Rod Morrell
Mark Morrisroe
Nicolas Moufarrege
Jeffrey Mzientz
Ray Navarro
Barry Nelson
Lowell Nesbitt
Mark Niblock-Smith
Robert Nyland
Robert Michael O'Brien
Gustavo Ojeda
Ken Olsen
Sam Orwen
Randal Pacheco
Felix Partz
Michael Paulson
Doug Pearl
Joseph A. Pecsenke
Angel Perez
Jay Phillips
Noland Poole
David Potash
Dennis Price
Carl Ramos
Rory Ransom
Robert Allen Reed
Joseph Reeds
Jim Reva
Rodrigo Reyes
Rod Rhodes
Beau Riley
Andy Roberson
Cory Roberts-Auli
Nelson Rodriguez
Stephen Romano
Miguel Ronguillo

Thomas Block Rubnitz
Randal Rupert
Daniel Salazar
Adolfo Sanchez
Rene Santos
Dean Savard
Ron Sawhill
Johnny David Scipio
Andreas Senser
Andrew Shea
Michael Slocum
Bebe Smith
Duncan Smith
Jersey Smith
Rupert Jason Smith Jr.
Huck Snyder
Don Sorenson
Daniel Sotomayor
Harry Soviak
Ted Spagna
Ted Stamm
George Stavrinos
David Stebler
Hugh Steers
Don Sterton
Hugh Sweeney
Bill Sykes
Steven Tangalakis
Warren Tanner
Tony Tavarosi
Paul Thek
Dennis Thibodeau
Michael Tiffany
William Lincoln Tisdale
Stanley Toplif
Tomas Touron
Fred Trant

Kwong Chi Tseng
Osman Tyner
Julio Ugay
Herk Van Tongeren
Stephen Varble
Chuck Vetter
Michael Vivo
Chris Von Wangenheim
Alan Walker
James O. Watson
Adam Waugaman
Bruce Weinberg
Bruce Witsiepe
David Wojnarowicz
Gordon Wolter
Martin Wong
Bill Wright
Jorge Zontal

FILM- AND VIDEOMAKERS

Peter Adair
Paul Bartel
Juan Saurez Botas
Arthur Bresson
Howard Brookner
David Carpender
Cyril Collard
Charles G. Cyberski
John Dorr
Marie Edwards
Henrique DeSouza Filho
Adam Gale
Leon Hirszman
Guy Hocquenghem
Derek Jarman
Roger Jacoby

Tom Joslin
Robert McDonald
Curt McDowell
Bill McNeill
Andrew Meyer
Andy Milligan
Ray Navarro
Costa Pappas
Erik Paulo
Marlon Riggs
Thomas Block Rubnitz
Richard Schmiechen
Bill Sherwood
Jack Smith
Warren Sonbert
Joseph Vasquez
Bill Vehr
Phil Zwickler

CHOREOGRAPHERS
AND DANCERS

Damian Acquavella
William Adair
Thomas Aguilar
Alvin Ailey
John Aller
Juan Antonio
John C. Attle
Arnie Armquist
Tony Azito
Antony Balcena
Art Bauman
Steve Bellin
Michael Bennett
Barry Bernal
John Jeffery Bernd

James Daniel Blanc
Fred Booth
Dennis Botutis
Bob Bowyer
William V. Boyd Jr.
Derek Brice
Bill Brown
Harriet Browne
Bob Brubach
Cisco Bruton
Dan Buelow
Edward Campbell
William Carter
Christopher Chadman
Stephen C. Coleman
David Corey-Vernon
Joey Cuevas
Kevin Daley
Nicholas Dante
Greg Davis
John Davis
Gary DeLoatch
Jose De Vega
Robert Angelo Dicello
Richard Doran
Harding Dorn
William Douglas
Ulysses Dove
Mark Dovey
Jeff Duncan
Vito Durante
Germaine Edwards
Michael David Eilart
Rick Emery
Michael Empero
Don England
Carey Erickson

Bruce Falco
Louis Falco
James Farnsworth
Ron Field
Robert Ronan Fisher
Ward Fleming
Paul Fonseca
Ronn Forella
Robert E. Fournier
Michael Fullington
Steven Gelfer
Roscoe Gilliam
Christopher Gillis
Phillip F. Gilmore
Miguel Godreau
Eleanor Goff-Doerfler
Choo-San Goh
Adam Grammis
Charles Eugene Grant
Curtis Gregory
Michael Scott Gregory
Larry Grenier
Morgan Grey
Rodney Griffin
Jerry Grimes
William S. Hayes
Spencer Henderson III
Victor Leo Heineman
Ted Hook
Ernie Horvath
Ian Horvath
Andy Hostettler
Donald Ives
James F. Jacobs
Jim Jeppi
Brian Jay
Howard Jeffrey

Philip Jerry
Tom Jobe
Robert Joffrey
Bernard Johnson
Bobby Johnson
Carlton Johnson
Tommy Johnson
Mark Jollie
Carld Jorel Jonassaint
Carlton T. Jones
Gib Jones
Jason Jones
Reed Jones
Tom Joyce
Ed Kerrigan
Bruce King
Austin Kirby
Chris Komar
Robert Kovich
Kenneth Kreel
David Landis
David Joseph Leahy
Kristofer Michael Leighton
David Lemos
William Patrick Leonard
Tony Lillo
Holgar Linden
Keith Locke
Roberto Lorca
Edward M. Love Jr.
Stephan A. Love
Cary Scott Lowenstein
Kenneth Macdonald
Loremil Machado
Alex Mackay
Mark Maples
Gary Mascaro

Cameron Mason
Gene Masoner
Tony Mastorilli
Wayne Mattson
James Maxwell
Dan McCoy
Alvin McDuffy
Shaun McGill
Heywood "Woody"
    McGriff Jr.
Timothy C. McInerney
Antonio Mendez
Steve Merritt
Daniel James Messett
Tanis Michaels
Prentiss "Mitch" Mitchell
Charles Moore
Jean-Louis Moran
Steve Musha
Edward Myers
Gerald Nobles
Edward J. Nolfi
Rudolf Nureyev
Michael O'Gorman
Dale Orrin
Thomas Jullian Pazik
Ricardo José Peinado
Al Perryman
Michael Peters
Alan Peterson
Pete Peterson
Darryl Phelps
John Preston
Michael Radigan
Walter Raines
T. Michael Reed
Luis Rivera

Greg Rosatti
Danny Rounds
George Russell
Paul Russell
Jorge Samaniego
Craig Sandquist
Danny Scarborough
Michael Schwartz
Timothy Scott
Stuart Sebastian
Michael Shawn
Harry Sheppard
Roy Smith
Allan Sobek
Frank Solis
Vernon Spencer
Edward Stierle
Ron Stafford
Philip Stamps
Danny Strayhorn
Gary Sullivan
Swen Swenson
Brian Taylor
Burton Taylor
Danny Taylor
Leon Taylor
Bert Terborgh
Claude Tessier
Toney Thompkins
Robert Thompson
Clark Tippet
Christopher Todd
Gabriel Trupin
Antony Valdor
Jeff Veazey
Axel Vera
Buddy Vest

Mark Villa
Peter Vincent
Peter Wandel
Randy Wander
Randy Warner
Robert Warners
Tim Wengerd
L. Edmond Wesley
Glenn White
Larry White
Stuart White
Marc Wilder
Billy Wilson
John Wilson
David Steiger Wolfe
David Wolff
Derek Wolshonak
Travis Wright
Arnie Zane

ARCHITECTS
AND LANDSCAPE
ARCHITECTS

Alan Buchsbaum

Roger Ferri
Kevin George
Kenneth Halpern
Mel Hamilton
Simon Hart
George Howe
Philip Housewirth
Frank Israel
Mark Kaminski
Bruce Kelly
Tim Lanahan
Gerald B. Olanoff
Robert Pierson
Thomas H. Struth
Fiortio Tritia
Phillip Winslow

INTERIOR DESIGNERS

Robert Currie
Robin Jacobsen
Charles Pfister
Jay Spectre
Michael Taylor

NOTES

Chapter 1. The Great Experiment

1. Huey Newton, "Huey Talks about Gay and Women's Liberation," *Gay Sunshine* (October 1970), p. 8.

2. Carl Wittman, "Refugees from Amerika: A Gay Manifesto," in *The Homosexual Dialectic* (Englewood Cliffs, N.J.: Prentice Hall, 1972), p. 159. Originally published in *Berkeley Tribe,* December 26, 1969, p. 21.

3. Unsigned editorial, *Fag Rag* (February/March 1978), p. 1.

4. Charles Shively, "Incest as an Act of Revolution," *Fag Rag* (fall/winter 1976), p. 3.

5. Charles Shively, "Cosmetics as an Act of Revolution," *Fag Rag* (spring 1977), p. 15.

6. Charles Shively, "Self-Indulgence as an Act of Revolution," *Fag Rag* (1980), p. 2.

7. Ibid.

8. Peter Pehrson, "The Gay Male Feminist—A Personal Account," *Fag Rag* (1978), p. 13.

9. Unsigned editorial, *Fag Rag* (February/March 1978), p. 1.

10. John Stoltenberg, "Exploring Radical Feminism: An Interview with John Stoltenberg by Allen Young," *Fag Rag* (February/March 1978), p. 16.

11. Shannon Austin, "The Pink Scare," *Fag Rag* (1979), p. 3.

12. John Preston, "What Happened," in *Leatherfolk: Radical Sex, People, Politics and Practice,* edited by Mark Thompson (Los Angeles and New York: Alyson, 2001), p. 212.

Chapter 2. Theater of Pleasure: The Mineshaft

1. Mark Thompson, introduction to his *Leatherfolk: Radical Sex, People, Politics and Practice* (Los Angeles and New York: Alyson, 2001), pp. xi–xxiv.

2. Ray Ryan, "Advice to the Wartorn," *Gay Sunshine* (November 1970), p. 4.

3. Guy Baldwin, "A Second Coming Out," in Thompson, ed., *Leatherfolk*, p. 171.

4. Ibid., p. 172.

5. Unless otherwise noted, quotes from Guy Baldwin are from an interview I conducted in Los Angeles on 3 October 2001.

6. Wayne Hoffman, "Mineshaft Manager Wally Wallace Dies," *New York Blade,* 17 September 1999, p. 8.

7. Laud Humphreys, *Tearoom Trade: Impersonal Sex in Public Places,* 2d ed. (Hawthorne, N.Y.: Aldine de Gruyers, 1975), p. 48.

8. Brad Gooch, *The Golden Age of Promiscuity* (New York: Knopf, 1996), p. 155.

9. Ibid., p. 173.

10. Quotes from Ira Tattleman are from "Staging Masculinity at the Mineshaft," an unpublished essay provided to me by the author.

11. Quotes from Arnie Kantrowitz are from an interview conducted by my research assistant, Brennan Gerard, on my behalf in New York City on 4 October 2001.

12. Joel I. Brodsky, Ph.D., "The Mineshaft: A Retrospective Ethnography," *Journal of Homosexuality* 24, no. 3/4 (1993), p. 235.

13. Ibid., p. 247.

14. Edmund White, *States of Desire: Travels in Gay America* (New York: E. P. Dutton, 1980), p. 292.

Chapter 3. Another World: San Francisco and the Catacombs

1. Mark Thompson, introduction to his *Leatherfolk: Radical Sex, People, Politics and Practice* (Los Angeles and New York: Alyson, 2001), p. xxi.

2. Ibid., p. xi.

3. Ibid., p. xxiii.

4. Bill Brent, "Queer American," *Black Sheets* 12 (1997), p. 29.

5. Quotes from Guy Baldwin are from an interview I conducted in Los Angeles on 3 October 2001.

6. Gayle Rubin, "The Catacombs: A Temple of the Butthole," in Thompson, ed., *Leatherfolk*, p. 124.

7. Ibid., p. 130.

8. Ibid., p. 131.

9. Rita Mae Brown, "Queen for a Day: A Stranger in Paradise," in *Lavender Culture,* edited by Karla Jay (New York: NYU Press, 1994), p. 75.

10. Ibid., p. 74.

11. Quotes from Kantrowitz are from an interview conducted by my research assistant, Brennan Gerard, on my behalf in New York City on 4 October 2001.

Chapter 4. The Saint and the Beginning of the End

1. Quotes from Felice Picano are from an interview I conducted in Los Angeles on 14 September 2001.

2. Quotes from Kathy Watt are taken from an interview I conducted in Los Angeles on 26 September 2001.

3. Unless otherwise noted, quotes from Kantrowitz are from an interview conducted by my research assistant, Brennan Gerard, on my behalf in New York City on 4 October 2001.

4. Quotes from Marisa Cardinale are from a telephone interview I conducted on 17 October 2001.

5. Quotes from Richard Peters are from a telephone interview I conducted on 14 November 2001.

6. Quotes from Susan Tomkin are from an interview I conducted in New York City on 10 February 2002.

7. Unsigned editorial, *Fag Rag* (summer 1973), p. 2.

8. Percy Deane Young, "So You're Planning to Spend a Night at the Tubs?" *Rolling Stone* 128 (15 February 1973), p. 50.

9. Ibid.

10. Arnie Kantrowitz, "A Gay Struggles with the New Acceptance," *Village Voice* (17 November 1975), p. 39.

Chapter 5. Gathering Darkness

1. Quotes from Felice Picano are from an interview I conducted in Los Angeles on 14 September 2001.

2. George Whitmore, "After a 'Career' in Suicide: Choosing to Live," *The Advocate* (1982), p. 73.

3. Ibid.

4. Quotes from Ferd Eggan are taken from an interview I conducted in Los Angeles on 2 October 2001.

5. Unsigned editorial, "What Is Is What Needs to Be Destroyed," *Fag Rag* (1979), p. 17.

6. Quotes from Guy Baldwin are from an interview I conducted in Los Angeles on 3 October 2001.

7. Quotes from Kathy Watt are from an interview I conducted in Los Angeles on 26 September 2001.

8. Michel Foucault, *History of Sexuality*, Vol. 1, *An Introduction* (New York: Random House, 1978).

9. Ibid.

10. Bill Brent, "Queer American," *Black Sheets* 12 (1997), p. 31.

11. Ibid., p. 32.

12. Bill Brent, "Interview with Pat Califia by Bill Brent," *Black Sheets* 15 (1999), p. 30.

Chapter 6. The Life and Films of Fred Halsted

1. Quotes from Durk Dehner are from an interview I conducted in Los Angeles on 18 October 2001.

2. Quotes from Roger Earl are from an interview I conducted in Los Angeles on 6 November 2001.

3. Quotes from Jeanne Barney are from an interview I conducted in Los Angeles on 30 November 2001.

Chapter 7. What Might Have Been

1. Edmund White, *The Farewell Symphony* (New York: Vintage Books, 1998).

2. Quotes from Arnie Kantrowitz are from an interview conducted by my research assistant, Brennan Gerard, on my behalf in New York City on 4 October 2001.

3. Quotes from Felice Picano are taken from an interview I conducted in Los Angeles on 14 September 2001.

4. Michel Foucault, *Foucault Live: Interviews, 1961–1984* (New York: Semiotext[e], 1996), p. 383.

5. Ibid., p. 331.

6. Jacques Barzun, *From Dawn to Decadence: 1500 to the Present* (New York: Harper Collins, 2000), p. xv.

Chapter 8. The Rise of the East Village

1. Frank Rich, "The Gay Decades," *Esquire* (November 1987), p. 88.

2. "The Creative Engine: How Arts & Culture is Fueling Economic Growth in New York City Neighborhoods," Center for an Urban Future, November 2002, p. 1.

3. Ibid., p. 3.

4. Quotes from Sarah Schulman are taken from an interview I conducted in New York City on 12 February 2002.

5. Rene Ricard, "Pledge of Allegiance," *Artforum* 23 (November 1982), p. 42.

6. Walter Robinson, "The East Village Goes to School: History, Geography, Civic Economics," in *Neo York: Report on a Phenomenon* (Santa Barbara: University of California/University Art Museum, 1985), p. 15.

7. Carlo McCormick, "Guide to East Village Artists," *Neo York: Report on a Phenomenon* (Santa Barbara: University of California/University Art Museum, 1985), p. 1.

8. Ricard, "Pledge of Allegiance," p. 43.

9. From an e-mail message from Musto to me on 30 November 2001.

10. Ibid.

11. Gary Indiana, "Crime and Misdemeanors," *Artforum* 38 (October 1999), p. 117.

Chapter 9. New Role Models: Cookie Mueller and David Wojnarowicz

1. Cookie Mueller, *Ask Dr. Mueller: The Writings of Cookie Mueller* (New York and London: High Risk Books, 1997), p. v.

2. John Waters, introduction to *Ask Dr. Mueller: The Writings of Cookie Mueller* (New York and London: High Risk Books, 1997), p. xi.

3. Ibid., p. xii.

4. Linda Yablonsky, *The History of Junk* (New York: Farrar, Straus, Giroux, 1997), p. 36.

5. Waters, introduction to *Ask Dr. Mueller*, p. xi.

6. Yablonsky, *The History of Junk*, p. 148.

7. Mueller, *Ask Dr. Mueller*, pp. 292–293.

8. Ibid., p. 70.

9. David Wojnarowicz, *In the Shadow of the American Dream: The Diaries of David Wojnarowicz* (New York: Grove, 1999), p. 153.

10. David Wojnarowicz, *Close to the Knives: A Memoir of Disintegration* (New York: Vintage, 1991), p. 22.

11. Ibid., p. 29.

12. Dennis Cooper, "Odd Man Out," *Artforum* 38 (October 1999), p. 130.

13. Quotes from Tom Rauffenbart are taken from an interview I conducted in New York City on 15 February 2002.

14. *Artforum* 38 (October 1999), cover image.

15. Wojnarowicz, *In the Shadow of the American Dream*, p. xiii.

Chapter 10. The Sexual *Flâneur*

1. Quotes from Carolyn Dinshaw are taken from an interview I conducted in New York City on 15 February 2002.

2. Quotes from Felice Picano are from an interview I conducted in Los Angeles on 14 September 2001.

3. Quotes from Susan Tomkin are taken from an interview I conducted in New York City on 10 February 2002.

4. Quotes from Jonathan Weinberg are taken from an interview conducted by my research assistant, Brennan Gerard, on my behalf in New York City on 16 October 2001.

Chapter 11. ACT UP

1. From an e-mail from Chris Hennelly to me on 20 March 2002.

2. Ibid.

3. "ACT UP Working Document," www.actupny.org./documents/firstworkingdoc.html.

4. "ACT UP Civil Disobedience Manual," www.actupny.org/documents/CDindex.html.

5. Laraine Sommella, "This Is about People Dying: The Tactics of Early ACT UP and Lesbian Avengers in New York City," *Queers in Space: Communities/Public Places/Sites of Resistance* (Seattle: Bay Press, 1997) p. 418.

6. ACT UP Treatment and Data Teach-In, www.actupny.org/documents/T&DTI.html.

7. Ibid.

8. Ibid.

9. Quotes from Ann Northrup are from an interview I conducted in New York City on 14 February 2002.

10. Quotes from Sarah Schulman are from an interview I conducted in New York City on 12 February 2002.

11. Quotes from Ferd Eggan are from an interview I conducted in Los Angeles on 2 October 2001.

12. Quotes from James Wenzy are from an interview I conducted in New York City on 14 February 2002.

13. Quotes from Michelangelo Signorile are taken from an interview I conducted in New York City on 15 February 2002.

14. "Demonstrations," www.actupny.org/documetns/cron-91.html.

15. Jeff Kelley, "The Body Politics of Suzanne Lacy," in *But Is It Art?* (Seattle: Bay Press, 1995), p. 224.

16. Ibid., p. 239.

17. Ibid., p. 241.

18. John Greenberg, "ACT UP Explained," www.actupny.org/documents/greenbergAU.html.

19. Ibid.

20. Ibid.

Chapter 12. Owning AIDS

1. Lawrence K. Altman, "Many Gay Men in U.S. Unaware They Have H.I.V., a Study Finds," *New York Times* (8 July 2002), p. A13.

2. Ibid., p. A1.

3. Centers for Disease Control, *Morbidity and Mortality Weekly Report* 50, no. 21 (1 June 2001), p. 431.

4. Quotes from Kathy Watt are from an interview I conducted in Los Angeles on 26 September 2001.

5. Troy Suarez, Ph.D., and Jeffrey Miller, MSN, ACRN, APNP, "Negotiating Risks in Context: A Perspective on Unprotected Anal Intercourse and

Barebacking among Men Who Have Sex with Men—Where Do We Go from Here?" *Archives of Sexual Behavior* 30, no. 3 (2001), p. 288.

6. Lawrence K. Altman, "Swift Rise Seen in H.I.V. Cases for Gay Blacks," *New York Times* (1 June 2001), p. A1.

7. Ibid.

8. David Mixner, "Phill Wilson targets solutions to HIV problems," Gay.com Network (http://content.gay.com/channels/news/mixner/mixner_wilson.html).

9. Quotes from Collin Robinson are from a telephone interview I conducted on 11 October 2002.

10. Quotes from Ferd Eggan are from an interview I conducted in Los Angeles on 2 October 2001.

Chapter 13. Hope and Caution:
Assotto Saint and Felix Gonzalez-Torres

1. Assotto Saint, "Addendum," in *Spells of a Voodoo Doll* (New York: Richard Kasak Books, 1996), p. 9.

2. Assotto Saint, "Haiti: A Memory Journey," in *Spells of a Voodoo Doll*, p. 230.

3. Ibid., p. 233.

4. Ibid.

5. Assotto Saint, "Miss Thing/for Marcia Johnson," in *Spells of a Voodoo Doll*, p. 209.

6. Quotes from Walter Holland are taken from a telephone interview I conducted on 9 October 2002.

7. Assotto Saint, "Black Fag," in *Spells of a Voodoo Doll*, pp. 393–394.

8. Assotto Saint, "Why I Write," in *Spells of a Voodoo Doll*, p. 7.

9. Ibid., p. 5.

10. Quotes from Andrea Rosen are from a telephone interview I conducted on 11 April 2002.

11. Tim Rollins, "Interview with Felix Gonzalez-Torres by Tim Rollins," in *Felix Gonzalez-Torres,* monograph (New York: Art Resources Transfer, Inc., 1993), p. 43.

12. Ibid., p. 45.

13. Robert Storr, "Setting Traps for the Mind and Heart," *Art in America* (January 1996), p. 89.

14. Quotes from Jim Hodges are taken from an e-mail from Hodges to me received on 15 August 2002.

15. Storr, "Setting Traps for the Mind and Heart," p. 89.

16. Ibid.

17. Text taken from photocopies faxed to me by Bill Bartman on 12 May 2001.

18. Ibid.

19. Quotes from Bill Bartman are taken from a telephone interview I conducted on 12 May 2001.

20. Rollins, "Interview with Felix Gonzalez-Torres by Tim Rollins," p. 43.

Chapter 14. "Contact" and the Dangers of Assimilation

1. Fran Lebowitz, "The Impact of AIDS on the Artistic Community," *New York Times* (13 September 1987), p. 22.

2. Jane Jacobs, *The Death and Life of Great American Cities* (New York: Random House, 1961), p. 15.

3. Ibid., p. 55.

4. John Rechy, "Interview," *Gay Sunshine* (May 1974), p. 3.

5. Jacobs, *The Death and Life of Great American Cities,* p. 50.

6. Ibid., p. 58.

7. Ibid., p. 62.

8. Samuel R. Delany, *Times Square Red, Times Square Blue* (New York: NYU Press, 1999), pp. 148–149.

9. Rem Koolhaas, "Regrets?" *Grand Street* 57 (April 1996). Text also archived online (http://www.grandstreet.com/gsissues/gs57/gs57d.html).

10. Delany, *Times Square Red, Times Square Blue,* p. 122.

11. Ibid., pp. 56–57.

12. Arnie Kantrowitz, "A Gay Struggles with the New Acceptance," *Village Voice* (17 November 1975), p. 39.

13. From an interview with Signorile that I conducted in New York City on 15 February 2002.

14. D. W. Seal, J. A. Kelly, F. R. Bloom, L. Y. Stevenson, B. I. Coley, and L. A. Broyles, "HIV Prevention with Young Men Who Have Sex with Men: What Young Men Themselves Say Is Needed," AIDS *Care* 12 (2000), p. 8.

15. From an interview with Baldwin that I conducted in Los Angeles on 3 October 2001.

16. From an interview with Watt that I conducted in Los Angeles on 26 September 2001.

17. D. W. Seal et al., "HIV Prevention with Young Men Who Have Sex with Men," p. 21.

18. Sheryl Gay Stolberg, "Grants Aid Abstinence-Only Initiative," *New York Times* (28 February 2002), p. A16.

19. Quotes from Lynn Ponton are from a telephone interview I conducted on 13 November 2001.

20. Stolberg, "Grants Aid Abstinence-Only Initiative," p. A16.

Epilogue. The Estate Project for Artists with AIDS

1. Patrick Merla, *Boys Like Us: Gay Writers Tell Their Coming Out Stories* (New York: Avon, 1996).

2. Jonathan Weinberg, *Ambition and Love in Modern American Art* (New Haven, Conn.: Yale University Press, 2001), p. 242.

INDEX